Around the Absurd

Around the Absurd

Essays on Modern and
Postmodern Drama

Edited by
Enoch Brater and Ruby Cohn

Ann Arbor
The University of Michigan Press

Copyright © by The University of Michigan 1990
All rights reserved
Published in the United States of America by
The University of Michigan Press
Manufactured in the United States of America
1993   1992   1991   1990   4   3   2   1

Library of Congress Cataloging-in-Publication Data

Around the absurd : essays on modern and postmodern drama / edited by
   Enoch Brater and Ruby Cohn.
       p.   cm. — (Theater — theory/text/performance)
   Includes bibliographical references.
   ISBN 0-472-10205-2 (cloth : alk. paper)
       1. Drama—20th century—History and criticism. 2. Theater of the
   absurd.   I. Brater, Enoch.   II. Cohn, Ruby.   III. Series.
   PN1861.A76   1990
   809.2'045—dc20   90-43740
                                                                   CIP

For
Martin Esslin

"... whom else ..."

Contents

1, 2, 4, 239, 270, 271

Introduction: Around the Absurd

RUBY COHN

Martin Esslin opens his *Theatre of the Absurd* with a vivid account of the Actor's Workshop performance of *Waiting for Godot* in the maximum-security prison of San Quentin, California. The date was 1957—three years after Brecht's Berliner Ensemble first traveled west (to Paris), one year after *Look Back in Anger* erupted on the London stage, three years before the American permissive sixties freed theater and habits (temporarily). The Actors' Workshop has gone the way of underfunded theaters, and prisoners have occasionally performed Beckett's plays in San Quentin, while Beckett himself wrote "on" for another three decades. *Waiting for Godot*, bleak through its humor, became the talismanic play of the modern repertoire. *The Theatre of the Absurd* has reached its third edition, and Martin Esslin remains devoted to theater, ever hopeful of "a Protean avant-garde"—the last phrase in his book.

The theater of the absurd did not begin either in 1957 or 1961, the date of Esslin's first edition of his book. A handier figure is 1950, exactly at mid-century, five years after the close of World War II. In 1950 two of Esslin's four major absurdists (Adamov, Beckett, Genet, Ionesco) played in Paris—two plays for Adamov, and *The Bald Soprano* for Ionesco. By mid-century, Beckett had completed *Godot*, although it was still seeking a theater. Most successful of the quartet was the imprisoned Genet, since Louis Jouvet had commissioned and produced *The Maids* in 1947. It was that production, on a double bill with Giraudoux's *Apollo of Bellac*, that first lured Esslin to the absurd. On his way from his London home to Zurich, to see his father for the first time since they were separated by World War II, Esslin had to change trains and stay overnight in Paris. Being Martin Esslin, he went to the theater, where the names of Jouvet and Giraudoux beckoned to him. But Genet, the then-unknown newcomer, enthralled him.

I choose mid-century as the birthdate of the theater of the absurd on personal as well as critical grounds. I arrived in Paris too late to see the Jouvet/Genet *Maids*, but I did, to my consternation, see the Left Bank Adamov—*The Large and the Small Manoeuvre*—and Ionesco's *Bald Soprano*. I sought meaning in these plays of acrid humor, which I naively took to be French. By the time Esslin's book appeared, a decade later, I had read (but not seen) Genet, and I had been present at that first indelible *Godot* (as I have boasted ad nauseam). By that time, too, embarked upon a dissertation on Beckett, I had found (or imposed?) meaning through the optics of Sartre, Camus, and the medieval morality *Everyman*. I had a vague notion that transcendence and agnosticism meet theatrically when an absurd Everyman faces death, but it was Esslin's book that sharpened my focus.

Unlike most early readers of *The Theatre of the Absurd*, I already had a nodding acquaintance with Esslin's Big Four. (Only in later editions does he allot Pinter a full chapter, but the first edition is already sensitive to East European absurdists.) What instructed me by surprise was Esslin's chapter titled "The Tradition of the Absurd." It was easy enough to agree with him about the drama of the 1950s: "The Theatre of the Absurd has renounced arguing *about* the absurdity of the human condition; it merely *presents* it in being—that is, in terms of concrete stage images" (25).[1] Esslin's quartet of absurdist playwrights was not new to me, but his quartet of absurdist techniques made me re-view drama:

"Pure" theatre; i.e. abstract scenic effects as they are familiar in the circus or revue, in the work of jugglers, acrobats, bullfighters, or mimes

Clowning, fooling, and mad-scenes

Verbal nonsense

The literature of dream and fantasy, which often has a strong allegorical
component. (328)

The list highlights the absurdity of the absurd, downplaying its
metaphysical dimension. The list furnished me with a wedge into
unfamiliar pre-absurdist drama, which, more important, was unfamiliar to most students of drama (with the durable exception of Eric
Bentley). Should I blush in admitting that Esslin introduced me to
Buchner, Grabbe, and Wedekind? "From Grabbe and Buchner,"
wrote Esslin, "the line of development leads straight to Wedekind,
the Dadaists, German Expressionism, and the early Brecht [about
whom Esslin had published the first book in English]" (339). Slowly,
I traced that line, which no longer seems "straight" to me, and I
should like here to retrace it, looking backward from the absurd and
adding stops along the way.

Birthdates of cultural phenomena are arbitrary, and although my
predilection runs to round numbers, I cite 1887 as the birth of modern
theater—when André Antoine, the first modern director, opened
the Théâtre Libre in Paris, to stage adaptations of realistic fiction.
We can all recite the litany of his naturalistic techniques: slice of life,
fourth wall removed, set and three-dimensional props true to the
milieu (climaxed by fountains and carcasses), and actors who *inter-
acted* as though the audience were absent. In short, Antoine pio-
neered the realistic theater that still dominates the stages of the West.
In 1887, too, Strindberg completed his realistic *Father*, while for Ibsen,
often called the father of realism, it was a fallow year between *Rosmer-
sholm* (1886) and *The Lady from the Sea* (1888), dramas whose mysterious atmosphere was alien to a realistic stage that was brightly lit in
the first darkened theaters. 1887 was also the year when Chekhov
produced his realistic pre-Stanlislavski *Ivanov*.

Even in 1887 short-lived journals struck out against realism, or the
naturalism that was sometimes understood as its synonym, but in the
last decade of the nineteenth century, when theater realism radical-
ized Berlin and Moscow, discordant voices arose in opposition. In
Paris, teen-ager Paul Fort founded the Théâtre d'Art for the self-
designated symbolists. In Berlin, bohemian Central Europeans mixed
with Slavic or Scandinavian refugees to become the precursors of

expressionism. In London a poetic reaction against the new realism was delayed until the new century.

Theatrically, the last century went out with a series of bangs rather than a whimper. Strindberg spent much of the 1890s in Berlin, but he wrote no plays until 1898, when *To Damascus* (part 1) offered a road for the spiritual quest in drama—a model not lost on Adamov and Beckett. Also in end-of-the-century Berlin was Frank Wedekind, some fifteen years Strindberg's junior, whose *Spring's Awakening* (1891, but not produced until 1906) brought dead characters to life on the stage, and whose "Lulu" plays (later "Englished" by Peter Barnes) lampooned bourgeois clichés as mercilessly—and as comically—as Ionesco was to do a half-century later. Both Strindberg's dismantling of traditional dramatic conflict and Wedekind's blend of lyricism and violence contributed to the expressionism of the following generation, but only obliquely to the absurdists.

Although the word *surrealism* was not coined until the twentieth century, supernatural shadows occasionally darkened late nineteenth-century theater. In the two years of existence of the Théâtre d'Art, Paul Fort staged a number of dreary symbolist plays, but he also produced *The Blind Ones* by Maeterlinck, whose atmosphere we can now breathe through Beckett. Although Aurélien Lugné acted in the realistic productions of Antoine, he added the Poe to his name before he directed Maeterlinck's *Pelléas et Mélisande* (1893)—at age 24. Thus linked to the brooding American, Lugné-Poe salvaged Paul Fort's failing symbolist theater, renamed it Théâtre de l'Oeuvre, and moved it to the Bouffes du Nord, where Peter Brook works today. The physical stage of Antoine was opposed (for a few years) by the metaphysical stage of his erstwhile student. What the realists and the symbolists had in common was respect for a superhuman law—heredity and environment for the realists, a mysterious transcendence for the symbolists. Moreover, Antoine and Lugné-Poe both directed Ibsen in their respective theaters, but not the same plays of Ibsen.

Lugné-Poe, as the name suggests, was partial to mysterious symbols, dreamlike moods, and rhythmic patterns. Against the grain, then, he was importuned to produce the play of his embattled assistant, Alfred Jarry. Neither symbolist nor naturalist, but prophetically absurd, *Ubu roi* burst out of the theater on December 10, 1896, into the press and thence into our cultural legacy. Although Jarry sets his *Ubu* in Poland, or Nowhere, he did not suspect that a nonrealistic

Polish drama would be nourished by his monster. Jarry was closer in spirit to the dadaists than the surrealists of the twentieth century, but it was the latter who beatified him, long after his death in 1907. As Esslin points out, Jarry's 'pataphysical aesthetics "anticipates the tendency of the Theatre of the Absurd to express psychological states by objectifying them on stage" (361). A member of the post–World War II College of 'Pataphysics, Ionesco has often doffed his cap to Jarry, but similar dunce caps occasionally adorn the characters of Adamov and Genet as well.

In that dusk of the nineteenth century, Russian Chekhov, far from the high jinks of Paris and the desperate bohemianism of Berlin, wrote *The Seagull*, the first of his four masterpieces that straddle the old and new century, weaving the grotesque and the atmospheric upon the sturdy loom of realism. What Chekhov's realism, Maeterlinck's symbolism, and Strindberg's intimate and less intimate theater shared was a de-emphasis on plot and a fragmentation of dialogue that would become the lingua franca of the absurdists.

The very title of Ibsen's *When We Dead Awaken* in the last year of the nineteenth century seemed to promise new life for twentieth-century drama, but, except for Chekhov and Strindberg—gigantic exceptions, to be sure—the new century did not immediately herald new theater. In the last year of the old century, the Irish Literary Theatre (later the Abbey) was founded, enfolding an old form into its name, while the Irishman Shaw raised hackles in London by pouring new subjects into old forms. The new century slowly assimilated the avant-gardes of the 1890s.

Queen Victoria died in 1901, but her unpuritan son brought no vigor to the British theater. Across the Channel, where *la belle époque* entrenched the well-made play, the painter Hervé coined the word *expressionism* to distinguish his bright colors from the subtle tints of the impressionists. Soon crossing national and genre frontiers, expressionism exulted in its own unbridled emotion. Although a few expressionist dramas predate World War I, most of them bear the scars of that war. Rebelling against the decorum of the Hohenzollern Empire, the expressionist playwrights staged skirmishes between sexes, classes, and generations. In the typical expressionist play short scenes zigzagged into a quest, where the protagonist met type-characters, whom he harangued either in staccato phrases or rhapsodic monologues. Outside of central Europe, expressionist drama, in contrast to expressionist staging, had little impact. But one expressionist, Yvan Goll, a bilingual Alsatian, translated his German *Methusalem* into French, which facilitated a penurious Paris production. Of Esslin's Big Four, Adamov alone borrows from expressionism the quest structure (with gaps), type-characters (with exceptions), and splashes of emotion.

If we pause before World War I—say, in 1913—Eugene O'Neill, having survived a suicide attempt and tuberculosis, resolved to become a playwright, and he would prove the richest heir of expressionism. In the United States and in western Europe, realism ruled the theater, and yet Jacques Copeau chafed against its bonds when he opened the Vieux-Columbier in Paris, with his ideals of purity and a bare stage. In contrast, Central European expressionists attracted directors who explored every physical dimension of the stage, and actors who explored every diapason of emotion. When World War I ended, directors on both sides of the Rhine extended their idiom to Shakespeare, Greek tragedy, and European classics. The line of descent is fuzzy, but Genet somehow combines Copeau's purity with expressionist turgidity.

Embryonic expressionists were killed on the German front, but some artists of diverse nationalities escaped World War I in neutral Zurich. Surrounded by bellicose madness, these artists were heady with life, and they viewed all art with a jaundiced eye. Choosing the name Dada, apparently when the Romanian Tristan Tzara randomly thrust a paper cutter into a dictionary, the Zurich group rallied to unmatrixed performances at the Cafe Voltaire—harbingers of the unscripted theater and the performance art of the late twentieth century. According to the fictionalized Joyce of Tom Stoppard's *Travesties,* "this local bourgeois-baiting pussy-cat, Dada, had grown into a tiger standing for scandal, provocation, and moral outrage through art."

Once the war was over, Tzara, having corresponded with André Breton in Paris, moved Dada to that city, where Breton had already accepted Aragon as his colleague. Proud of their theatrical flare, Breton and Aragon were hostile to theater, and yet they, as well as Tzara, Artaud, and Vitrac, wrote disjunctive plays. In homage to Apollinaire (dead on Armistice Day, 1918), Breton adopted the neologism invented by that poet in the preface of his *Breasts of Tiresias:* "When man wanted to imitate walking, he created the wheel, which does not resemble a leg. He thus made surrealism without being aware of it." The surrealists resembled the symbolists in hostility to reason and realism. Like Dada, surrealism valued the unconscious, the erotic, the shocking. Breton, loathing theater, soon excommunicated Artaud and Vitrac, who thereupon founded the short-lived Alfred-Jarry Theater. While expressionism seduced such theater directors as Reinhardt and Jessner in central Europe, where even the young Brecht wrote his first play *Baal* in that frenzy of feeling, the plays of Dada and surrealism were relegated to audiences invited to the paris attic of Edouard Autant and his wife, Louise Lara. Even the anticommercial directors of the Cartel (Baty, Dullin, Jouvet, Pitoeff) were cold to such flippancy about plot, character, and coherent dialogue. Only after World War II did the playwrights of the absurd assimilate surrealism, but I speed too quickly past World War I.

In spite of *A Farewell to Arms*, Italy was relatively unaffected by World War I, and it was at that time that Pirandello, already successful as a fiction writer, turned first to Sicilian one-acters, and then to Italian adultery dramas. In 1921 his *Six Characters in Search of an Author* caused an uproar in Rome, but European notoriety came in 1923 when the Russian émigré Pitoeff directed it in Paris. Trained by Stanislavski, Pitoeff founded an antirealist theater in St. Petersburg, much as Lugné had done two decades earlier in Paris. Like the Dada group, Pitoeff sought refuge in Switzerland during World War I—in Geneva rather than Zurich. In 1921 he moved his company to Paris. Always in financial difficulties, he nevertheless directed a determinedly international repertory, highlighted by Chekhov and Pirandello, but he also encouraged new French playwrights—notably Anouilh and Lenormand. Authoritatively though Pitoeff may have directed his countryman Chekhov, it was Pirandello who indelibly stamped both boulevard and avant-garde French theater in dramatizing the conflict between the flux of life and the fixity of art.

European theater between the two world wars is often described as a directors' rather than a playwrights' domain, but this ignores Polish Witkacy, Spanish Lorca, Irish Yeats, German Brecht, and Italian Pirandello. Scenography was internationalized between the two wars, but an international repertory was only beginning to seep into European theaters. For anglophone audiences, the two giant interwar playwrights are Shaw in Britain and O'Neill in the United States. Unlike the international names mentioned—diversely antirealistic and diversely suggestive of the absurd—neither Shaw nor O'Neill broke free of the exigencies of plot, and yet each of them strayed from realism. Shaw fashions a ship of England in *Heartbreak House*, he accommodates the supernatural voices of his St. Joan, and he ornaments his "political extravaganzas" with absurd touches—or so they now seem. After O'Neill's expressionist plays of the early twenties, he experimented with masks, asides, and doubles. Although none of the absurdists borrowed from these two playwrights, today's productions of Shaw and O'Neill might well borrow from the absurdists a raucousness of comedy and an incisiveness of stage imagery.

Shaw died at mid-century, the year I arbitrarily chose as the birthdate of the absurd. A decade earlier, O'Neill, terminally ill, had stopped writing. Realism continued to dominate Anglophone commercial stages, as well as the Paris boulevard theater, which had rarely closed during World War II. Slowly, the subsidized theaters of central Europe were rebuilt, and even more slowly they opened their stages to new voices. Among these voices were those of Swiss Max Frisch and Friedrich Dürrenmatt, whose plays exhibit grotesque elements, analogous with those of the absurd. In the United States Arthur Miller and Tennessee Williams were successful as realists, but their late plays—*Two-Way Mirror* and *Out Cry*, respectively—carry traces of the absurd in their symbolic ubiquity.

Perhaps my line of tangents to the absurd should end on that note. A short-lived Paris theater called itself symbolist in the last decade of the nineteenth century, but the mid-twentieth-century dramatists of the absurd—preeminently Beckett—vitalized symbols theatrically. Not only were wild ducks or cherry orchards symbolic, but also the set, the props, the actors' gestures, and virtually every line of dialogue. Although Martin Esslin points to subordination of dialogue as a quality of the absurd—"In its devaluation of language, the Theatre of the Absurd is in tune with the trend of our time" (407)—it is so only by comparison with the discursive causality of the realistic play. In the most concentrated drama of the absurd, however, linguistic structures are symbolic—negation, interrogation, and above all repetition. Preceding poststructural criticism that reduces the world to language, the drama of the absurd stages language as paradigm.

The editors of this collection, appreciative of the formative impact of Martin Esslin's *Theatre of the Absurd*, invited a number of critics to reflect, some three decades after his book's publication, upon the absurd. It will be apparent that the reflections are sometimes direct, more often oblique; that the contributors examine plays, playwrights, performances, audiences, politics, critics, muses, artists, fictions, styles, themes, words, movements, and phenomena. In proper absurdist fragmentation, they cohere only in their debt to and admiration of Martin Esslin. The absurd is around.

NOTES

1. All citations in my text from Martin Esslin's *The Theatre of the Absurd* are taken from the first edition of his book (Garden City, N.Y.: Anchor, 1961).

Dagny and Lulu

Jan Kott

In the 1905 Vienna premiere of Wedekind's *Pandora's Box*, the second of his Lulu plays, a young woman named Tilly Newes played Lulu. On the second day after the premiere, Wedekind wrote to her rapturously, saying that she had portrayed Lulu "like a Madonna." My colleague, Leo Treitler, a musicologist writing on Berg's *Lulu*, has amplified this to say, "like *Munch's* Madonna."[1] He was referring to one of Munch's best-known pictures, which exists in at least five versions—in oil and in lithograph. Munch depicts a young woman at the peak of sexual ecstasy, naked to the loins, a red halo around her head, blank eyes looking without seeing. In one version, a shrunken embryo is seen in the left corner, and around the rim of the painting drift spermatozoans. "Woman, who gives herself up whole and discovers in this surrender the painful beauty of the Madonna," Munch wrote of this picture. Sigbjorn Obstfelder, a poet and friend of Munch and Strindberg, wrote in 1896: "For me, [Munch's] Madonna shows the essence of his art. She is the Earth Mother."[2]

But that is only part of the story. The youthful Tilly Newes played Lulu, the earth demon *(Erdgeist)*, as if she were Dagny Juel. Early in the spring of 1893, in a Berlin tavern called the Little Black Pig, Munch introduced this young woman to August Strindberg and to Stanlislaw Przybyszewski, whom Dagny would marry the following

September. The German art historian Julius Meier-Graefe writes in his memoirs:

> In a first-floor room on Louisenstrasse in North Berlin, the red light from an alcohol lamp would burn the entire night. . . . It was here that the Przybyszewskis lived. . . . He, a pure-blooded Pole who wrote avant-garde novels in German and suffered from hallucinations. . . . She, a Norwegian, very thin, with the slender face of a fourteenth-century Madonna and a smile that drove men mad. She was called "The Spirit." She was able to drink a litre of absinthe and not get drunk. . . . An upright piano stood in the exact center of this shabby room. While one of the men danced with The Spirit, the other two sat at the table and eyed her intently. The first was Munch, the second, as often as not, was Strindberg. All of them, each in his own fashion, were in love with this woman, but they never openly showed it.

The "earth demon" was twenty-six years old, the "brilliant Pole" a year younger. It was at this time that Przybyszewski coined the phrase "In the beginning there was lust."

It may be well to review briefly the German and Polish chapters of Dagny Juel's life, before her tragic end in Tiflis.[3] Strindberg had a stormy three-week affair with Dagny in the spring of 1893, when his fiancée and future wife, Frida Uhl, was away in Munich. Strindberg later came to hate Dagny, slandering her in letters, often calling her "a common slut." In his attacks of dementia during his Inferno period, he dreamed that she and Przybyszewski poisoned him. Even in letters to distant acquaintances, Strindberg was merciless about Dagny, describing their relationship in detail as if they were still intimate. Nor did Frida have any warm feeling for Dagny. In *Marriage to a Genius*, which she wrote near the end of her life, she described a possibly fictional account of Strindberg's first night with Dagny, who had led him drunk to her hotel room. Since everyone lived in similar shabby rooms, Strindberg woke at daybreak and thought he was at home. He drove the naked Dagny out of bed and into the hallway.

Frida's marriage to Strindberg did not last long. After a little over a year she left him, taking up almost immediately with Wedekind, who had created a sensation with his *Spring's Awakening*. Frida became pregnant by Wedekind before his divorce (in all these fin de siècle romances the women immediately became pregnant!), but they never married. Wedekind did not need to ask Frida about Dagny. In 1893–94 in the tavern that Strindberg himself named the Little Black Pig (Zum Schwarzen Ferkel), on a side street off Unter den Linden, the most celebrated German and Scandinavian bohemians gathered, and for them "Fru Dagny" was the leading demon, at once Aspasia and Madonna. Religious connotations were absent from this Madonna, at once the title of Wedekind's portrait and the title given to Dagny. Rather, the name was conceived as *ma donna* or "my lady," as in Shakespeare's *Twelfth Night*, when the Clown addresses Olivia: "Good madonna, give me leave to prove you a fool" (1.5.55).

Wedekind's Lulu plays were completed in 1895, but the second part of his *Pandora's Box* was too scandalous to be staged or published. In it Lulu is a common London streetwalker who ends up being murdered by Jack the Ripper. Similarly, Dagny perished in a shabby hotel in Tiflis, shot by the Polish Count Emeryk, a young companion in this desperate exile. It is possible that they were not lovers. He shot her and then himself, admitting that he was one of the sons of "sad Satan." Dagny was a femme fatale who victimized herself rather than the men who were infatuated by her paradoxical blend of earthy otherworldliness and carnal spirituality, even though Przybyszewski called her "Spirit."

More than the relevant anecdotes and even the factual drama itself, what is important to me is the conjectural history: Lulu more than Dagny. This Aspasia (as Dagny was called by Strindberg) who took off her green wool stockings under the intent gaze of the men at the Little Black Pig—it was this woman whom Wedekind had seen earlier in Munch's paintings. He knew her from Munch's Madonnas, which in subsequent versions of this sexual descent from heaven have pursed lips and drooping eyelids; he knew her also from compositions such as *Jealousy*, with the triangular head of Przybyszewski, and a slim, nude, long-haired woman under the biblical Tree of Knowledge, next to a man in a black suit who bears a striking resemblance to Strindberg. From this period also dates Munch's *Three Stages of Woman*: a young woman in white with a wedding bouquet and flowing hair; an old woman dressed in black; between the two, a nude standing with her legs apart. In yet another painting, there is a half-nude woman in a dress that has fallen to her thighs, and hands reach out to her from all sides. And again there is the triangular face of Przybyszewski with a short beard and a thin trimmed moustache, but this time surrounded by a woman's hair. Perhaps the most significant of all for Munch is *The Vampire*, an oil painting of 1893 (and a lithograph two years later), showing a woman with long red hair, her lips pressed against the neck of a man bent over her breast. Dagny had light hair, but with auburn highlights; in the sun it looked red.

Among the characters of the two parts of Wedekind's *Lulu* are probably many faces of the regular patrons of the Little Black Pig. One of them was surely Dr. Carl Ludwig Schleich, later to be famous for his work with local anesthetics. He was a friend of Strindberg and especially of Frida, whose dreams he pronounced to be sexual in nature. She at first denied this, but later admitted it, and Strindberg shouted: "Women play with truth as they do with dolls." The tone is that of Dr. Goll and Dr. Schoen in the first scene of Wedekind's *Lulu*, when Lulu poses for the painter. In the memoirs of Meier-Graefe Dr. Schleich is called "the fourth friend" of Dagny.[4]

The Przybyszewskis and Munch often went hungry, and were therefore invited by acquaintances to lavish meals. But more important than such anecdotes are the thematic shifts and stylistic transformations in the work of that period. In Wedekind's *Lulu*, "artists" and "philistines" for the first time mirror and need each other, not only because the artists are always impoverished and their "patrons" hold the purse strings. Wedekind, in his great perspicacity, noticed that the philistines had long ago stopped fearing the artists, just as the artists no longer spurned the philistines. Both the aristocracy, though of course only its "decadent" fringe, and the bourgeoisie, though of course only its "progressive" fringe, co-opted not only the sexual morals of the bohemians, but also their language and worldview. They all despised philistines. Jerzy Stempowski, in his vignette *The Chimera as a Beast of Burden*, relates how a famous tycoon, known for lucky but risky transactions, confided to him that the surrealists had inspired his financial imagination. In *Lulu* Wedekind showed that the editorial office, the stock exchange, and the painter's studio are inhabited by the same cast of characters. However, in contrast to Strindberg, there is no longer room for tragedy; even though people drop dead all around, they are only characters in a comedy. The Polish writer Witkacy would later call one of his plays *(The Water Hen)* "a spherical tragedy" and his theatrical style "formism."[5]

Wedekind entitled the first part of *Lulu Erdgeist*, which is sometimes translated as *The Earth Demon*. This "demon of the night,"
which sometimes appears in *Isaiah* as an owl screeching in the desert,
is Lilith, the first wife—or rather the female counterpart—of Adam,
formed out of sediment. Wedekind's play is venomous, stripped of
metaphysics and symbols, ironic to an almost grotesque degree, bordering on cabaret, already pre-Brechtian. Why this mythic paradigm
of Lulu/Lilith and Lulu/Madonna?

Lulu destroys all men who find themselves in her embrace. She
terrifies and fascinates. Like the Babylonian and Hebrew Lilith, she
is the personification, or rather the embodiment, of lust. She *is* sex.
For the Scandinavian misogynists Strindberg and Munch, sex was the
vulva dentata, a devouring womb, both desirable and dangerous. The
human female in these sexual obsessions is Virgin, Mother, or
Whore. In Strindberg's plays, and even more in his prose writings
and journals, a dance of life and death is obsessively repeated. This
dance is repeated just as obsessively in Munch's canvasses and litho-
graphs. Images of birth and death bound together often appear in
Mediterranean carnival rites. In this tradition, which certainly derives
from the saturnalias, wedding and funeral are of the same order; sex
is delight, and death arouses no dread. In Strindberg and Munch, sex
smells of cadavers. But perhaps this makes it all the more fascinating.
The secret of life and death is contained in the vagina. It seems as if
Wedekind took possession of both Strindberg's wife Frida and his
demons.

In this tangle of the history of behavior, painting, and literature,
Dagny's role remains astonishing. The daughter of a provincial Norwegian doctor, she danced barefoot at the Little Black Pig, and she
fought for free love a bit prematurely—fragile and tender, naive and
oversensitive, as one can deduce from her letters and novels. Dagny
unexpectedly became the most prominent figure of "demonic modernism" in Berlin, Munich, Vienna, and Krakow. She had blond hair,
but Munch set it ablaze. She was first transformed into a Madonna
and later into Lulu, the Lilith of the end of the nineteenth century.

"Look, Spirit, come to me, give me your hands, give yourself
fully," Stanislaw Przybyszewski wrote to Dagny Juel in his last letter
before they were married; "I'm the only man in the European style
and the only true 'blond beast,' born for one woman only—for You."[6]
"The blond beast" is from Nietzsche. Obviously, Przybyszewski was

not the only one to read him; there was also Witkacy. In 1919, in the manifesto *On New Forms in Painting*, Witkacy wrote: "It is necessary to unfetter the slumbering beast and to see what it will do." I don't know if anyone has written about the impact on Witkacy of Przybyszewski, the man and the legend. But it is enough to alter slightly and heighten the style of this passage from his letter to Dagny, to recognize the dialogue of Witkacy's plays and his novel *Insatiability*. This is because "insatiability," as it appears in Witkacy's painting and at the very core of his personality, is always portrayed in the guise of monsters. It was perhaps unfortunate that Witkacy called this insatiability "form," because it was also content, life, painting, women, and himself—or rather something that Witkacy had within himself.

This insatiability is derived from Przybyszewski. And if something remains of Przybyszewski and his followers, and perhaps of the entire modernist period, which can still grip us, it is precisely this "hunger" of these artists of the Young Poland, Young Scandinavia, and Young Germany movements. Witkacy's Satans and Titans are rather pitiful, even with his Hyrcanian worldview, and they are often comical, as when they foam at the mouth and he provides in a footnote the appropriate instructions for the desired effect. His "demon women," though sexually insatiable and well versed in perversions, are no longer "earth spirits."

For a long time the theater has recognized only what is absurd in Witkacy's plays. With their frantic theatricality, his works play best as comedies, and they often unexpectedly reveal a quite realistic and sometimes prophetic timeliness. On a considerably higher plane, it is more difficult to stage Witkacy's *Angst*. Perhaps only Tadeusz Kantor has seen the images of death in these "whimsical" plays. In my opinion, what is impressive and perhaps unique in this eternally serious Witkacy, his true and inimitable *teatrum absurdu*, is precisely this hunger of the modernist avant-garde. To understand this, it is perhaps necessary to return to these early modernists, to their symbols and paintings. I see Munch's *Madonna* under the gaslight as the Duchess of Nevermore in Witkacy's *Water Hen*. Perhaps a profound source of the theater of the absurd should be sought in the milieu that Munch and Wedekind shared with Strindberg, which revolved around the transformation of Dagny Juel into this icon of Lulu.

NOTES

Translated by Allen Kuharski.

1. Leo Treitler, "The Lulu Character and the Character of Lulu," in *Music and the Historical Imagination* (Cambridge: Harvard University Press, 1989).

2. Ibid.

3. In Poland the last to write on Dagny Juel were Maria Szczepanska Kuncewicz in *Fantasia alla polacca* (Warsaw: Czytelnik, 1979) and Krystyna Kolinska in *Przybyszewski: His Women, His Children* (1978). Ragna Stang writes a great deal about Juel's Berlin period in her superb study of Munch (1979), as does Reinhold Heller in *Munch: His Life and Works* (Chicago: University of Chicago Press, 1984). Michael Meyer and Olaf Lagerkrantz also write of Juel in their recent biographies of Strindberg.

4. Michael Meyer, *Strindberg* (London: Secker & Warburg, 1985), 268.

5. See *The Illustrated Encyclopaedia of World Theatre* (London: Thames and Hudson, 1977), p. 289.

6. See note 3, above.

Maeterlinck in the Light of the Absurd
KATHARINE WORTH

The stone of the absurd thrown into the stream of modern thought by Martin Esslin has sent ripples spreading into all sorts of unlikely places. One of these is the twilight terrain held sacred to Maeterlinck; that unique theater kingdom of mists and shadows where walls and doors are the boundaries between the living and a mysterious other world that surrounds them. Viewed from the sharp, saturnine viewpoint of the absurd, Maeterlinck's strange oeuvre can take on a new look, even perhaps seem ripe for a major theatrical revival.

The Maeterlinckian world went out of fashion shortly after its heyday around 1900–1910. We need to start by taking a look at this heyday.[1] It was a considerable affair, with repercussions in many countries outside France and Belgium, notably in England and Russia and also in America (where Robert Edmond Jones created exciting designs for plays such as *The Seven Princesses*). Maeterlinck's fame spread within three or four years of the first production of any of his plays: *The Intruder (L'Intruse)*, directed by Lugné-Poe at the Théâtre d'Art, Paris in 1891. A major cause of the public interest that soon developed was the impact made by *Pelléas and Mélisande* in 1893. Its romantic love story, unlike the austere fables of *The Intruder* or *The Blind Ones* (1891), undoubtedly helped to move it out of the avant-garde into more fashionable domains.

Between 1898 and 1904 *Pelléas and Mélisande* could have been seen in London on two separate occasions, performed by some of the greatest stars of the time. In the glittering production at the St. James's Theatre in 1898, Mrs. Patrick Campbell presented her waiflike Mélisande—"a plaintive figure out of tapestry, a child out of a nursery tale"—in exquisite costumes by Burne Jones.[2] Her Pelléas, John Martin-Harvey, a much-adored romantic actor, himself adored Maeterlinck's drama. *Pelléas and Mélisande* was for him the "beloved work": he thought the part of Pelléas fitted him so well it might have been written for him. Maeterlinck, who came from Paris to see the production, did not disagree. Martin-Harvey's Pelléas, he said, was "the unlooked-for but unimistakable soul of my dream."[3] He might not have said this about the French production of 1904 when Londoners again saw Mrs. Patrick Campbell as Mélisande, this time costarring with a still more prodigious enchantress, Sarah Bernhardt, in a travesti role as Pelléas. Reviewers were inclined to be sarcastic about the two odd phenomena: Mrs. Patrick Campbell performing in French (apparently just adequately) and Sarah Bernhardt, at her mature age, playing the stripling Pelléas. (Maeterlinck had said, when asked by Martin-Harvey if Pelléas represented his author, "Yes, at eighteen"). Nevertheless the production was an occasion, socially as well as theatrically; even, according to the *Times* reviewer, politically: "This is the heyday of the *entente cordiale* and Anglo-French activities are in fashion."[4]

A huge increase of theatrical fame was injected into Maeterlinck's reputation in 1902 when Debussy's operatic version of *Pelléas and Mélisande* (with the Scottish soprano, Mary Garland, as Mélisande) had its first performance at the Opéra-Comique, Paris. The glorious work thus launched was destined never to lose its place in the international operatic repertoire (a fate unlike that of the play in the theater). Powerful new talents have continued to be attracted to the opera: in 1969, for example, it was with *Pelléas* that Pierre Boulez made his first appearance at Covent Garden, for which Josef Svoboda created one of his most exquisite designs: brilliant, impressionistic transparencies continually changing under a subtle light to suggest a fragile background of forest, park, and castle. It might be (indeed has been) said that the music carries a play that can no longer stand on its own: it is too romantic for our day, romantic to the point of absurdity, as in the scene when Mélisande at her window lets down her hair to be grasped and raved over by Pelléas standing below. The word *absurdity* brings us to the brink of the question to be explored in a moment. First, however, we need to conclude this rapid view of Maeterlinck's golden era with a glance at its last phase.

The Maeterlinck rocket continued to trace a starry trajectory until just after the First World War when it began a downward descent. Before the decline there were one or two plays that had an immediate popular success, starting their stage life not in the "poor" theater of the avant-garde but in the sort of theater where audiences came in expectation of polished entertainment performed by well-known actors. One such play was *The Burgomaster of Stilemonde*, a realistic piece about the heroic behavior of a peaceable, garden-loving burgomaster during the German occupation of Belgium. Martin-Harvey produced it (and played the burgomaster) in 1918, encouraged to undertake a part so different from his Pelléas by Granville Barker, who hinted that it might receive official support as a kind of contribution to wartime propaganda. Martin-Harvey himself was attracted by the "philosophy of mercy" and the transcendent values expressed through the story of the gentle, unassuming hero. The play was another aspect of Maeterlinck, a clear proof that he could make contact with an audience in straightforward realistic terms when he found that the appropriate method. It has relevance here as a reminder that Maeterlinck always sought a language that *would* communicate. The reason for the "other" style of the symbolist plays was an attempt to express something that was in a way inexpressible.

The most spectacular popular success Maeterlinck enjoyed in these years was undoubtedly *The Blue Bird*, produced first by Stanislavski in Moscow in 1908 and in London the following year. People who know nothing else of Maeterlinck often identify him through this play. It was produced regularly in London for many years after its first triumphs, acquiring a status comparable to that of *Peter Pan* as a Christmas entertainment. This suggests that it succeeded as a children's play that could also be enjoyed by the grownups. Magical design effects, clever costumes (some humorous, some glamorous, like those for Light or the Queen of Night), and grand transformation scenes were an important feature of all the early productions. The designs by Egorov for Stanislavski or the distinctively English treatment of sets and costumes for the 1909 production at the Haymarket Theatre, London (still on view in the foyers of that theater), show

how much designing talent went into the realization of Maeterlinck's dream play. It is easy to understand how audiences were charmed by the colorful stage fantasies made out of the journey of the young brother and sister, Tyltyl and Mytyl, in search of the blue bird of happiness. Their companions on the journey, the "souls" of the creatures, objects, and elements that are part of their life, inspired some inventive design and performance, as lavishly revealed in pictorial and critical records. On the stages of Moscow and London (Paris followed Moscow's designs) some wonderful creations appeared: Fire, a dancer in flame-colored gauzes; Sugar, tall and thin with elongated fingers representing sugar sticks; Bread, a stout figure in crust-colored tights decorated with pretzels; Dog, with an appealing face halfway between man and dog, like one of the companions following the yellow brick road in *The Wizard of Oz*.

Was the play any more than a sentimental fantasy for children, with an appropriate mix of humor, dream adventures, and moral sentiment? Stanislavski thought it reached much beyond this.[5] He tried to bring out the spiritual quality that had moved him in first reading the play. The Moscow production was to be "delicate as lace": he envisaged a setting "naive, simple and light," in tune with the "happy illusion" of a childish dream but also suggestive of a deeper vision. He applied his usual method of training actors (as for playing Chekhov) to this otherworldly material. The actors in *The Blue Bird* were to work seriously at the task of imagining themselves into nonhuman modes of being. They were to study the individuality of some animal, or try to feel themselves limited to one essential attribute—the sweetness of sugar, the flow of water. They were to transport the audience into a dimension that might seem by the end of the play to be somehow "real"—more real than what is ordinarily called reality.

Stanislavski sensed in Maeterlinck a visionary mode of thought in which "absurdity" was an integral element. For an actor to imagine himself a loaf of bread or a tree could be seen as absurd (and often has been, in sarcastic criticism of Method exercises). But for Stanislavski this kind of imaginative exercise was the only way to a true rendering of Maeterlinck's vision. The aim was to capture the sense of things as they are, or as they might seem to the eye of innocence, viewing with simple immediacy: a childlike, not childish, view. The odd, bizarre, sometimes comical incidents of the play (like Sugar breaking off its long sugar-stick fingers for the delectation of the children) were not to be mere jokes. They were also intimations of a perspective on the universe.

Responses to the early productions, English as well as Russian, were clear about the moral notes in this perspective. Audiences appreciated that Tyltyl and Mytyl were meant to learn important lessons from their dream: that happiness is always there waiting to be realized, even in the poorest circumstances; that everything has a life of its own and everything is connected. The play was taken (perhaps especially by the English and Americans) as an edifying, optimistic morality—one that offered justifiable opportunities for heart-warming sentiment. Here again we must put the same question that arose apropos the romanticism of *Pelléas and Mélisande:* whether the moral sentimentalism brought out in early interpretations of *The Blue Bird* cuts the play off from modern audiences. Crucially, is that really the only way in which the play can be taken? Or has the recurrence of the word *absurd* in contemporary reactions to Maeterlinck some possible relation to the absurd of Martin Esslin's concept?

Stage history appeared at one time to supply a very negative answer to questions about Maeterlinck's continuing appeal. In the decades following 1918, a period inimical to symbolic dream plays, Maeterlinck steadily lost ground as a playwright whose work was performed, though he remained celebrated and read (his *Life of the Bee,* for instance, has never gone out of fashion). The plays did not cease to exert their influence. They helped to mold a context for Beckett and Pinter in the second half of the twentieth century, as earlier for Strindberg, Wilde, Yeats, and Synge. But with the exceptions of *The Blue Bird* and the operatic version of *Pelléas and Mélisande,* his drama was less and less frequently performed on the professional stage after the 1920s.

In the last decade or two, however, a change has occurred. Interesting new productions are increasingly seen, especially in Belgium and France. As the country of his birth and upbringing, Belgium might indeed be expected to honor him, but the style of some of these productions suggests something more than pious recognition of a national figure. A new, modern kind of interest is being shown in the theatrical potentialities of plays like *The Intruder* and *The Blind Ones.* The enterprising Henri Ronse has twice directed the latter play in Brussels within a period of two years (in 1980 and 1982). A text so loaded with symbolist decoration that it might have seemed to belong inexorably to the past proved capable of attracting two remarkably different styles of design and production. It was a live event, open to controversy.

This is more than a question of putting the plays into unexpectedly modern design styles, although that has proved an important starting point. The blind people's elegant white suits and white sticks in Ronse's production might have had a shock effect for anyone expecting to see a more traditional realization of Maeterlinck's stage directions. He envisaged his twelve blind characters sitting among the dead leaves of an ancient forest on stumps of trees and stones, dressed in "ample garments, sombre and uniform." Not a description to conjure up the cool, sophisticated image Ronse projected.

Yet the image was not inappropriate. Arguably, the brilliant clarity of Ronse's stage scene brought out Maeterlinck's theme—the painful and absurd incomprehensibility of life—better than a more muted, conventionally dreamy approach. In the hard bright light of a modern stage scene (with that modern idea of the absurd in the background) the odd, awkward moments of *The Blind Ones* can be played for all they are worth, for their absurdity value, so to speak. It is absurd, for instance, that everything is so symmetrical. The lost blind ones, just a little like Beckett's despairing seekers in *The Lost Ones*, are desperate for a system. They sit drawn up in neat rows, twelve in all, six of each sex, facing each other; frozen in a pattern we may come to feel is partly of their own making (the degree of their deprivation varies, the women being allowed more experience of "vision," a word whose double meaning is apparent from almost the start). It is also absurd, in a chilling way that takes us very close to the dark absurdities of Ionesco or, again, Beckett, that the blind are unaware of the presence among them of their sighted guide, the priest. He is sitting there, dead, hence undetectable by those for whom identity is determined by words and sounds. This makes a black joke of their irritated talk about him:

> Third Blind Man: It seems to me that he is leaving us alone too long.
> First Blind Man: He is growing too old. It appears that he has hardly been able to see for some time himself. He will not admit it in case someone else should take his place among us. I suspect that he can't see any more.[6]

Most absurd of all is the moment of discovery that he is still—in a way—among them. It is brought about by the irruption onto the stage of a dog that bounds unhesitatingly up to the dead man. In the first production of 1891, absurdity of the wrong kind resulted when the dog, instead of dragging the actor to the corpse, had to be pulled by him in the right direction. It was a droll demonstration at the start of his career of how dangerously narrow a track Maeterlinck was to tread in his departures from the "reasonable" convention—and, too, of how he needed to do this, for the correspondences between the nonhuman and the human world were deep at the heart of the mystical philosophy he espoused in the days of *The Blind Ones*. The animal has a natural knowledge from which the humans are cut off; some such message, uncomfortable to many, no doubt, was carried by the awkward dog.

It is just this element of danger that might now attract to Maeterlinck modern directors familiar with the absurd. In the last fin de siècle his plays came out under a different banner. The symbolist theater had deep-rooted associations with mysticism on the one hand and luscious pre-Raphaelite and art nouveau styles on the other. The pioneer audiences to Maeterlinck's drama often gained access to it through aesthetic associations. They submitted to a hypnotic artistic persuasion: seductive pre-Raphaelite versions of medieval costumes by Burne-Jones in *Pelléas and Mélisande* (with romantic acting to match by Martin-Harvey and Mrs. Patrick Campbell), or, in more austere form, the impression of dreamlike distance created by Lugné-Poe's gauzes, which kept the stage scene dim and mysterious. This could work very well, and Lugné-Poe created some mesmeric effects by such means. His production of *Interior* in 1895 seemingly realized Maeterlinck's attempt to cast a veil of strangeness over ordinary, day-to-day life by showing a family behind glass. (They are viewed, unknown to them, by someone aware of a tragedy, the death of a daughter of the house, of which they are ignorant).

Maeterlinck's stage direction for that particular effect creates a dreamlike impression that could well be served by a romantic symbolist approach:

When one of them rises, walks or makes a gesture, the movements appear grave, slow and apart, and as though spiritualised by the distance, the light and the transparent film of the window-panes.[7]

But there are other effects in *Interior* that call for a more saturnine modern approach: an Ionesco-like style would suit the Old Man, hovering and wavering before he can screw up courage to leave his onlooker's role, and the grotesque scene at the close when the silent garden is suddenly flooded with a crowd of people, all straining to look into the house and see the reactions of the stricken family.

In the theatrical ambience of the 1890s no chances could be taken with the odd and awkward elements in Maeterlinck's curious art. Early audiences and critics were sometimes uneasily aware of this aspect of his drama, but the object of the actors usually was to gloss over or avoid it. Directors normally cut from *Pelléas and Mélisande* the opening scene in which the unseen servants are heard inside the castle, trying with enormous difficulty to push open the great door; later they are seen trying to wash ever-resistant stains from the steps. The scene is never explicitly explained, but a strange explanation suggests itself at the end of the play, when the focus falls again on the servants and we hear how the wounded Mélisande and Golaud had been discovered by a servant "lying, both of them, in front of the door! . . . Just like poor folk that have been hungry too long. . . . There was blood on the stones." The play has gone round in a circle, it seems; the end was at some deep level known at the start.

Mrs. Patrick Campbell would not have been alone in finding the opening scene, as she said, "eccentric." Plot of a more or less realistic kind still ruled, for her as for most theater people of the time. Perhaps for that reason she also cut the scene in the castle vaults where Golaud takes Pelléas to the edge of the "little underground lake" that infects the whole castle with its deathly stench—and does no more than watch him intently, warning him of his nearness to the abyss. Nothing happens, nothing in terms of plot, that is. For a modern director this dip into the dark unconscious would present no problem. The lack of obvious connection with the advancing plot would give an opportunity to highlight not only the emotional understanding implicit in the characters' inarticulacies, but also the pattern of the unknown fate that lies beyond that fragile understanding and seems to mock it. Such scenes must surely take on for us the color of the absurd, with its black jokes, its freewheeling audacity.

A bold experimental approach, eschewing gauzes and medieval fairy-tale effects and seizing on the odd or bizarre elements in the plays, has been a feature of some recent French and Belgian productions of Maeterlinck. The stormy horrors of *La Princesse Maleine* have been located in a hospital, drawing the tale of the poor little princess and her world of castles, wicked stepmothers, and demented kings explicitly into the domain of the unconscious. *Aglavaine and Sélysette* has had its soulfulness put under a jaunty scrutiny, with a steel scaffolding to represent Sélysette's tower, and actors of acrobatic agility who changed clothes in front of the audience with indifferent aplomb as the text dictated their mercurial changes of heart.

The admittance of the absurd, as in this latter production by Françoise Merle (Théâtre d'Athenée, Paris, 12 January 1988) need not obliterate the psychological credibility that is an important source of Maeterlinck's power, but it is likely to change our perspective on the psychology, as on other features of the drama. In Merle's production Sélysette lost her aura of passive, pre-Raphaelite helplessness and was allowed some energetic encounters with her husband and with the friend who draws him from her supposedly by virtue of a superior personality. The audience was encouraged to think iconoclastically about the romantic aspects of the drama, including, crucially, the grand gesture made by Sélysette when she throws herself from her tower to leave the way free for Aglavaine and Meléandre. Why did she need to do this? Why did she not simply go away? enquired an early Aglavaine, Georgette Leblanc. Modern productions can afford to fasten onto such questions, following up hints provided by Maeterlinck himself (almost, indeed, against himself) in his risky admission of things that are freakish and odd.

Maeterlinck in English has had a poorer showing in the postabsurd theater than Maeterlinck in French. Among the reasons must be the awful Edwardian translations to the modern ear. The BBC took an important step to free Maeterlinck from this handicap when it commissioned a translation of *Pelléas and Mélisande* from Timberlake Wertenbaker for a new production of the play by Radio 3 in August 1988. It was the start of a Maeterlinck week. The BBC's broadcast of the play was followed later the same day by a partly staged concert version of Debussy's opera, and during the week music written for the play by Fauré, Sibelius, and Schoenberg was performed in the Promenade Concerts at the Royal Albert Hall.

In a preview to this remarkable week the BBC broadcast a discussion on Maeterlinck between Timberlake Wertenbaker and myself. Wertenbaker remarked that she felt the French were more ready than the English to accept plays about men loving women. The English liked their plays to be about women loving men. This interesting idea draws some reinforcement from the kind of hostility *Pelléas and Mélisande* met in England. Johnston Forbes-Robertson, who played Golaud (powerfully) in Mrs. Patrick Campbell's 1898 production, thought the play "weak and morbid." His brother Ian agreed, demanding, so the actress reported, "Why do you want to make such a damned fool of Forbes?" For this Englishman, it seems, there was something sickening in the sight of two grown men, and brothers at that, at the mercy of obsessive desire for a woman. Golaud is a mature man, almost old enough to be Pelléas's father; he has a young son by his first marriage. Yet he gives way so helplessly to desire for Mélisande that he marries her without knowing anything about her. He kills her (in effect) and Pelléas, without ever knowing whether they really are lovers. As she lies on her deathbed he is still ignorantly seeking: "It is time! It is time! The truth! The truth!"[8]

In such moments as this—when the desperate question receives only its own echo for answer (Mélisande repeats "The truth . . . the truth")—the play makes a characteristic move into modernity out of the rhetoric and melodrama that attaches it to the nineteenth century. The death of Mélisande is poignant, but the poignancy is inseparable from absurdity. Golaud comes to see himself as absurd when he accepts that he is "blind"; Maeterlinck's favored image for human incomprehension of life's mysteries. After his frustrating final conversation with the dying woman, he diagnoses his own condition with a generality that brings the modern absurd into the play:

> Yes, yes; you can come in . . . I know nothing; it is useless . . . It is too late; she is already far from us . . . I shall never know! . . . I shall die here like a blind man.

Pelléas too is enmeshed in absurdity. The celebrated scene, already mentioned, where, Rapunzel-like, Mélisande lets down her hair and Pelléas luxuriates in it, commonly drew some snickering from early audiences. This could no doubt be ascribed to philistinism, as irritated lovers of the play maintained, but still, it is an awkward scene, even in the operatic version where it is immeasurably helped by Debussy's persuasive music. Here again, however, the concept of the absurd suggests a way in for modern stage interpretation. Admit the absurdity in the episode, exaggerate perhaps the wildness of the youthful high spirits that produce it, instead of trying to enter into the romanticism (an impossible task for moderns); recognize its childishness. Golaud actually does perceive this for a moment when he moves out of the shadows to confront the pair. "You are children," he says, and "Don't play like this in the dark."

What is this dark but the dark of an unknowable universe that is the real ambience of the play? A coherent modern production of *Pelléas and Mélisande* would project this shadow, not by playing down the absurd but by registering it as the trap in which all are caught. They are groping after meaning in a world that yields no meaning. So a new emphasis would fall on the kaleidoscopic aspect of the play; its fascination with randomness, with apparently unrelated or inconsequential scenes; its bleak, ironic, and pitying view of the blindness inherent in the human situation.

In this perspective of the absurd there would be a vital role for the humble minor characters and the crowd scenes that often carry Ionesco-like undertones of the existential bizarre. The servants would figure here importantly: toiling to open the door so the play can begin—at the point where it might be supposed to have ended—and filing into the room where Mélisande is dying, to stand silently around the walls, returning blank silence to Golaud's question, "Why have you come here?—Nobody asked for you." There would be a sharp light on the young boy, Yniold, laboriously working away to lift a piece of rock ("It is heavier than all the world") or naively questioning an offstage shepherd about the reason for the sheep suddenly falling silent. The sense of a whole world waiting to be pieced together, if only one could do it, might be made to come through such incidents as the grotesque encounter in the sea cave with the three old beggars asleep on a ledge. A Beckettian image, almost, comically absurd and yet dark and disturbing.

The human drama of *Pelléas and Mélisande* need not lose its pathos if the emphasis is made to fall more aggressively on the absurd, grotesque, and impersonal elements in the story. We might in fact find it easier to feel sympathy with these fey, emotional beings if we, like them, were exposed in the theater to the full force of the menacing, indecipherable universe they inhabit, with its seeming penchant for grim jokes. The 1980 performance of *The Blue Bird* by the Rideau de Bruxelles gained immensely in human feeling as well as in intellectual vivacity by the mordant treatment of scenes that were once handled more sentimentally. Shades of *Endgame* hovered in the Land of Memory scene, which in the first London production had been played for nostalgia, with the grandparents, storybook rustics, inhabiting a dream cottage with roses round the door. In the Rideau production, when the children leave and the grandparents too must go (the dead have no existence outside the memory of others), the old pair step into the ominously bare box that had represented their living place. It is on castors, so they can be wheeled away, as if back to their dustbins. No cosy nostalgia here as in the first production. Maeterlinck's bleaker vision had been effectively realized in the form of a wry joke—for it was funny as well as disturbing when they were disposed of so smartly and economically.

A simplicity of approach that takes advantage of modern lighting and sound techniques but eschews elaborate sets is one way in to a more biting and stimulating treatment of the plays. Recognition of the humor—a quality Maeterlinck has sometimes been said to lack—is another. His is not exactly the sort of humor that causes delighted laughter, but it is there—in plenty in *The Blue Bird* but also lurking in the droll or absurd moments of the other plays: the frustrated effort to close a door in *The Intruder* or to open one in *Pelléas and Mélisande;* or the quirkiness of the blind grandfather, insisting that he can tell differences in the strength of light from the lamp beside him. (The first actor to play the grandfather in England, Beerbohm Tree, in 1892, recognized opportunities for expression of his own famously idiosyncratic personality: the long waiting of the blind for the invisible arrival of death in the house was not to be an entirely somber experience.)

The comedy in *The Blue Bird* was of course obvious to anyone who produced the play. For the producers at the Haymarket in 1909 it was a particularly appealing feature, promising great jollity in the style of English Christmas pantomime of the period. Maeterlinck's talking animals—faithful Dog, treacherous Cat—fitted easily into a tradition that accommodated the adventures of a female Dick Whittington, battling on the side of Good with the aid of a magic lamp and an accomplished talking cat. English pantomime delighted in mercurial changes of mood that brought the supernatural or magical elements into sharp contact with the comical. Maeterlinck allows many opportunities of this kind. The two children's ignorance of life produces some droll gaffes, as when they penetrate into the awesome Palace of Night (described in the stage direction as formidably austere and metallic) and humanize it a little with their naive greeting of the deity who presides there: "Good-day, Mrs. Night." "Good-day?," she snaps, "I am not used to that . . . You might say, Good-night, or, at least, Good-evening. . . ."[9]

The fun is real but to an eye or ear turned to the absurd the special interest of the comedy in *The Blue Bird* must be the affiliation it so often displays with that mode we think of as modern. Tyltyl's naïveté leads into some very black jokes on occasion, jokes that totter on the edge of horror. There should be something of that vertigo—so familiar in the theater of today—in the encounter of the children with the aggressively misanthropic trees, led by the blind and ancient Oak, and the animals that support them. "What have I done to you?" Tyltyl shouts, as an increasingly militant horde, freed to show its rage against humankind by the soul-releasing power of the magic diamond, closes in on him and his sister. The Sheep provides a reply that has a fearful kind of jocularity:

Nothing at all, my little man . . . Eaten my little brother, my two sisters, my three uncles, my aunt, my grandpapa and my grandmamma. Wait, wait, when you're down, you shall see that I have teeth also. . . .

Early audiences may have found it possible to dismiss this as "only" a nightmare that is dissipated when Light enters the stage as dawn breaks. Maeterlinck intended them not so easily to minimize his brooding fears about a universe in which human beings are newcomers, in some ways aliens. When Light saves the children, she only shows them how to silence the dread force of offended nature, not how to placate it. "They will return into silence and obscurity," she says, "and you will no longer perceive their hidden feelings." The feelings are still there, however, to be recalled the more easily for having found expression in the tart jokes the nonhuman world is shown to have at its disposal.

Maeterlinck would have recognized the opportunities offered by today's theater, with its experience of the absurd, for capturing his strange dramatic world. He looked back on his early plays from the mentally more comfortable position of his later life with a kind of shock that is exactly the feeling they should induce in audiences:

The keynote of these little plays is dread of the unknown that surrounds us. I . . . seemed to believe in a monstrous, invisible fatal power. . . . Its intentions could not be divined but the spirit of the drama assumed them to be malevolent always. . . . The problem of existence was answered only by the enigma of annihilation.[10]

This sounds like a manifesto for the absurd. Nowadays we have techniques well adapted to realizing Maeterlinck's staging concepts, but the subterranean depths he explores in acting out his metaphysical questioning present many pitfalls to modern directors, actors, and audiences. If the perspective of the absurd can help to restore a neglected theatrical treasure to English-speaking audiences, we will have yet one more reason for being in Martin Esslin's debt.

NOTES

1. For detailed accounts (with slide illustrations) of early productions mentioned in this article, see Katharine Worth, *Maeterlinck's Plays in Performance* (Cambridge, Eng.: Chadwyck-Healey, 1985).

2. Arthur Symons, *Plays, Acting, and Music* (London, 1903), 73–74.

3. *The Autobiography of Sir John Martin-Harvey* (London, 1933), 198–201.

4. *Times* (London) review of *Pelléas*, 2 July 1904.

5. Konstantin Stanislavski, *My Life in Art*, trans. J. J. Robbins (London, 1924), 498–504.

6. *Pelléas and Mélisande and The Sightless*, trans. Laurence Alma Tadema (London, 1895).

7. *Interior* is in *Three Plays by Maurice Maeterlinck*, trans. William Archer (London, 1911).

8. *Pelléas and Mélisande and The Sightless*, op. cit.

9. *The Blue Bird*, trans. Alexander Texeira de Mattos (London, 1909).

10. *The Buried Temple / Le Temple Enseveli*, trans. K. A. Sutro (London, 1902).

O'Neill and Absurdity

Linda Ben-Zvi

Four people pace back and forth on the stage. They talk, eat, sing, tell stories, emote, quote, and drink. Their words concern the mundane events of the day—weather, chores, neighbors. However, underlying the interminable small talk, and constantly surfacing when the action and the conversation cease, is the one reality they share: the pull of the past, or rather *pasts*, since all carry memories of an earlier time and an earlier self that make it impossible for them to participate fully in the present moment. Although they move in the same physical space, the four appear strangers to themselves and to each other, "irremediable exiles" from a lost time to which they desire to return, but cannot. The present cannot be lived because of the past; the past cannot be reclaimed because of vagaries of memory and the weight of the present. The future does not exist.

As if to mirror their situation, the play in which they appear takes on a particular shape. It circles in on itself. Just as the action is unresolved, the day fading to night and then to early morning, the play ends where it begins: in the same room at almost the same time. Yet nothing has changed. No one comes, no one goes. At the end they are as they were at the beginning. Nothing happens because there is nothing to be done. The only positive thing one can say is that their words passed time, but as another playwright noted, in a work written five years later, "it would have passed in any case."

33

Although set in the year 1912, the play, which took four years to write, was completed in 1941, four years before the date Martin Esslin uses in *Theatre of the Absurd* as the beginning of the epoch that produced what he calls absurd drama. Esslin argues that until the end of World War II "the decline of religious faith was masked . . . by the substitute religions of faith in progress, nationalism, and various totalitarian fallacies" (5). World War II, he says, gave rise to the "sense that the certitudes and unshakable basic assumptions of former ages . . . have been tested and found wanting . . . discredited as cheap and somewhat childish illusions" (4–5).

The playwright who wrote the work described above knew the absurdity of life and the loss of faith from an earlier age. The war only confirmed what he had experienced personally. "Senseless," "absurd," and "useless"—the words, taken from Ionesco, that Esslin uses in his introduction to demarcate the plays he is discussing— were the vocabulary of Eugene O'Neill as far back as 1901, when he discovered his mother's morphine addiction and lost his belief in God. A key document in the shaping of the absurdist vision, Nietzsche's 1883 *Thus Spake Zarathustra*, which Esslin cites at the beginning of his chapter "The Significance of the Absurd," was already familiar to O'Neill by 1908. "It has influenced me more than any book I've ever read. I ran into it . . . when I was eighteen and I've always possessed a copy since then and every year or so I reread it and am never disappointed," he wrote a friend in 1927 (Sheaffer, *S&P*, 121). Repeatedly throughout his career, when asked for his literary idol, he answered, "Nietzsche" (122).

Personally and intellectually, O'Neill, early in his life, renounced the possibility of a saving grace and a divine power. A lapsed Catholic from the age of thirteen, he found intellectual confirmation of his own apostasy and began to use the ensuing skepticism about easy answers or sham religions in his plays, starting with the Glencairn cycle first performed in 1916, in which a group of men spend their time talking, telling stories, singing, waiting for time to pass. Even in these early plays, one can find what Esslin describes as the element of the absurd, deriving from Nietzsche:

An effort to make man aware of the ultimate realities of his condition, to instil in him again the lost sense of cosmic wonder and primeval anguish, to shock him out of an existence that has become trite, mechanical, complacent, and deprived of the dignity that comes of awareness. (Esslin, 351)

O'Neill, like the playwrights of the absurd, was aware of the pain of existence in a postlapsarian world, where the possibility of salvation is absent, God dead, and human beings strangers to themselves, to each other, and to the physical world in which they live. His Tyrones, while fictive embodiments of the O'Neills, are also depictions of the modern family crushed by regret, recrimination, and aimlessness; playing what Kenneth Tynan called "the blame game," trying to fix responsibility for their present condition, while yearning for a past they only dimly remember.

The quotation that Esslin cites from Camus's *The Myth of Sisyphus* on the nature of the modern stranger—a quotation that has become something of an epigraph for Esslin's entire study—can be used, as I did above, to describe the characters in *Long Day's Journey into Night*. What is striking, however, is that O'Neill penned almost the same words as Camus, not in 1942, the year *Sisyphus* was written, but in 1922, and he placed them in the mouth of a coal stoker in the bowels of an ocean liner: "But me—I ain't got no past to tink in, nor nothin' dat's comin', on'y what's now—and dat don't belong" (O'Neill, *Hairy Ape*, 230).

The Hairy Ape and *Long Day's Journey* share many points of similarity with the plays Esslin labels absurdist. O'Neill uses as his theme the same metaphysical dilemma. He also fulfills the other requisite Esslin states: he attempts—sometimes successfully, sometimes not— to find a form to accommodate his vision and to present in "concrete stage images" (6) the "absurdity of the human condition" (5). Esslin's initial description of the form such a theater would take covers the majority of plays O'Neill wrote:

If a good play must have a cleverly constructed story, these have no story or plot to speak of; if a good play is judged by subtlety of characterization and motivation, these are often without recognizable characters and present the audience with almost mechanical puppets; if a good play has to have a fully explained theme, which is neatly exposed and finally solved, these often have neither a beginning nor an end; if a good play is to hold the mirror up to nature and portray the manners and mannerisms of the age in finely observed sketches, these seem often to be reflections of dreams and nightmares; if a good play relies on witty repartee and pointed dialogue, these often consist of incoherent babbling. (Esslin, 3–4)

O'Neill recognized that if he were to offer his particular vision of life on the stage, he would have to break with the dramatic traditions he had inherited: the melodrama, the well-made play, the farce. Working against restrictive forms, he was forced to invent his models, freed from all limitations except those of his own talent. In so doing he cleared the way for himself and for others to follow. To Russel Crouse, to whom he sent a copy of his Nobel address, he added his awareness of his legacy to other playwrights: "My pioneering . . . busted the old dogmas wide open and left them free to do anything they wanted in any way they wanted. (Not that many of them have had the guts to try anything out of the ordinary—but they could have)" (quoted in Sheaffer, *S&A*, 463).

It is not surprising that in his experimentation he turned to another iconoclast of the stage: August Strindberg. If Nietzsche was mentor for O'Neill's metaphysical nihilism, Strindberg was father to his experimental stagecraft. When O'Neill made his Nobel acceptance speech, he acknowledged both men. Esslin also credits Strindberg as an antecedent for the theater of the absurd who, like Nietzsche, began "the exploration of the reality of the mind" (355).

In his choice of mentors and in his plays O'Neill seems to follow closely the absurdist pattern Esslin describes. However, when making his choices of representative playwrights, Esslin does not include O'Neill; in fact, O'Neill is mentioned only once in the study, and this in relation to a much younger writer. It is easy to conjecture about the omission. Those playwrights Esslin analyzes began to write after 1945, the demarcated year; O'Neill had already written his last plays by that date. Also, he was too directly connected with an earlier school of writing, so that to see him as in some way related to absurdism would have muddied the very distinctions Esslin was attempting to establish between the old and the new theater.

What Esslin might well have done, however, was include O'Neill—as he did Strindberg and Ibsen—in that list of forerunners of absurdist theater, acknowledging O'Neill's kindred worldview and some of his dramatic experimentation that helped pave the way for later writers. Instead, O'Neill is absent from *Theatre of the Absurd*, and such was the immediate power of Esslin's seminal study and its continuing sway that O'Neill has remained on the other side of the critical divide. There are the absurdist dramatists—Beckett, Ionesco, Pinter, Albee—and there are the "others," who, for want of a more precise term, are generally labeled "realistic writers." O'Neill is usually consigned to the latter, nebulous category. Critics, by and large, are drawn either to one group or the other; few tastes spread wide enough to bridge the chasm that theater of the absurd opened.

Those critics who have suggested affinities among O'Neill, Beckett, and Pinter have been chary in their comparisons. For example, Normand Berlin begins a recent essay entitled "The Beckettian O'Neill" by saying that he doesn't want to push his thesis "so far that it seems absurd" (28). Jean Chothia, in the concluding chapter of her book *Forging a Language: A Study of the Plays of Eugene O'Neill*, is equally tentative. However, both add an "And yet." Chothia goes on to argue that, in fact, the reason that O'Neill gained an audience for his posthumously performed *Long Day's Journey into Night* and for the 1956 staging of *The Iceman Cometh* was that O'Neill's was not "a quaint voice but an urgent one . . . one that sounds both of and outside of its own time and presents us with pressing questions about our own being"—like that found in *Waiting for Godot* (Chothia, 187–88). She cites O'Neill's experimentation, which pushed realism "to the edge" and threatened it—again like the work of Beckett. Berlin shares her views, arguing that the 1956 production of *The Iceman Cometh* played to an audience more prepared than in 1946 to accept its nihilistic message, precisely because of the advent of *Godot*, published in English three years earlier.

Catherine Mounier, writing of a 1975 French production of *Iceman*, also notes the similarities between the play and *Godot*, which, she says, it seems to "anticipate." The comparison between the two plays becomes even more striking when Mounier lists the notes that director Gabriel Garran made concerning the costumes for the production—notes that could well have come from a directorial *regiebuch* for *Godot*:

> realistic, poetic, and burlesque conception of the costumes;
> deterioration, wear and tear, the bottom of the social ladder, slovenliness;
> must preserve individuality of each character;
> must suggest remnants of former stations in life;
> must suggest that clowning is part of attire;

midway between lost petit-bourgeois universe and more or less pronounced process of becoming derelict. (Mounier, 165).

These studies that place the theater of O'Neill, at least *The Iceman
Cometh*, in juxtaposition to Beckett's dramas are still, for the most
part, apologetic about the implied critical heresy—again a sign of the
resiliency of Esslin's initial categories. Yet the very power of a literary
movement is precisely that it illuminates not only those works included; it also illuminates what was present but not named—or recognized—in works of the past. One of the great contributions of
feminist criticism has been its reading or "re-vision," to use Adrienne
Rich's word, of past works in light of the critical tools and "visions"
of the present. Esslin's ideas in *Theatre of the Absurd* provide a means
for discovering possible absurdist elements in those plays that ante-
dated his discussion. Among the most interesting possibilities for
such a re-visionist reading are the works of Eugene O'Neill.

I am not trying to reinvent O'Neill as an absurdist. What I am
suggesting is that an analysis of O'Neill's canon in light of the work
of contemporary playwrights discloses themes and dramatic techniques of staging and language that O'Neill developed and that
would have corollaries in forms that flourished after 1945. Also, once
O'Neill is placed in conjunction with Beckett and with the theater of
the absurd, his plays become provocative in entirely new ways; readings become possible that were precluded before. In many ways the
Irish-American O'Neill, like the Irish Beckett, was attempting to
break with the dramas of the past and to forge a new language, and
was working fully aware of the limits of his craft and of himself.

Many elements in O'Neill's plays lend themselves to a comparative analysis; I will suggest only a few key areas, however, that indicate the connections between O'Neill and the absurdist theater. More
exist. The list derives from the central categories Esslin isolates as
characteristics of the absurd:

1. Stage and visual imagery
2. Character delineation
3. Dramatic language
4. Theatrical artifice

1. The obvious place to begin looking—as the critics cited above do—
for O'Neill images that most directly point to absurdist forms would

be in the late works *Long Day's Journey into Night* and *The Iceman Cometh*, written at a time when playwrights sensitive to the growing shadow of fascism would tend to produce similar works. Such imagery appears, however, far earlier in the O'Neill canon and is central to his vision from the very beginning of his career. For example, a rereading of O'Neill's sea plays in light of Esslin's discussion takes on a new, exciting configuration and reveals how early the playwright was experimenting with absurdist themes in new dramatic forms.

Too easily placed in the Jack London school of "sea adventures," O'Neill's sea plays are images of the awareness of a lost Eden. To reinforce this interpretation O'Neill employed a particular type of stage design. His sea plays—as most of his other works—are set in small, confined areas: forecastles, bunks, small rooms, stokeholes. The promised openness and desired freedom the sea should bring are always negated by the actuality of confinement or dispossession. Rather than escape, the characters seem exiled from a home they cannot recover, condemned—like Yank in *Bound East for Cardiff* and his namesake in the later *The Hairy Ape*—to fashion a surrogate home, salvaging the only dignity they can muster in a cold, hostile world. The settings are early stage metaphors for the enclosed spaces of Beckett, the tomblike rooms of Pinter. They are skullscapes as much as landscapes, where characters, when they talk at all, seem to be conversing with themselves.

In these sea plays almost nothing happens. Visual images of confinement act as metaphors for the ennui of the characters trapped in their cell-like rooms, waiting for their watches to end or for night to come. In *Bound East* O'Neill specifies the time: "It is nearing the end of the dog watch—about ten minutes to eight in the evening," that gray time of *Godot*, before the rise of the moon, of waiting.

The cramped forecastle is the only set visible in the play. The "outside," however, is signified repeatedly by the blast of the steamer's whistle. The sound summons the men to their rounds, punctuates their words, and underlines their silences. It is an early version of what O'Neill describes as the "inexorable whistle" that performs the same function in *The Hairy Ape*, a sound emanating from an unseen source. Its function is similar to Beckett's use of the whistle in *Act Without Words I*, or the bell in *Happy Days*: it controls but cannot be controlled by those who hear it. It is an aural reminder of the undemarcated "outside" just as the drumbeats of *The Emperor Jones* are a metaphor for the pulse within.

Presumably controlling the whistle in *Bound East*, but offering no assistance or comfort—no assuagement for grief or imminent death— is the impotent authority figure in the play, the captain, a visual image of the death of God. Before he arrives, he is already described as ineffectual. In this play there are no illusions about a Godot who will matter.

SCOTTY (sardonically):   He gave him a dose of salts, na doot?

DRISCOLL: Divil a thing he gave him at all, but looked in the book had wid him, and shook his head, and walked out widout sayin' a word. . . . (*Seven Plays of the Sea*, 37)

When the captain appears below deck, he is an old man with gray mustache and whiskers who talks in platitudes—"And how is the sick man" (43)—and who offers only a thermometer from his pocket and the warning "Here. Be sure and keep this in under your tongue, not over it" (43). In response to Driscoll's pleas for some help for his dying friend, the captain impatiently responds, "But, my good man, I'm not a doctor." All he can offer is the platitude "Keep up your courage! You'll be better tomorrow" (45). After he leaves, the dying Yank does not castigate the captain or even bemoan his own state. Instead he simply offers a prayer echoed in most of O'Neill's works: the desire for death, which will end the hell of living. "Whatever it is what comes after it can't be no worser'n this. I don't wanta leave you, Drisc, but—that's all" (46).

Seen in the context of absurdist drama, O'Neill, even as a young playwright, was already aware of the impossibility of warding off death or of finding solace from God or humans. The best that could be hoped for was the company of "buddies" who might somehow temporarily mitigate the sin of being born, which so many of O'Neill's characters recognize as their primary transgression. Moreover, O'Neill was already struggling with a dramatic form that would offer a concrete stage image of the situation of metaphysical angst. The small, cramped world of the bunks becomes a surrogate home. Outside is fog—the unknown in much of O'Neill; within is the solace of companionship.

A similar, concrete embodiment of the meaningless nature of life is presented in another Glencairn play, *The Moon of the Caribbees*. In it there is not even a death to move the plot forward. Out of the dark, sounds are heard; women appear, they board a ship, sell drink, sing and dance with the sailors, and leave. That is all. A mood piece, it, too, is a picture of what one does to pass time. And again O'Neill breaks stage conventions. At one point in the action all the characters go below; the stage remains empty, with noises barely audible from some unseen space. And again the nihilistic philosophy that O'Neill had already formed in 1916 is articulated, this time by Smitty, in perhaps the first speech in modern drama self-consciously deconstructing the platitudes and language of the period, an appropriate bit of cynicism by an expelled Ivy Leaguer, placed as it is in the mouth of the seaman: "We're poor little lambs who have lost our way, eh, Donk? Damned from here to eternity, what? God have mercy on such a we! True, isn't it, Donk," to which the Donkey Man responds, "Maybe; I dunno" (*Seven Plays of the Sea*, 19).

One of the best examples of what Esslin labels the "realities of vision" (Esslin, *Seven Plays of the Sea*, 372) of absurdist theater appears in another early O'Neill work, a play usually dismissed as his most narrowly drawn and clichéd realistic drama. O'Neill himself labeled *Anna Christie* a failure because it seemed to hew too closely to traditional plot constructions with its happy ending. Although he attempted to explain the fourth act reversal as "life flowing on, of the past which is never the past . . . of a problem solved for the moment but by the very nature of its solution involving new problems" (Gelb and Gelb, 481), he omitted the work from his collected plays and disparaged it in his later years. Yet a revisionist reading of *Anna Christie* offers some surprising nuances not immediately apparent if it is seen as just another version of the popular theater of the period. Instead, it can be read—and played—as an ironic commentary on the clichés of the melodrama from which it springs: the physical, handsome hero; the prostitute reformed by love; the comic father figure; even the happy ending, which O'Neill recognized is usually not very happy. As Esslin suggests, one of the functions of absurdist drama is precisely the parodying of clichéd life and of the clichéd dramatic forms that hold sway in conventional drama. More important, however, is the other goal Esslin describes: to offer visual images that indicate the struggles of humans in an absurd world, that dramatically present not just their foibles but their pain. *Anna Christie*, in one striking visual image, offers both the anticipated "happy ending" cliché *and* the very impossibility of any absolutes, surety, or easy happiness.

The scene takes place once more on the sea, again in the small, confining womb/room of a boat, this time a coal barge. Matt Burke, the romantic hero—an ironic throwback to the melodrama heroes of the earlier tradition—has returned to Anna, the reformed prostitute, another stage symbol reshaped by O'Neill. Matt's dilemma is how to determine whether Anna is honest when she says that he is the only man she has ever loved; moreover, how to be sure of the word *love*. In his anguish, he suddenly fixes on the crucifix his mother has given him, an icon he imbues with powers to save. "Would you be willing to swear an oath, now—a terrible, fearful oath would send your soul to the divils in hell if you was lying?" he asks Anna (155). Only after she eagerly agrees does Matt realize that her oath is meaningless; she no longer has religion. Even worse, when she did, it was Lutheranism. "Luthers, is it?" he explodes (159), usually causing laughter in the audience. Then with a grim resignation, slowly to himself he adds, "Well I'm damned then surely. Yerra, what's the difference?" (159) The moment is comic, as O'Neill, aware of the blend of the comic and the tragic in life, intended it to be. However, it also marks the recognition of the impossibility of surety–particularly of religious or iconic surety—in the modern world, a realization that is not so funny and that is at the heart of most absurdist works. It is Anna who offers the philosophical implications of such a position: "We're all poor nuts, and things happen, and we just get mixed in wrong, that's all" (142), a variation of what Beckett would later write: "That's how it is on this bitch of an earth."

I describe this scene at length because it is part of the problem with O'Neill. Even O'Neill critics tend to squirm at its "sappiness" and its echoes of set, formulaic drama. What I suggest is that O'Neill, like later playwrights, is playing with the very traditions he is exploding, and is doing so by making his characters just recognizable enough to point to the earlier forms he is parodying. At the same time he is also painfully sharing their dilemma. More like Beckett in *Godot* than Ionesco in *The Bald Soprano*, he positions himself with his characters, in the confusion, not looking down cynically from some elevated perch at their floundering. He, too, is "a crazy nut," "all mixed up." And he too keeps himself—at least in this scene, in this play—from pontifical language. Anna's "that's all," echoing the "that's all" of Yank in *Bound East*, is the simple, unadorned language of Didi and Gogo.

While O'Neill's early plays tend to be dismissed today by all but O'Neill lovers as "too easy," too realistic, it is instructive to remember that the first critical reviews they received echoed almost verbatim the initial reactions to absurdist postwar drama whose stage experimentations left the viewers confused and shocked. One critic writes of *The Emperor Jones*, "Absolutely nothing happens . . . yet by his vivid imagination and relentless power the author casts his spell over even the most pedestrian listener" (Miller, 23). Another, writing about *The Hairy Ape*, notes, "This certainly is not drama as we have known it; it is neither drama of realism nor of poetic suggestion. It is something new, something strange and something so profoundly theatrical that it can not be expressed or even imitated in a printed text" (Miller, 34).

Later O'Neill plays continue to employ equally arresting stage images: the brooding elms that "bend their trailing branches down over the roof" of the Cabot farmhouse in *Desire under the Elms*; Lavinia Manon, in *Mourning becomes Electra*, ascending to the portico of the Manon house, about to enter its tomblike interior for the last time; the drunken habitués of Harry Hope's bar, mechanically returning to their narcotized state at the end of *The Iceman Cometh*; Mary Tyrone, in the last moments of *Long Day's Journey into Night*, holding a visual image of her dream of youth in her arms: the tattered wedding dress in which she married James Tyrone. More than the words any O'Neill characters speak, it is the evocative power of the stage and visual imagery that O'Neill creates that shapes his plays. Like absurdist drama, as Esslin describes it, the plays of O'Neill are "not intended to tell a story but to communicate a pattern of poetic images" (Esslin, 354); they proceed "not by intellectual concepts"; they are "concerned essentially with the evocation of concrete poetic images designed to communicate to the audience the sense of perplexity that their authors feel when confronted with the human condition" (368). For Esslin, more than any other quality, it is the playwright's ability to capture metaphysical uncertainty in stage images that characterizes absurdist drama. Such stage images are O'Neill's most successful achievement.

2. A second characteristic of the plays described in *Theatre of the Absurd* is their particular delineation of characters that are usually not three-dimensional figures but tend to be generalized and flat, "almost mechanical puppets" (4), not "objectively valid" (354), "whose motives and actions remain largely incomprehensible" (361). Rather than trailing personal biographies behind them, people in absurdist plays are more often generalized representatives of the modern period, and are given few specific distinguishing personal features. The same could be said for most of O'Neill's characters, a fact that is often overlooked in the rush to connect O'Neill's dramas with his life. Jones, Yank, and the Glencairn sailors, for example, are as much specters of modern alienation as they are personae representing actual people O'Neill knew, the Tyrones as much the modern family as they are the embodiments of O'Neill's own.

O'Neill's characters tend to be modern mythic figures. They share another attribute of absurdist characterization: they are usually fragmented personalities. In the preface to *Miss Julie*, Strindberg called attention to the implications of the new psychology—particularly of the fractured nature of the self—for theater. Following Strindberg, O'Neill recognized that personality could best be shown as a series of sometimes contradictory faces and voices held together by the controlling image of the external self. He worked on depicting the dualities of self on the stage throughout his career, but particularly during the years from 1924 to 1939—commonly referred to as his middle period—during which he produced *The Great God Brown*, *Lazarus Laughed*, *Mourning Becomes Electra*, *Strange Interlude*, *Marco Millions*, and *Dynamo*. In these works, O'Neill is at his most lugubrious, least absurdist, most turgid. Such works may be the reason that Esslin dismissed him out of hand as having no connection with the playwrights he discusses. Yet even in these plays, in works that often fail painfully, one can still see the playwright struggling toward a theater where a character's inner thoughts can be staged, and where the dualities of self can be incorporated into a new theatrical form— all goals of the absurdist dramatists. Like Beckett after him, O'Neill recognized that a person is a simultaneity of selves and that a character could not with impunity use the first-person pronoun without acknowledging a *me*, unseen but existing under the imprint of an *I*.

The masks of *The Great God Brown* are one way that O'Neill found to indicate on the stage the multiple nature of the self. In his essay

"Memoranda on Masks," written in 1932, O'Neill discussed the technique:

> One's outer life passes in a solitude haunted by the masks of others; one's inner life passes in a solitude hounded by the masks of oneself. . . . what, at bottom, is the new psychological insight into human cause and effect but a study in masks, an exercise in unmasking? (quoted in Sheaffer, *S&A*, 403)

Masks, first used by O'Neill in *The Emperor Jones* and *The Hairy Ape*, become the central device of character portrayal in *The Great God Brown*, where all the characters indicate their public and private natures by their use. While the stage business is awkward in its execution, O'Neill is struggling to be true to his conception of the self as fragmented and the obligation of the playwright to show—not deny—this fragmentation. Later plays abandon actual masks, but they continue to indicate through the stage directions that actors are to assume masklike expressions that are constantly to be readjusted to protect them from revealing too much of their inner feelings or of the often contradictory nature of their personalities. Much of the action of *Moon for the Misbegotten*, for example, involves shifts in facial expressions as the Hogans and James Tyrone mask their feelings.

A second technique O'Neill experimented with in his search for authentic character delineation was what he called "thought asides," in which characters speak their thoughts directly to the audience. They are attempts to introduce traditional asides and soliloquies into modern psychological drama, freezing the action while long speeches indicate the complex motivations and desires of characters. In *Strange Interlude*, the only play in which O'Neill used the device, the speeches are awkward at best, but they once more indicate O'Neill's continual search for means to externalize the inner self—something later playwrights will continue to try to do.

The asides also point to another, later development in absurdist theater: the blurring of genre distinctions. O'Neill described the nine-act, seven-hour *Strange Interlude* as "wedding the theme for a novel to the play form" (Sheaffer, *S&A*, 288). In attempting to do on the stage what novelists do in fiction—allow the characters an outlet for their private thoughts as well as for their public utterances—O'Neill is experimenting with the coalescence of genre forms, something that

Beckett will do with far more success, using narrative in his dramas and dramatic devices in his prose.

A third attempt to depict the inner and outer self on the stage was O'Neill's experimentation with monologues. O'Neill was fascinated with the form. He realized, before Beckett and Pinter, that often what passes for dialogue is at best mutual monologue, two conversations that go on sometimes simultaneously, sometimes sequentially. Like Chekhov before him—whose work also prefigures absurdist writing—O'Neill wrote speeches where characters are actually talking not to the ostensible recipient of the discourse but to themselves. They either relive their pasts, as the Tyrone family does in *Long Day's Journey*, or speak their inner thoughts aloud like Emperor Jones. Throughout his career, O'Neill reworked the monologue: in *Before Breakfast* (1916), *The Emperor Jones* (1921), *Strange Interlude* (1927), and his last completed one-act play, *Hughie* (1941), where he finally achieved a successful rendering of the technique. Yet even in his failures he pointed the way to later dramatists who could find means—as Beckett does in *That Time* and *A Piece of Monologue*, or as Pinter does in *Monologue*, for example—to offer a character's thoughts superimposed on an external image of the self.

Hughie is O'Neill's most successful attempt to push the bounds of character delineation on the stage in the direction later writers will take. Less a contrived tour de force, as in *Jones*, the monologue of Erie Smith, addressed ostensibly to the night clerk, seems a natural extension of the character's need to be heard and understood. Like so many of Beckett's characters, Erie must have an audience to validate the self he wishes to project: reminiscent of Hamm in *Endgame*, he needs someone to hear his chronicle; like Winnie in *Happy Days*, he cannot bear to be alone. He is a big-time, successful gambler only if his touchstone, Hughie, believes in him. Having lost Hughie, Erie has lost himself. With the advent of the second Hughie, the next in a string of night clerks who seem to wend their way westward like so many interchangeable Beckett figures, Erie once again finds solace and hope in the discovery of a compliant audience for his "act" (what O'Neill, in professional eclipse, might well have wished for himself in 1941).

O'Neill also experiments with monologues in other plays that are not given over entirely to the form: the memories of each of the

Tyrones in *Long Day's Journey,* Hickey's long "confession" in *The Iceman Cometh,* and James Tyrone's equally long "confession" in the last act of *Moon for the Misbegotten* clearly point the way to the embedded monologue forms of Pinter and even beyond to the plays of Sam Shepard, for whom O'Neill also acts as an antecedent.

3. If character depiction clearly links O'Neill to those playwrights Martin Esslin discusses, language is a more thorny problem. On the surface, the subject of O'Neill and language would seem the area most difficult to reconcile with the practices of the absurdists. In his book Esslin makes clear that the absurdist playwright "tends toward a radical devaluation of language, toward a poetry that is to emerge from the concrete objectified images of the stage itself" (7). O'Neill, as I have shown above, creates arresting stage images, but he seems not to offer a commensurate displacement away from traditional stage language. Rather than "devaluing language," O'Neill offers a reified vocabulary, not held in check but often allowed unbridled excess.

It is not that O'Neill bore any illusions about the power of words to convey meaning; what he wrote about language could have been written by any whom Esslin included in his study:

> One gets weary and bewildered among the broken rhythms of this time. One misses one's beat and line of continuity, one gets the feeling of talking through a disconnected phone, foolishly to oneself. (quoted in Chothia, 41)

In O'Neill's case, however, his own frustration over what he called his "tin ear" made him often place the failure of his words on his personal limitations. "Oh, for a language to write drama in! For a speech that is dramatic and isn't just conversation," he wrote (Gelb and Gelb, 698). O'Neill believed his stage language to be his weakest area. Critics have agreed. Some, like Bernard DeVoto and Mary McCarthy, fault his endless repetitions; others, like Eric Bentley (an early champion of O'Neill), criticize his unnecessarily long speeches (Miller, 108–12; 146–57).

O'Neill *is* windy, repetitive, verbose. The exclamation point *is* his favorite mark of punctuation. However, O'Neill's logorrhea may be

a response to the same problem absurdist playwrights and all modern
writers face: the limits of, and possible human bewitchment by, language.

As much as O'Neill faulted himself for his linguistic limitations,
he was also aware of the banality of much that passed for communication in his own day:

> And, by way of self-consolation, I don't think from the evidence of all
> that's being written today, that great language is possible for anyone
> living in the discordant, broken, faithless rhythm of our time. The best
> one can do is be pathetically eloquent by one's moving dramatic inarticula-
> tions. (quoted in Chothia, 106)

O'Neill reflects the disenchantment with language expressed by
linguistic philosophers Ludwig Wittgenstein and Fritz Mauthner,
thinkers who influenced the theater of the absurd by their critiques
of the limits of language, critiques that underscored the impossibility,
finally, of extracting oneself from what Beckett would call the "unalterable whey of words" (Beckett, *Collected Poems*, 30). Thinking, they
argued, was impossible without speaking, words being vague refer-
ents of already receding memories of the sensory world. To describe
this entrapment by language, Esslin uses this quotation from
Wittgenstein's *Philosophical Investigations:* "A picture held us captive.
And we could not get outside it, for it lay in our language, and
language seemed to repeat it to us inexorably" (Esslin, 358). "We are
incapable of keeping silent," Gogo tells Didi in *Godot.* For Pinter, words
become stratagems to cover the nakedness silence uncovers.
Implicit in the writing of both playwrights is the recognition that language
says little; rather, it serves to illustrate the little that can be said.

In many ways, O'Neill's stage language does similar service; his
"pathetic" eloquence provides yet another response to the same linguistic collapse. In his plays, particularly the later ones, characters
talk endlessly so that they will not have to think. They engage in
dialogues so that they will not have to be alone and hear themselves
in the silence. O'Neill's famous retort to those who said that the
characters in Harry Hope's bar repeat ideas eighteen times—"I meant
for them to say the same thing eighteen times"—points to his awareness of the necessity for repetition in his plays, as a mirror of the
repetitions in normal conversation. In the same way that characters

in a Pinter play will repeat words and phrases almost as incantations, often fixing on sound rather than sense to establish signification, O'Neill's characters, in his middle and late plays, blabber on and on in repetitive and revealing patterns of discourse. They cannot seem to stop themselves from speech. "For god's sake be quiet," James Tyrone tells his wife, but she cannot stop replaying the memories of the past in the worn rhetorical phrases she uses. She can no more be quiet than she can stop sinking into her morphine haze, for without both words and drugs she must face the realities of the present.

Linguistically, Mary Tyrone is sister to many of the women in Beckett. She resembles Maddy Rooney, in *All That Fall*, who calls herself "just a hysterical old hag" who cannot stop talking, to herself or to others, and who—like Mary—is not understood. "I use none but the simplest words, I hope, and yet I sometimes find my way of speaking very . . . bizarre," she says (Beckett, *Collected Plays*, 35). Mary also has much in common with that unseen, unnamed woman in *All That Fall*, whose musical sign, "Death and the Maiden," marks Maddy's outward and homeward trip and whose plight causes Maddy to commiserate: "All alone in that ruinous old house" (Beckett, *Collected Plays*, 12). Beckett's use of music to indicate the loneliness that cannot be put into words is echoes by the foghorns that punctuate the talk in *Long Day's Journey*, aural equivalents of Mary's nonverbal cries.

Mary prattles like Maddy. Like Winnie in *Happy Days* she touches her hair, makes small talk, and relives her past, more to herself than to her husband. However, for both women there are times when even words fail. It is then that the rituals of daily life must suffice. O'Neill, like Beckett, provides his women with stage business to fill the interstices between words. For Mary Tyrone, it is the overseeing of meals; for Winnie the rummaging in her capacious bag. For both, the physical actions are reminders of the failure of language to fill time completely while waiting and to completely express their needs.

This failure of language is not gender-specific in either playwright. O'Neill also gives the Tyrone men individual monologues in which they struggle to find words to explain their deepest desires. Talk is the "dope" on which they, too, are hooked. And they, too, go through established routines when words fail: cutting the hedges, and going into town, the latter possible since they, like Beckett's Willie, are afforded a mobility precluded for Winnie and Mary. "Will you never finish," Hamm asks Clov in *Endgame*. "Will this never finish?" (23). Underlying the four hours of *Long Day's Journey* are the same questions. O'Neill's characters, even more than Beckett's, are "inexhaustible."

Another linguistic connection between O'Neill and the absurdists is their shared recognition of the relation between language and memory. "Yesterday"—"that bloody awful day, long ago, before this bloody awful day" (*Endgame*, 43–44) is the stage time for all O'Neill characters: Jones, Yank, Lavinia Manon, Nina Leeds, the Tyrones, and especially the habitués in *Iceman*. Jimmy Tomorrow's name may point to a future for himself and his friends, but the advent of Hickey reveals that tomorrow, "the Feast of All Fools" as Larry Slade calls it, will never come since the characters' language is frozen in some memory of yesterday. The perpetuation of the group pipe dream— and by extension, O'Neill indicates, the American societal pipe dream of the 1940s—is dependent on a shared language of clichés and euphemisms, of frozen forms; a language of the past. Memory is finally only a construct of language; it exists in no other form. Yet by the evocative power of words, it can submerge all attempts to live in the present or move into "tomorrow." "I can remember," Edmund Tyrone tells his father as he recreates the feelings of life on a sailing ship. "It was in those days," James Tyrone begins when he sketches the events of his childhood to his son. For them, as much as for Mary Tyrone and Jamie, language is all that remains of the dreams of the past. And since they only seem alive in their memories, when they sink into silence, as the men do at the end of *Long Day's Journey* or the drunks do after they return from the "outside" in *Iceman*, they appear dead. O'Neill's stage directions indicate that the silent figures who have been forced by reality or booze to stop speaking are "corpses."

O'Neill's most famous director, José Quintero, may have been touching on some of these points of linguistic experimentation when he commented on his experience in directing the successful 1956 *The Iceman Cometh*, the production that seemed most nearly Beckettian in its tone:

> It resembles a complex musical form, with the themes repeating them-
> selves with slight variation, as melodies do in a symphony. . . . My work
> was somewhat like that of an orchestra conductor, emphasizing rhythms,

being constantly aware of changing tempos. . . . The paradox was that for the first time as a director, I began to understand the meaning of precision in drama—and it took a play of four and one half hours long to teach me, a play often criticized as rambling and overwritten. (Quoted in Raleigh, 32–33)

Unlike O'Neill, Beckett is brief; his brevity a part of what has been labeled Beckettian. And yet Quintero's words are strikingly similar to those of Beckett's directors, leading one to wonder if O'Neill's verbosity might not be a variation on the same theme Beckett develops: the impossibility of words to convey meaning. What O'Neill may be doing with his endless repetitions "with slight variations" is to underline the same verbal aimlessness, open-endedness, and meaninglessness that many of the absurdist dramatists achieve in their abbreviated works. Endless words or silences and pauses may come down to the same thing: "a stammer," as Edmund Tyrone, O'Neill's persona, explains to his Shakespeare-quoting father in *Long Day's Journey*, "faithful realism," since "stammering is the native eloquence of us fog people" (154).

4. The final area I wish to explore briefly has to do with O'Neill's use of what—for want of another phrase—I call theatrical artifice. By that I mean a self-conscious calling of attention to the dramatic form and dramatic devices. Absurdist playwrights often point to the fact that their plays are, at best, fictive renderings of some reality impossible ever to depict. For instance, rather than talk about issues, modern characters often talk about talk. Like the men in Pinter's *The Dumb Waiter*, they may make grammar the subject of their exchanges.

O'Neill's use of self-reflexive techniques can be seen in his stage dialogue. For example, in *The Iceman Cometh* the characters indicate the power of words to create images of reality and hold their speakers captive. Rocky fights to retain the title "bartender." As long as he is bartender he is not "pimp"; his "goils" are "tarts," they are not "whores." One of the first results of Hickey's appearance is the uncovering of delusions foisted by word choice. Joe Mott is not "the whitest man in the place"; he is black. The men are not "resting" while waiting for tomorrow; they are drunk, sunk into the torpor of yesterday. However, rather than disguise these plays of language,

O'Neill foregrounds them, nearly swamping the verisimilitude of his plot and his setting in the wake of his awareness that his play is at bottom a tale of words.

O'Neill calls attention to language as language; he also creates plays in which characters self-reflexively call attention to themselves as actors and the play as artifice. In scene 1 of *The Emperor Jones*, Jones tells Smithers how he has been "playin" emperor. He knows that it is a role whose options for renewal are limited. Dion Anthony is clearly playacting; beneath the masked face of the actor is the real person who is unseen by the audience for whom he plays. At the same time the other characters are playing roles: all actors who are acting actors acting. In a similar "metalevel" maze, the staged set of the back room of the Hope Bar is itself disclosed as a stage where actors take turns playing and replaying their pasts to an always acquiescent audience of drunks. And in *Long Day's Journey*, what do the Tyrones do but "act": for each other, for themselves. They quote, emote, and "play" roles. They even call attention to their artifice. For example, when Edmund hears Jamie enter, he calls out in the mock seriousness of the melodrama, "Well, that sounds like the absent brother" (154). When James Tyrone wants to make a point, he immediately turns to quotations: "There's nothing wrong with life. It's we who—[he quotes] 'The fault dear Brutus . . .'" (152).

Unfortunately, the manipulation of artifice in the work is often lost when critics choose to read the play only as biography. Mary Tyrone's character, for example, may derive from events in O'Neill's family, but the crafting of her last speech, where she is lost to the present and her familial audience, as they are lost to her and to each other, is pure stage artistry, and O'Neill seems to emphasize the fact by having Jamie herald her "stage" entrance—"The Mad Scene. Enter Ophelia!" (170)—and her perform her greatest conjuring routine herself: metamorphosing before their eyes—and our own—into the girl she wishes she were, just as completely—and miraculously—as Billie Whitelaw, at the end of *Rockaby*, returns to her girlhood as she sinks into death.

A Moon for the Misbegotten, O'Neill's last completed full-length play, is even more self-consciously theatrical. As James Robinson points out in a recent essay entitled "The Metatheatrics of *A Moon for the Misbegotten*," all the characters assume roles and make their roles apparent. Josie Hogan "plays" at being a whore, the Hogans play "politeness" and "argument." James Tyrone, in the last-act monologue embedded in the work, calls particular attention to his performance: "Rise of curtain Act four stuff" (*A Moon for the Misbegotten*, 111). As Robinson suggests, O'Neill, the playwright, is calling attention to his own act-four manipulations through his persona. He is also self-consciously poking fun at the dramatic form itself and its inability to stretch to fit the shape of human need and human suffering.

One intention of his premeditated undermining of dramatic techniques may be to shatter the parameters of traditional theater, particularly the melodramas on which he was raised. Edmund Dante's "the world is mine" is not so much banished in O'Neill's plays as it is exposed by O'Neill's repeated references to the creaky underpinnings of the form. In much the same way that Ibsen slyly dangled the question mark at the end of *Ghosts* in order to parody and thereby explode forever the tidy endings of the well-made plays of his time, O'Neill seems to tweak himself, his father, and his period by reminding audiences of what still passed for drama in 1945, the year he completed *Moon for the Misbegotten*. Just as Beckett will have his ham actor announce his final speech with "I'm warming up for my last soliloquy" (*Endgame*, 78), O'Neill will indicate to the audience, by means of the characters' histrionic flourishes, the self-conscious posing that masks and often causes their real suffering.

Besides these four areas, there are others that link O'Neill and the absurdist writers: the circular shape of many of the plays; the brooding sense of "nothingness" often denoted by stage lighting in "shades of the colour grey" (Beckett, *Collected Plays*, 248); the evocation of other places and people that are never seen on stage and exist only in the speeches of the characters; the nonverbal use of the voice—for example at the beginning of *The Hairy Ape*—indicating the cacophony from which speech emerges. There are more. Yet even this brief discussion should make clear that O'Neill has within the body of his work many elements that are early examples of the theater Esslin isolated for critical consideration in his 1961 study. Had Esslin chosen to, he could well have begun his discussion not with the San Quentin performance of *Waiting for Godot* but with selected O'Neill plays that indicate O'Neill's struggle to find a form to accommodate the mess of modern existence.

Like Beckett, Pinter, and other absurdist dramatists, O'Neill recognized the absurd nature of life:

> Life is a farce played by a baboon who feels in his invertebrate bones a vision that, being an ape, he cannot understand. He scratches his fleas absently, with melancholy eyes and then hangs upside down on the nearest branch and plays with his testicles. (quoted in Bogard, 419)

He also recognized the potential of the theater to comment on such existence:

> Life in terms of life cannot reveal more to us than our own bewilderment. Life in terms of the theatre, as an art separate from the simulacra of what we term reality may find expression in the great force of which that reality is but a symbol. . . . (quoted in Chothia, 38)

His plays have within them both the awareness of modern futility and the need to find dramatic articulation of this nullity. Although predating the period, they contain the kernel of what Esslin demarcates as absurdist, and gain in power, stature, and interest, I believe, when read as such. They are also important as historical foreshadowings of the theater that was to follow, the theater of Beckett, of Pinter, and later of Shepard and Mamet, a theater that O'Neill may in part be responsible for foretelling, even for influencing, but which has yet to train its gaze back on him and his plays.

Martin Esslin concludes his discussion in *Theatre of the Absurd* with the comment,

> Only when its inventions spring from deep layers of profoundly experienced emotion, only when it mirrors real obsession, dreams, and valid images in the subconscious mind of its author, will such a work of art have that quality of truth, of instantly recognized general, as distinct from merely private, validity that distinguishes the vision of a poet from the delusions of the mentally afflicted. (370–71)

In many of the best works of Eugene O'Neill the seeds of such a theater are present, and can be seen, retroactively, in light of Esslin's study.

WORKS CITED

Beckett, Samuel. *Collected Poems in English and French.* New York: Grove, 1977.
———. *The Collected Shorter Plays of Samuel Beckett.* New York: Grove, 1984.
———. *Endgame.* New York: Grove, 1958.
———. *Waiting for Godot.* New York: Grove, 1954.
Berlin, Normand. "The Beckettian O'Neill." *Modern Drama* 31 (1988): 28–34.
Bogard, Travis, and Jackson Bryer, eds. *Selected Letters of Eugene O'Neill.* New Haven: Yale University Press, 1988.
Chothia, Jean. *Forging a Language: A Study of the Plays of Eugene O'Neill.* London: Cambridge University Press, 1979.
Esslin, Martin. *Theatre of the Absurd.* Garden City, N.Y.: Anchor, 1961.
Gelb, Arthur, and Barbara Gelb. *O'Neill.* Rev. ed. New York: Harper, 1973.
Miller, Jordan Y., ed. *Playwrights Progress: O'Neill and the Critics.* Chicago: Scott, 1965.
Mounier, Catherine. "Notes on the 1967 French Production of *The Iceman Cometh.*" In *Eugene O'Neill's Critics: Voices from Abroad,* ed. Horst Frenz and Susan Tuck, 163–68. Carbondale: Southern Illinois University Press, 1984.
O'Neill, Eugene. *Anna Christie / The Emperor Jones / The Hairy Ape.* New York: Vintage, 1972.
———. *The Iceman Cometh.* New York: Vintage, 1957.
———. *Long Day's Journey into Night.* New York: Vintage, 1984.
———. *A Moon for the Misbegotten.* New York: Vintage, 1974.
———. *Seven Plays of the Sea.* New York: Vintage, 1972.
———. *Six Short Plays of Eugene O'Neill.* New York: Vintage, 1951.
———. *Three Plays of Eugene O'Neill.* New York: Vintage, 1959.
Raleigh, John Henry. *The Plays of Eugene O'Neill.* Carbondale: Southern Illinois University Press, 1965.
Robinson, James A. "The Metatheatrics of *A Moon for the Misbegotten.*" In *Perspectives: O'Neill, New Essays,* ed. Shyamal Bagchee, 61–75. English Literature Series. Victoria, B.C.: University of Victoria Press, 1988.
Sheaffer, Louis. *O'Neill: Son and Artist.* Boston: Little, Brown, 1973. Cited in the text as *S&A.*
———. *O'Neill: Son and Playwright.* Boston: Little, Brown, 1968. Cited in the text as *S&P.*

Tradition and Innovation in Ionesco's La Cantatrice chauve

JAMES KNOWLSON

Several decades separate us from the opening of Eugene Ionesco's first play, *La Cantatrice chauve*, at the tiny Théâtre des Noctambules in Paris in May, 1950, and that may help us to consider the play in theatrical as well as historical perspective. The main intention of this essay is to examine what was old and what new (as well as how the old came to be radically transformed) in a play that appeared startlingly innovative and which, after all this time, still strikes me as a surprising, challenging, but also extremely disquieting piece of theater. Looked at from this perspective, some of the predecessors of the theater of the absurd and the influences upon it, which were first analyzed by Martin Esslin, may emerge as rather more important than has so far been the case. By pursuing suggestive hints from Martin Esslin's book, I want to employ a number of parallels and comparisons with earlier drama to establish Ionesco's achievements in the play that continues a record-breaking run at the Théâtre de la Huchette.

La Cantatrice chauve is described by Ionesco on the title page as an antiplay, and he has often referred to it himself as "a true parody of a play, a comedy of a comedy" (*NCN*, 189). It is a complex interplay of theater and antitheater. The success of *La Cantatrice chauve* depends to a great extent on what the spectator brings by way of expectations relating to plot, character, and language, as well as on what Ionesco deliberately invokes within the play, by means of parody of conventional theatrical devices that were common to many earlier plays, and not only those of boulevard theater.

Beyond mere parody, Ionesco aims to mock, challenge, fragment, and, ultimately perhaps, explode a cozy, conformist, Cartesian view of reality. The dramatist has said as much himself in his critical writing and interviews, but these wider implications, as well as the humor of the play, depend on an unusual transformation of assumed norms—of theater just as much as of human behavior and rational thought. Within Ionesco's stage world, nonsense, fantasy, and nightmare are given "the concrete and obvious properties of ordinary reality" (Guicharnaud, 218). Partly through the apparent normality of response of his characters to the proliferation of words (or rhinoceroses), to bodies growing, or to a world that is in the process of contracting and crumbling, Ionesco questions, threatens, and sometimes undermines those norms that lurk behind the stage world or are brought to it from the outside by the spectator. (Samuel Beckett did something similar in *Happy Days* when he buried Winnie in her mound of earth, as if this were the most natural thing in the world— as, in Beckett's own terms, it was.) One of the effects of such assumptions of normality, as we are confronted by Ionesco's unusual approach to reality, is that "our world is neither more nor less justified than what unfolds on stage and can be considered quite as ridiculous" (Guicharnaud, 218). The starting point for such a challenge to accepted norms begins in Ionesco's first play, with the forms of its theater.

The most immediate and obvious feature of conventional theater that is presented in parodied form in *La Cantatrice chauve* is the setting. A mere glance at any collection of late nineteenth-century French *comédies* or *comédies dramatiques* by authors such as Augier, Sardou, Alexandre Dumas fils, Labiche, and Barrière shows plays that begin with the traditional box set, an "intérieur bourgeois" of a town or country house, "un salon donnant sur une salle à manger," "un salon de rez de chaussée," looking out sometimes on to a garden. Inside the proscenium arch stand the furnishings, drapes, and ornaments of a bourgeois interior. The conventionality of such a form of theatrical decoration was one of the reasons why the naturalism of André Antoine's Théâtre Libre, with its more authentic sets depicting a peasant cottage or a butcher's shop, caused such a stir in the early 1890s.

In *La Cantatrice chauve* the armchair and slippers, the newspaper and pipe, and the man's socks being darned by the fireplace of this "English interior" are far more cozy and "down-market" than the fluted champagne glasses and sumptuously laden tables of the earlier, upper bourgeois setting. Ionesco has merely substituted a mid-twentieth-century, supposedly English, stereotype for a late nineteenth-century French one. The Smiths and the Martins have all their own resolutely middle-class accoutrements and associations: a maid-cum-cook, but no other servants; good, solid English food (albeit with a decidedly French concern for the quality of the salad dressing!), washed down with English beer and served with a side order of prudential English morality.

At the opening of the curtain, the setting of the play and the appearance of its characters blend to suggest that this is to be yet another piece of comfortable, stereotyped family drama masquerading as naturalism. Indeed, it would be quite destructive of what follows if a director were to work against Ionesco's explicit stage directions and distort the conventional nature of this reality by creating a fantasy set that was not grounded in an accepted theatrical reflection of apparent normality.

Ionesco wastes no time at all in challenging and undermining these assumptions. Before Mrs. Smith opens her mouth to speak, the clock on the mantelpiece insists on being heard with its own noisy, alogical intrusion, from which Mrs. Smith nonchalantly draws her own quite unperturbed, normal conclusion—for alogic is an essential part of Mr. and Mrs. Smith's everyday diet. The opening line, "There it's nine o'clock," is a laugh line, since the audience recognizes this immediate deviation from the normal and the logical. Clocks in that kind of suburban setting do not strike seventeen times, or if they do, Mrs. Smith's words to her husband might be: "There goes that clock again. Why don't you get it fixed? I've asked you to do it a thousand times already!" Mrs. Smith reaches a conclusion that is satisfying to herself and in no way surprising to her husband. In this stage world the abnormal is treated as if it were thoroughly normal; the striking clock and the conclusion drawn from it reflect a conventional form of theater and a cozy, comforting reality that are distorted as they are being echoed.

Another object of parody is the theatrical device of the recognition scene. There are two recognition scenes in the play, which emerge from and hark back to examples of the same device in, for example, Shakespeare, Molière, Sheridan, and Beaumarchais. First, Mr. and Mrs. Martin recognize each other as man and wife. Second, the maid Mary and the visiting Fireman recognize each other as former lovers: "It was she who extinguished my first fires." And Mary responds: "I am his little firehose." Both recognition scenes belie their traditional role in drama, however, since neither one advances or resolves the plot. Mary's revelation is deliberately gratuitous, and the parody of a traditional device allows also for parodied responses on the part of her employers, the Smiths: "This is too much here in our home in the suburbs of London."

Earlier, Mr. and Mrs. Martin's own discovery that they are married and that they sleep in the same bed scarcely involves plot at all, but builds up by a series of coincidences: a stage-by-stage, apparently logical demonstration that is then totally undermined by Mary, in an intervention that in itself merges the traditional devices of the monologue and the aside. This recognition scene is riotously funny, but through its implications it also introduces a sense of the Proustian solitary nature of being, which confers at the same time a sense of unease. Following recognition scenes in which long-lost bonds are renewed and couples traditionally vow that they will never part again, Ionesco's reunited partners duly express their own dedication—not in this case to each other, but to their own former emptiness.

Into this family's "at home" enters the "handsome stranger" or the intruding visitor, who traditionally brings news of importance. Alternatively, such a visitor may seek something. Often, particularly in melodrama, the presence of such an intruder initiates a twist in the plot or introduces a threat to one or more of the protagonists. In creating his Fireman, Ionesco draws on such assumptions concerning role and significance. However, by giving his "fifth character" an irrational motive that equates him with a commercial traveler trying to drum up business ("You don't have a little fire . . . ?"), these assumptions are overturned to comic effect. The Fireman serves either as an object of desire or as an incitement to jealousy. Yet he is virtually the *occasion* rather than the *cause* of these quick outbursts of emotion—and such displays bear little or no relation to any form of psychological motivation.

The gathering of all the characters on stage recalls the importance of the *scène à faire* (obligatory scene) in nineteenth-century French theater. Eugene Scribe in particular developed this key scene in which all of the characters came together to sort out a complex situation that had evolved out of the intricacies of the plot. In Ionesco's play, since there is little plot, this scene, when all of the main characters are present, hinges not on any kind of resolution of difficulties but on the very entrance of their visitor. Is there or is there not someone there when a doorbell rings? They conclude with a total admission of rational failure: Sometimes there is and sometimes there is not! So the *scène à faire* becomes a *scène à ne rien faire*, in which what is done and said is merely a matter of filling in the time by recounting stories. These time-fillers echo another (nontheatrical) tradition in that the stories themselves are Aesopian fables that are grotesquely transformed and soon run wild. The final story, "The Cold," recounted by the Fireman, anticipates in its complex, self-proliferating genealogy the acceleration and final disintegration of language that its presence has initiated.

Although these parodied features represent an important element of the dramatic vitality as well as the humor of the play, *La Cantatrice chauve* is a parody of theater in a much more fundamental sense. Plot has been reduced to occasion, that of two visits, which (as Ionesco himself pointed out) serve merely to canalize the dramatic tension: "The aim is to release dramatic tension without the help of any proper plot or any special subject" (*NCN*, 187). And this is what happens in the play. Motivation for the visits is minimal. Yet reliance on traditional expectations has not been totally abandoned either, since the Smiths respond in their capacity as hosts (albeit in mutually contradictory fashion) to the Martins, and, as we have seen, the Fireman offers a form of explanation (if an illogical one) for his own unusual intrusion.

Instead of characters, Ionesco tells us also that he has offered us "characters without character. Puppets. Faceless creatures. Or rather empty frames, which actors can fill with their own faces, their own shapes, souls, flesh and blood" (*NCN*, 188). Thus, characters as such barely exist in *La Cantatrice chauve*, and all the elements that underlie the characterization of naturalistic drama, such as psychological coherence and rational behavior and discourse, are replaced by unpredictability, incoherence, and irrationality, which are nonetheless given the appearance of the former. So the Smiths and the Martins may say almost anything. Or again they may say one thing and do something quite different. At the end of the play Smiths and Martins are shown to be interchangeable, with the Martins repeating in a da capo conclusion the words that had been spoken by the Smiths at the beginning of the play. Yet even here the return to an apparent normality, following the extravagant violence and disintegration that have just occurred, is important to the incongruity that lies at the heart of the play.

In Ionesco's early plays his characters *are* their words. As he systematically parodies the mechanisms of theater, so he parodies its most obvious manifestation, in talk. Mrs. Smith prattles gaily on, although we can see that her husband is not listening. The Smiths and the Martins need to fill the silence with words, "talking for the sake of talking, talking because there is nothing personal to say" (*NCN*, 186). As plot has been reduced to occasion and characters have become empty frames, so dialogue has been made into mere exchange. Words are almost drained of content until, finally, they become particles of matter that are hurled across the stage from one physical presence at another.

The innovatory nature of Ionesco's approach to theater in *La Cantatrice chauve* did not emerge ex nihilo. It is in relation to Ionesco's attitude toward language that I want to look at various ways in which his play may be related to and distinguished from the work of a number of earlier dramatists with whom Martin Esslin in particular showed his close affinities. An exploration of these affinities (and differences) seems to me to point to what distinguishes Ionesco as a World War II, postexistential writer rather than a throwback to the earlier surrealist movement.

Questioned by Claude Bonnefoy as to the dramatists whom he regarded as the precursors of the new theater, Ionesco commented:

There were a number of attempts which did not come to fruition because they were too deliberate or too preconceived. There were the efforts of certain surrealists, Philippe Soupault, perhaps Desnos, perhaps Tzara, perhaps Picasso *(Desire Seized by the Tail)*, perhaps Vitrac. Above all there was Jarry. *Ubu roi* is a remarkable play where tyranny is not discussed, but it is *shown* in the form of this odious figure of Father Ubu who is the archetype of every kind of gluttony, material, political and moral. (quoted in Bonnefoy, 186)

One may speak of Jarry having influenced Ionesco in certain very specific ways, and almost all of them are relevant to the perspective that is being adopted here.

Ionesco's best plays, including his first one-acters, all use direct, concrete stage images in a way that is not only characteristic of Jarry in the *Ubu* cycle but that also echoes directly Ionesco's appraisal of Jarry's importance to the new theater. As Jarry shows tyranny in *Ubu roi*, so Ionesco shows the hollowness, emptiness, and monstrousness of language as it becomes a strange, uncontrollable object in *La Cantatrice chauve*. For Ionesco, speaking of both *La Cantatrice* and *La Leçon,* "the theater is finally concerned with the revelation of monstrous things, or of monstrous states without form, or of monstrous forms that we carry within us" (*NCN*, 6). In this way Jarry and Ionesco in his wake allowed the direct, physical nature of their own highly provocative dramatic imagery to work on the audience. Moreover, in this way, both dramatists were able to avoid being overexplicit and to allow the spectator to play his or her part in interpreting the stage images by an appeal to the imagination as well as to the senses.

In his interview with Claude Bonnefoy, Ionesco offered a further clue to the elements of Jarry's play that had most impressed him: "In Jarry we see a new research into language, into a concise, primitive, and caricatural language. His characters are powerful creations, violent, rich in color and true. King Ubu is a character who transcends time" (Bonnefoy, 190). It might appear that there is some degree of conflict here between Ionesco's own empty creations in *La Cantatrice* and Jarry's sharply outlined, caricatural, full-bodied ones, but Ionesco's play possesses the same broad, outrageous dimension that characterized Jarry's theater. In *Notes and Counter-Notes* Ionesco wrote that he wanted

to go all out for caricature and the grotesque, way beyond the pale irony of drawing-room comedies. No drawing-room comedies, but farce, the extreme exaggeration of parody. Humor, yes, but using the methods of burlesque. Comic effects that are firm, broad and outrageous. No dramatic comedies either. But back to the unendurable. Everything raised to paroxysm, where the source of tragedy lies. A theatre of violence: violently comic, violently dramatic. (*NCN*, 6)

What could be closer to Jarry's own approach as a dramatist than such a declaration of intent?

There are numerous occasions when the behavior or the language of Ionesco's own puppets in *La Cantatrice chauve* recalls specifically that of Père or Mère Ubu. Père Ubu's exaggerated, grotesquely comic outbursts against his wife, such as "I am going to sharpen my teeth on your shanks" or "I am going to tread on your toes," are of the same order of simple extravagance and pure violence as Mrs. Smith's sudden literal baring of her teeth or the rapid shifts of mood or violent, unmotivated verbal responses of several of Ionesco's characters. But what in Jarry's *Ubu* cycle appeared as puppetlike violence set in a context of broad caricature and psychological and moral simplicity has become in *La Cantatrice* a structural principle as the violence breaks through intermittently at first, then reaches a climactic paroxysm.

It is in their unusually bold use of language that Ionesco and Jarry have most in common. One of the best-known quotations from Ionesco concerns the way he envisages that the new theater uses words:

> First of all, there is a proper way for the theatre to use words, which is as dialogue, words in action, words in conflict. If they are used by some authors merely for discussion, this is a major error. There are other means of making words more theatrical: by working them up to such a pitch that they reveal the true temper of drama, which lies in frenzy; the whole tone should be as strained as possible, the language should almost break up or explode in its fruitless effort to contain so many meanings. (*NCN*, 27)

Jarry's own "concise, primitive, caricatural language" does not go quite as far as this, although he does emphasize sound and rhythm as much as he does sense. He comes very close to Ionesco's use of language as a battering ram.

I agree with Richard Coe on the importance of Jarry's legacy of 'pataphysics. It is well known that Ionesco was a "Transcendant Satrap of the Collège de Pataphysique," and that a number of his works were first published in the pages of either the *Cahiers* or the *Dossiers* of the college, which was dedicated to perpetuating Jarry's invented science. The 'pataphysician's emphasis on the dominance of the particular and the exceptional, rather than on general laws, certainly characterizes much of the dialogue and the approach to reality that is found in *La Cantatrice chauve*. Reality emerges as far too complex, involving far too much contradiction, to be explained by the acknowledged laws of science or by Aristotelian logic.

In *La Cantatrice chauve* the depiction of a world that has been released from the deterministic laws and the formulae that are commonly used to define it is a disquieting but also a liberating experience. Laughter inevitably arises out of the encounter with a world that, however strange, has nonetheless close relations with everyday experience. The laughter is then that of the sophisticated adult temporarily allowed the naïveté of the child, and we laugh at the extraordinary mixture of observed reality and apparent absence of logic as well as at sheer play in conversations that go nowhere, dialogues that are frequently monologues, logical attempts at explanation that reality constantly defies, and contradictory judgments appearing side by side in close juxtaposition.

The clearest and most explicit example of this occurs in Mrs. Smith's opinion of Mrs. Watson, the wife of the dead Bobby Watson: "She has regular features and yet one cannot say that she is pretty. She is too big and stout. Her features are not regular and yet one can say that she is very pretty. She is a little too small and too thin. She is a voice teacher." Such antithetical revelations about the human mind and about language go back at least to Flaubert's *Bouvard et Pecuchet* and the *Dictionnaire des idées reçues*, which are much admired by Ionesco. Ladies who are brunettes are there described as being "warmer than blondes (see blondes)." If one then turns to "blondes," one finds them described as being "warmer than brunettes (see brunettes)." Under "negresses" the entry says that they are "warmer than whites (see brunettes and blondes)." Bouvard and Pecuchet also spoke about women "whom they declared frivolous, petulant, stubborn. Nevertheless, they were often better than men; at other times they were worse." Ionesco takes similar antitheses and self-contradictions and proceeds to offer them as part of a consistent worldview that owed much to Jarry and the 'pataphysical tradition.

Another play, this time from the 1920s, provides an even more interesting point of comparison and contrast with Ionesco's first absurdist work. Ivan Goll's *Methusalem or the Eternal Bourgeois* was first written in German in 1919 and produced in Berlin in 1922. Goll was born French, but became German, as he himself phrased it, because of a "piece of stamped paper," since he was born in Alsace-Lorraine. He wrote in both French and German and was as much at home in German expressionist circles as he was among the Paris surrealists.

Goll's American translators, Clinton Atkinson and Arthur Wensinger, have described Goll's *Methusalem* as an "amazingly prescient work with entire scenes that reappear nearly verbatim in the much later work of Ionesco (particularly in *The Bald Primadonna*)" (Goll, 17). Martin Esslin also mentions Goll as one of the precursors of the theater of the absurd, but he does not point out that *Methusalem*, although originally written in German, was published in French in 1923 and produced in Paris with Antonin Artaud appearing as an actor in the filmed sections. Wolfgang Leiner's bibliography on Ionesco does not list Goll, and the affinities between the two writers have not been considered.

It is uncertain whether Ionesco knew Goll's play, to which he never refers in his critical writing. It does seem unlikely, however, that he was totally unfamiliar with a work that was available in French and that was well known among the surrealists. My personal view is that even if Goll's influence on Ionesco could be demonstrated, it would be an exaggeration to refer to *La Cantatrice chauve* as a virtual copy of Goll's dialogue. I want indeed to argue that it is precisely in the differences that exist between the two texts when they seem to be closest that the modernity as well as the quality of Ionesco's play may best be discerned.

Goll's preface to *Methusalem*, dated Berlin, 1922, restates an aim that was common to German expressionists and French surrealists:

Surrealism is the most forceful negation of realism. Surface reality is stripped away to reveal the Truth of Being. Masks: crude, grotesque, like the emotions they express. No more "heroes," just people, no more characters, just naked instincts. Quite naked. To know an insect you must dissect it.

From the outset of his theater career with *La Cantatrice chauve*, Ionesco too aimed at creating a grotesque form of elemental theater that would allow him to break down a dull, neutral, rational way of conceiving reality. In this way he aimed to portray a world that, however strange it might appear to many, might emerge as truer than the narrower, perhaps more comforting view of reality that naturalism and its offshoots had tended to encourage. In this respect Ionesco's aims have much in common with those of Jarry, Goll, Breton, Soupault, and Artaud. It is worth noting, however, that Ionesco has distinguished between surrealist theater and his own:

> I believe there must be in a writer, and even in a dramatist, a mixture of spontaneity, unawareness and lucidity; a lucidity unafraid of what spontaneous imagination may contribute. . . . We must first let the torrent rush in and only then comes choice, control, grasp, comprehension. (*NCN*, 124)

In spite of this distinction, Ivan Goll's emphasis on masks, on stripping away surface reality, and on the crude, grotesque presentation of naked instincts must now surely be taken, along with Jarry's reflections on the "Uselessness of the Theatre in the Theatre" and Artaud's recommendations for an intensely physical, gestural, elemental theater, as culminating in Ionesco's early plays.

Ivan Goll's preface to *Methusalem* looks forward to Ionesco's *La Cantatrice chauve* even more precisely:

> Alogic is today the most intellectual form of humour, and therefore the best weapon against the empty clichés which dominate all our lives. Almost invariably the average man opens his mouth only to set his tongue and not his brain in motion. What is the point of saying so much and taking it all too seriously? Moreover the average man is so sensitive that he takes any highly flavored word for an insult and will throw death on the scales to avenge it. Dramatic alogic must ridicule all our banalities of language exposing the basic sophistry of mathematical logic and even dialects. At the same time alogic will serve to demonstrate the multi-hued spectrum of the human brain, which can think one thing and say another and leap with mercurial speed from one idea to another without the slightest ostensibly logical connection. (80)

At first glance large sections of the social chatter in Goll's *Methusalem* closely resemble that of Ionesco's garrulous quintet. Like Goll, Ionesco mocks the empty banalities and the clichés that clutter up our lives. As he wrote, "The text of *La Cantatrice chauve* or the Manual for learning English (or Russian or Portuguese) consisting as it did of ready-made expressions and the most threadbare clichés revealed to me all that is automatic in the language and behavior of the people" (*NCN*, 26–27).

Closer analysis, however, reveals a number of striking differences. First of all, Ionesco employs a wider variety of linguistic sources than does Goll, drawing on proverbs and common sayings in both English and French. Second, sentences are invented by Ionesco as much for their sounds and their rhythms as for their banality and their lack of sense. Utterances of the Smiths and the Martins have a frenzied, wild quality, so that the humorous effect is mingled with a distinct feeling of unease and menace. So sentences such as "Take a circle, caress it, and it will become vicious" or even "Paper is for writing, the cat is for the rat, cheese is for scratching" tend to swim out of the other platitudes and apparent nonsense phrases, to create miniature eruptions of violence and disquiet that anticipate the active disturbance and hostility that follow later in the scene. There is also less continuity of thought and actual exchange of dialogue in Ionesco than there is in Goll. Ionesco's protagonists appear to be more isolated in the emptiness of their inner selves than are any of Goll's more social caricatures. It soon becomes clear that Ionesco's interest extends beyond the mere satire of bourgeois tittle-tattle to encompass a vision of individuals who are almost totally immured in their own consciousnesses. Ionesco himself pointed out that what was surprising about his characters was that any form of communication at all between them was possible. Ionesco, at this stage of his career, would have agreed with Beckett's account of Proust's view of human exchange: "There is no communication, because there are no vehicles of communication. Even on the rare occasions when word and gesture happen to be valid expressions of personality, they lose their significance on their passage through the cataract of the personality that is opposed to them" (Beckett, 47).

The major difference between Ionesco's and Goll's play is that in *La Cantatrice chauve* a compelling and coherent vision lies behind the banalities of language. Goll looks at these banalities only in terms of their relations with social discourse or as indications of the surprising dexterity and possible illogicalities of which the human brain is capable. In Ionesco what emerges is not simply the hollowness and the emptiness of the language and lives of the Smiths and the Martins. It is also an overt manifestation of the quite extraordinary nature of human existence itself. Ionesco shows himself to be fully conscious of the nature of his achievement in this respect when he writes

> In my first play, *La Cantatrice chauve* which started off as an attempt to parody the theatre and hence a certain kind of human behavior, it was by plunging into banality, by draining the sense from the hollowest clichés of everyday language that I tried to render the strangeness that seems to pervade our whole existence. (*NCN*, 26–27)

The characters can therefore react with unanimous surprise at the spectacle of a man tying his shoelaces, whereas they have reacted quite naturally to a clock that strikes seventeen times or to a fireman who goes around actively seeking out fires. As Richard Coe explained: "The discovery that every phenomenon is totally unpredictable and therefore totally surprising means that there is no real distinction between the utterly fantastic and the unspeakably banal" (Coe, 51). The ordinary, everyday world appears then as utterly incomprehensible. Ionesco wrote: "To me it is existence itself that seems unimaginable; and that being so there is nothing within existence that has the power to startle my credulity" (*NCN*, 164). This offers more of the *feeling* of the absurd than any philosophical elaboration could possibly do.

With Ionesco's plays we find ourselves then in a very different world from the banalities and the dramatic alogic of Ivan Goll, however close in some ways they may seem to be to each other. With Ionesco we are firmly situated in a post-Kafka, post-*La Nausée*, post-*Le Mythe de Sisyphe* world. And it is surely one of Ionesco's most remarkable achievements—clearly visible now from our present moment in time—that he created, in the wake of Camus's awareness of the alien nature of the world, a dramatic experience that is at once riotously funny and profoundly disquieting, even totally horrifying: "For me what happened was a kind of collapse of reality. The words turned into sounding shells devoid of meaning . . . and the world appeared to me in an unearthly perhaps its true, light, beyond understanding and governed by arbitrary laws" (*NCN*, 185). By the conclusion of the play, humor has been joined to, or perhaps replaced by, horror at the unleashing of the blind forces being exercised in a totally directionless way, with the characters hurling first words at each other, then not even words but syllables, consonants, and vowels. Meaningless and destructive forces take over the language, just as they have threatened to do at different times and in minute flashes throughout the entire play.

Looking at Ionesco's entire dramatic output now, we can see the ambivalence of his attitude to the astonishing fact of being: wonderment, joy, light, weightlessness, and color on the one hand; yet oppression, fear of death, destruction of the self, darkness, and vacuity on the other. It is worth stressing in conclusion that the very sharpness with which these two responses to the extraordinary spectacle of human existence appear in Ionesco's plays would in itself be enough to distinguish his theater from that of some of his related predecessors. His first play focuses on the negative side of the vision. The very intensity of the horror and fear that is built up by the proliferation and disintegration of language in *La Cantatrice chauve*, although it draws on attitudes to the theater that are common to Jarry and Vitrac, Apollinaire and Goll, is enough then to show that Ionesco's play derives not merely from a postexistential but also from a post-Hiroshima world. Ionesco's disquiet may well have found its seed in the disturbing figure of Jarry's King Ubu. Yet invasion, proliferation, and disintegration have become key structural elements, causing, in the case of *La Cantatrice chauve*, a veritable explosion of meaninglessness that still from this distance seems to be very much Ionesco's own.

Anguish, with a desire for a lost wonderment and wholeness, runs through one of the author's most revealing comments on his own work:

> At certain moments the world appeared to me emptied of meaning, reality seems unreal. It is this feeling of unreality, the search for some essential reality, nameless and forgotten—and outside it I do not feel I exist—that I have tried to express through my characters, who drift incoherently, having nothing of their own apart from their anguish, their remorse, their failures, the vacuity of their lives. . . . As the world is incomprehensible to me, I am waiting for someone to explain it. (*NCN*, 193)

This text was written by Ionesco as a program note for *Les Chaises*, but it relates equally to his first play, where for the first time his striking theatrical imagery articulated that sense of profound disorientation and disquiet that seems now always to have been at the very heart of his comedy.

BIBLIOGRAPHY

Beckett. *Proust.* London: Chatto and Windus, 1931.
Bonnefoy, Claude. *Entretiens avec Eugène Ionesco.* Paris: Editions Pierre Belfond, 1966.
Coe, Richard N. *Ionesco, A Study of His Plays.* London: Methuen, 1971.
Goll, Ivan. *Methusalem.* In *Seven Expressionist Plays,* ed. J. M. Ritchie. London: John Calder, 1980.
Guicharnaud, Jacques. *Modern French Theatre from Giraudoux to Genet.* New Haven: Yale University Press, 1967.
Ionesco, Eugene. *Notes and Counter-Notes.* London: John Calder, 1962. Abbreviated in the text as *NCN.*
Leiner, Wolfgang. *Bibliographie et index thématique des études sur Eugène Ionesco.* Fribourg: Editions universitaires, 1980.

Late Modernism: Samuel Beckett and the Art of the Oeuvre

H. PORTER ABBOTT

On and on, anyhow onward . . .
                    —Browning, "Martin Relph"

One of the historically interesting things that has happened to Beckett since Martin Esslin situated him so firmly and usefully in the history of theater is the way his oeuvre has become a site of the modernist/postmodernist turf war. Unlike Virginia Woolf (modernist) or John Cage (postmodernist), Beckett is still at large, a kind of categorical rift, giving the lie to categories.[1] Yet in the turf war, steadily and, it would seem, inexorably, the postmodernist categorizers have been gaining the high ground. The advantage of armament in this contest has come from the apparent fit between Beckett's writing and poststructuralist theory. Foucault's early appropriation of Beckett in an effort to abolish essentialistic notions of authorship is frequently invoked, and much has been written on how Beckett provides, to use Herbert Blau's term, a "gloss" on deconstruction. Now, with the publication of Steven Connor's *Samuel Beckett: Repetition, Theory and Text*, the case for Beckett as postmodern *bricoleur*, Derridean in his bones, gains powerful support.[2] With all due acknowledgment of the frailty of categories, I want to argue in what follows that the deconstructive Beckett is, in his bones, a modernist Beckett. I am tempted to use the label John Fletcher almost used for Beckett: postmodern modernist.[3] But late modernist is better; it indicates where Beckett's center of gravity can be found. Indeed, if I am not mistaken, a center of gravity is something a modernist has.

When, over twenty years ago in his essay "The Culture of Modernism," Irving Howe called Samuel Beckett the last modernist,[4] he meant to underscore Beckett's fidelity to the modernist spirit of opposition and his consistent refusal to decline into one or another mode of intellectual or aesthetic fixity (primitivism, nihilism, political ideology) or, worse still, to sell out to a commercial culture in which "the decor of yesterday is appropriated and slicked up; the noise of revolt, magnified in a frolic of emptiness; and what little remains of modernism, denied so much as the dignity of opposition" (*Decline of the New*, 33). In so defining modernism, Howe came as close as anyone has to identifying one of the deep structures of modernism, one that holds for the greatest number of candidates and that the intervening years have done little to challenge: exceptional fidelity to the spirit of opposition. As such, modernist art goes beyond satire, carrying the spirit of opposition everywhere into the form as well as the content of art. The term in the wings here is irony,[5] but I avoid it to keep the stress where Howe placed it—on earnest opposition. Fredric Jameson uses basically the same idea to distinguish the modernist from the postmodernist. In Jameson's version of postmodern art and culture, the modernist device of parody gives way to pastiche, a value-neutral mashing together of styles, "without parody's ulterior motive, amputated of the satirical impulse, devoid of laughter. . . . Pastiche is . . . blank parody, a statue with blind eyeballs."[6] Like kitsch, pastiche thrives on a cultural technology of rapid reproducibility.[7]

The great challenge, then, faced by an art founded on the principle of opposition, is finding ways to resist the neutralizing effect of repetition, whether repetition is imposed from without or arises from within. From without, repetition is inflicted through the various cultural agencies of appropriation, duplication, and veneration. Commentary on modernism has frequently observed what Lionel Trilling noted in 1961 in his anxious reflections on the teaching of modern literature: that the familiarity bred and enforced by canonization robs the modernist "classic" of the very element that originally gave it life.[8] But the normality enforced by cultural repetitions parallels what modernists themselves have often sensed as a threat from within: the danger of self-repetition. In Howe's words, "modernism does not establish a prevalent style of its own; or if it does, it denies itself, thereby ceasing to be modern" (*Decline of the New*, 3). It was this dilemma of naming that led Jean-François Lyotard to his elegant inversion of terms whereby modernism would denote nameable styles (for example, cubism) and postmodernism their unnameable precondition (Picasso and Braque, reacting to the now recognizable, and hence modernist, style of Cézanne, but not yet arrived at cubism).[9]

Let us accept modernism (*pace* Lyotard, and numerous others) as designating an oppositional art so thoroughgoing as to require continual attention to the dilemma of repetition and the nameable. This quality lies as much behind the transformations of Proust's characters as it does behind the succession of new formal departures that characterize such modernist oeuvres as those of Woolf, Joyce, Stein (especially her work between the years 1905 and 1915), and, to a proportional degree, authors in the middle ground between modern and traditional realism such as Thomas Mann. This internal self-scrutiny of one's evolving oeuvre was brought to what will probably remain its historical apex by Beckett, who continues to manifest it, both through his formal experimentation in piece after piece and through a deliberate process of recollection by distortion. The latter is a technique of deliberate metamorphosis, a kind of misremembering in successive works of elements from those that went before. If it has the look of the postmodern, my case is that in Beckett it is a concentrated refinement of modernist practice. This is basically the same practice that Steven Connor in his study of Beckett called, drawing on the terminology of Gilles Deleuze, "clothed" (as opposed to "naked") repetition. Naked repetition is so blatant a repetition it gives the illusion of some essential reality—what Molloy called "the principle of advertising."[10] By contrast, clothed repetition puts difference on display; it is repetition that signals the impossibility of repetition— that, even as it indicates what is repeated, insures its absolute indeterminacy.[11] I shall return to Connor's important study later, but first I want to focus on this process of recollection by distortion, which was, I think, Beckett's most significant refinement of mod-

ernist oppositional practice in that it allowed him to create and maintain a web of resistances out of which his art gains its life. The Beckettian oeuvre, to adapt the phraseology of Lacan, operates as a language; but one that seeks never to allow us to forget that meaning is
a matter of difference and deferral. Beckett has always situated his
art against our expectations, but it is in the preemptive vigilance he
exercises on his own work that he has raised to a new level the
oppositional character of classical modernism.

In *Happy Days*, well on in act 1, Winnie, finding herself incapable
of putting her parasol down, says, "No, something must happen, in
the world, take place, some change, I cannot, if I am to move
again,"[12] and shortly thereafter her parasol bursts into flame. Again,
late in act 2, Winnie says, "No, something must move, in the world,
I can't any more" (60), and shortly thereafter Willie, for the first time
in the play, comes from behind the mound and out into full view.
Both events are rich parodies, drawing oppositional life from a variety of conventions: the answered prayer, the deus ex machina, the
catastrophe (flames, possible death-dealing by Willie), and most
broadly the dramatic mythos itself (Aristotelian action). But they also
take place in an aesthetic field that has been more recently fashioned
by Beckett's own work for the theater, most notably by *Waiting for
Godot*. By the fall of 1961, when *Happy Days* was first performed,
Godot was in serious danger of becoming a classic, having advanced
to that status through what could be called the law of retrospective
comparative advantage.[13] Beckett had become "the author of *Godot*,"
the man who wrote the play in which "nothing happens, twice."[14]
Happy Days, then, creates its effects not simply against Greek tragedy
and Protestant devotional practice, nor (to go on) against *Hamlet*,
Romeo and Juliet, *Cymbeline*, *Paradise Lost*, Gray's "Ode on a Distant
Prospect of Eton College," and *The Rubaiyat of Omar Khayyam*—to
name a few of the classics against which the play also situates itself
(one *never* "loses one's classics")—but against as well the emerging
classic *Waiting for Godot*.

In so doing, *Happy Days* is the play in which something happens,
twice. Like Winnie's femininity and her relentless cheerfulness, the
structure of the play draws energy from *Godot*'s countervailing field
of influence. *Godot*'s absolute absence of the long-awaited one is
undercut in the later play first by an unaccountable flame (bringing
incidentally to mind storied flames in which the deity appears or

from which it speaks), and second by the vivid manifestation of Willie, "dressed to kill." These subversions are not reversions (the deity is no more recoverable than orthodox Aristotelian form). Rather, in contradicting our dramatic expectations, they sustain in the later play the condition of unknowing that is so powerfully evoked in the earlier one. But to emphasize the main point here: one has only to imagine a *Happy Days* in which Willie never appears and is never seen by Winnie to appreciate at once how boldly opportunistic Beckett's oppositional art is (the fine embellishments of Willie's hairy arm, his newspaper, the words he says, Winnie's ability to rap him on the skull) and how oppressive *Godot* might have become in the oeuvre of a lesser artist.

Beckett's art, then, fuels itself. And the brilliance with which it burns is directly proportional to the threat of familiarity from which it seeks to escape. Familiarity and habit were defined as threats to art in Beckett's earliest published writing. At the time, he was advancing an aesthetic argument implicit in the art of the modernist masters (Proust and Joyce) who had the greatest influence on him and who, in their turn, were recapitulating an antagonism to habit one can find well back in Baudelairean *modernité*. Beckett's turn of this modernist screw consists in the keenness of his attention to the emergent familiarity of his own work and his ability to make of it—through the method of distorted self-recollection—occasions of renewed surprise. In consequence, the gathering intertextual complexity of Beckett's oeuvre is marked by a double action: *Happy Days* takes its life in opposition to *Godot* and in so doing gives new life to the earlier play. Beckett, in short, is always writing everything he has written.

Such an approach to one's art puts into question the idea of the progress or development of an oeuvre. By the time he had begun his theatrical work in earnest, Beckett had become fully absorbed by this question. Indeed, there are signs that Beckett began thinking in terms of a total oeuvre quite early in his writing, but it was in the forties, when he began repeatedly to elaborate the Victorian trope of onwardness, that his collected achievement began to take on its unusual combination of coherence and unravelment. This trope is worth dwelling on not only because it foregrounds the question of whether oeuvres progress but because the trope itself, in Beckett's hands, participates as an element in the complex web of resistances that Beckett creates through the method of recollection by distortion.

The textual history of the trope is closely bound up with that of the dead metaphor of progress. Its prehistory seems to lie mainly in the language of combat, a usage that is itself revived, often with symbolic suggestiveness, in nineteenth-century literature of the battlefield ("En avant, Gaulois et Francs!" "Forward, the Light Brigade!"). In the nineteenth century, it can be found spread out over a great range of discourse—poetry, devotional literature, political oratory, social commentary, the novel. In its characteristic manifestation, the trope was distinguished by three features: (1) the exhortative mood, bearing with it the sense of obligation, duty, moral imperative ("Onward!"); (2) linear directionality, or the sense of a progressive, usually ascending, advance toward an objective that lies ahead, both in space and time; and (3) processionality, or an orientation toward the ennobling and arduous process of advance rather than the final objective, which, like the end of a story, is less interesting in itself than in what it enables. It was the sufficiency of the process of onwardness that made, in an age that glorified the exploratory voyager, Scott's doomed 1912 expedition to the South Pole a kind of apotheosis of the trope.

All the major Victorian poets yield examples of the trope of onwardness:

> To strive, to seek, to find, and not to yield
>
> (Tennyson, "Ulysses")

> Not enjoyment, and not sorrow,
>   Is our destined end or way;
> But to act, that each tomorrow
> Find us further than to-day.
>
> (Longfellow, "A Psalm of Life")

> *Roam on! the light we sought is shining still*
>
> (Arnold, "Thyrsis")

In cadence and diction, this poetic language matches very closely that of nineteenth-century Christian hymnody ("Onward, Christian soldiers") as well as the political and social rhetoric of a society that conceived of itself as engaged in righteous movement and in which one's individual being found its validation in the degree to which one shared or imitated that movement:

A sacred burden is this life ye bear,
Look on it, lift it, bear it solemnly,
Stand up and walk beneath it steadfastly;
Fail not for sorrow, falter not for sin,
But onward, upward, till the goal ye win.
(Frances Anne Kemble, "Lines to the Young Gentlemen Leaving Lennox Academy")

Modernist parody made considerable capital out of the trope of onwardness, and in so doing thematized modernism's rejection of both linearity and the Victorian moral imperative. Perhaps the most undisguised subversion of the trope occurs in Woolf's *To the Lighthouse* in her representation of Mr. Ramsey's intellectual expedition to the end of the alphabet ("On, then, on to R").[15] The chapters of Joyce's *Portrait* present Stephen's immersion in successive transformations of the figure ("A wild angel had appeared to him, the angel of mortal youth and beauty, an envoy from the fair courts of life, to throw open before him in an instant of ecstasy the gates of all the ways of error and glory. On and on and on and on!".[16] The long last chapter of this book can be read as one final, difficult gestation of the figure, which at the very end makes its appearance in a dingy, battered improvisation: "Away! Away! . . . Welcome, O life! I go to encounter for the millionth time the reality of experience and to forge in the smithy of my soul the uncreated conscience of my race" (252–53). Coming now from Stephen's pen, the trope announces in its parodic style the birth of Stephen's own modernist awareness.

Beckett's adaptation of the trope begins implicitly in the novel he wrote during World War II *(Watt)* with the imperative yet obscurely destined journeying of its protagonist; is sustained in *Mercier et Camier*, the *Nouvelles*, and *Molloy*; and is finally given explicit development toward the end of *Malone Dies*. The striking variation on the trope that Beckett introduces through Malone is its reflexive application to the writing of which it is a part. Malone, struggling to bring on the catastrophe of his story before expiring himself, exhorts his pen to greater effort: "On. One morning Lemuel, . . ." and later, "But

what matter about Lady Pedal? On" (*Three Novels*, 280, 281). Since
then, Beckett has so frequently restated the trope that it has become
one of the commonest Beckettian markers. In the very next book of
the trilogy, it is transferred from the task of narration to that of
self-formulation:

> ... strange pain, strange sin, you must go on, perhaps it's done al-
> ready, perhaps they have said me already, perhaps they have carried me
> to the threshold of my story, before the door that opens on my story, that
> would surprise me, if it opens, it will be I, it will be the silence, where I
> am, I don't know, I'll never know, in the silence you don't know, you
> must go on, I can't go on, I'll go on. (414)

In the recent text *Worstward Ho* (1983), Beckett has built a forty-page
tone poem out of the trope, beginning with a fanfare so brazen as to
suggest not a little self-conscious irony: "On. Say on. Be said on.
Somehow on. Till nohow on. Said nohow on."[17] The title of this
piece, at first blush a bad joke, sustains the figure's Victorian em-
beddedness, evoking both the westward course of empire and, more
specifically, Charles Kingsley's classic tale of adventure and combat
on the Spanish Main.[18]

In the trope of onwardness, Beckett appears to have come upon
something that matched his obsessions so closely that it may have
presented a serious threat to the oppositional character of his art,
something on the order of an invariant repetition or signature. That
this was not going to be the case can be seen by noting how, once
Beckett had fastened it to the business of narrative composition at the
end of *Malone*, he had, within a matter of months, redeployed it in
Pozzo and Lucky as an outrageous caricature of the westward course
of empire (complete with baggage, bearer, and whip). In all productions of *Godot* that I have seen, the two enter from stage left, which
is appropriate as the position corresponds (for the audience) to the
cartographical index of westward movement. That they should enter
from the same side twice suggests the possibility that in the interval
they went clear round the world. Pozzo's first word is "On!"—announcing the arrival of the metaphor even before his appearance on
stage.[19] And as he departs in the first act, raising the cry with which
he entered, Pozzo seems to infect the waiting, unjourneying pair
with the trope:

Pozzo: I need a running start. *(Having come to the end of the rope, i.e. off stage, he stops, turns and cries.)* Stand back! *(Vladimir and Estragon stand back, look towards Pozzo. Crack of whip.)* On! On!
Estragon: On!
Vladimir: On!
Lucky moves off.
Pozzo: Faster! *(He appears, crosses the stage preceded by Lucky. Vladimir and Estragon wave their hats. Exit Lucky.)* On! On! (31)

Part of the comedy here turns on the imitation of a wagon train and the colonial departure for long expeditions to distant lands, embellished with nice touches in the standing back of onlookers and the waving of hats. And part of the comedy turns on the stark severity with which Estragon and Vladimir have been deprived of any vestige of forward movement. Nevertheless, the trope expands over the course of the play to cover as well their endurance of the sheer deprivation of physical onwardness. Vladimir, concluding his final soliloquy, exclaims, "I can't go on!" (58); and in the last lines of the play, Estragon echoes him: "I can't go on like this" (60). In yet another elaboration of the figure, Beckett enfolds within Pozzo's march of physical mastery a reapplication of the trope to the march of intellectual inquiry in Lucky's oration: "I resume alas alas on on in short in fine on on abode of stones . . ." (29).

In at least three different ways, then, *Godot*'s deployment of the figure of onwardness pushes against the way in which Malone had made use of it several months earlier. In the following years, Beckett was to redeploy the trope again and again, each time altering it or introducing new elements—of idiom, image, or grammar. In *Endgame*, a play that takes place entirely within its denouement, onward becomes both the mysterious working of time ("Something is taking its course") and the effort to bring time to an end, to "finish." In this context, Hamm's motif—"We're getting on"—inevitably calls to mind the business of aging (getting on). In *All That Fall*, the trope is reworked as leading and being led on, keyed to John Henry Newman's nineteenth-century variant of the trope, which Maddy Rooney tries to sing: "Lead, Kindly Light, amid the encircling gloom, / Lead Thou me on!" In *Happy Days*, the figure is split, its imperative mood given to the bell that rouses Winnie when she nods off and the sign of onwardness given to the earth that rises to swallow her.[20] In

Krapp's Last Tape, the trope receives its most thoroughgoing revision. Here the forwardness of time is played off against an insistent drive back and in. With bold economy, the play aligns the quest backward in time with Krapp's male drive into the eyes and womb of the loved figure—back in effect to his first home. "Onward!" becomes "Let me in," and the moment in the play that finally absorbs our attention is the anti-onward, a point of (fetal) stillness in random movement, repeated three times: "my face in her breasts and my hand on her. We lay there without moving. But under us all moved, and moved us, gently, up and down, and from side to side."[21]

Deleuze's metaphor—"clothed" or "masked" repetition—contains, despite (or perhaps because of) its deviser's best intentions, essentialistic implications that Beckett clearly sought to avoid in his successive distortions of the trope of onwardness (what is it that is being clothed?). There is, in fact, nothing under the trope. This is what gives it its great flexibility. And the theater, precisely because it is a medium ill-disposed to any representation of voyaging (on stage, all ships stand still), provided a "dramatic" enlargement of Beckett's capacity to elaborate the emptiness of the trope. If the characters in much of his prose fiction (Watt, Mercier and Camier, Molloy and Moran, and the narrators of the *Nouvelles*) are all at least on the move, the characters in Beckett's work for the stage are most emphatically going nowhere. What stunned the world in 1953 was the radical plotlessness of Beckett. Sheer Heideggerian "thrownness" displaced any sense of origins or historical chains of cause and effect. *Godot, Endgame, Krapp,* and *Happy Days* (despite its two surprises) were plays in which nothing really happened at all.

Beckett's method of recollection by distortion, in its refinement of modernist opposition, is the continual and vigorous reconstruction of tropological emptiness. Onwardness is only one of many blanks around which Beckett's texts, translations, and productions hover, but the process I have outlined here shows why Beckett must keep on writing. Going on, he wards off encroachments on these vital absences. The threat of content is ever-present and only waits upon an author's death, silence, or naked self-repetition. Beckett's oeuvre, then, operates like the life of Krapp, whose successive self-recordings and transcriptions (like his author, Krapp works in more than one medium) alter as they recall what went before and are in turn recalled and altered by those to come.[22] Pressing on, Beckett keeps the shape of his oeuvre, and the relations of all its elements, at play. Such a going on is both a going back and also a kind of spreading out. His oeuvre itself transmutes the trope of onwardness.

My argument so far, then, is that if Beckett's work glosses deconstruction, it is a modernist scribe who writes the gloss. What Beckett does, more thoroughly than any modernist, is at once concentrate and extend the modernist spirit of opposition, so that it is spread everywhere in his language. In the process, Beckett has turned the spirit of opposition perhaps most keenly upon himself—himself as, in effect, a maker of language. As he constructs his language in successive works he must be ever alert against its potentially deadening or imprisoning effects—which means, in turn, keeping that language from coming to an end. The function of writing is to avoid having written. Like Proust before him, who argued that great authors are always writing the same book, Beckett has made his "work" of art his uncompleteable oeuvre.

Of course, the best intentions of any author are no proof against the readership. In the last chapter of his book on Beckett, Steven Connor develops a stinging critique of the immense structure of critical discourse that has grown up around Beckett's work over the last three decades. Abetted, he argues, in curious ways by Beckett himself, this "discursive formation" has in its cultural effect run exactly counter to the kind of complex indeterminacy I have just been discussing. According to Connor, discourse about Beckett has served the function of completing Beckett, in effect taming him by making and maintaining a "Beckett" who by the very unity of being implicitly attributed to him reaffirms the essentialistic assumptions of the humanistic tradition. "What gives Beckett criticism such importance and cultural centrality is the continued reassertion in that discourse of the myth of the author as creator, source and absolute origin" (*Samuel Beckett*, 191). Beckett's long and difficult management of the repetitions in his work is thus converted, in the interests of cultural authority and power to a more limited and less disruptive kind of repeatability:

The discourse of Beckett criticism has a special, representative place within discourses of culture as a whole, for it is a site in which cultural

values of great importance may be repeated and recirculated with authority. What is extraordinary is that all the breaks which Beckett's writing
practice makes, or attempts to make, with these traditions and the power
relations which they encode can be so effectively contained and rewritten
as repetitions. (199)

The argument Connor makes is a powerful one, and in the course
of making it he touches on many all-too-familiar aspects of Beckett
criticism. But to begin with, it is not at all clear that what Connor
criticizes can, finally, be avoided. He himself does not avoid it. His
book is yet one more act of veneration; it is a reading, offered up, of
culturally important texts—all of them, moreover, attributed to the
same man. It presumes to its own superior penetration, to have
found a truth about these texts that has been hidden from others.
Perhaps most insidiously, the book's consistent use of the name
Samuel Beckett (along with grammatically appropriate pronouns),
both as a person and a maker of texts, and its blazoning of that name
in the title and on the cover, just encourage us to persist in our
essentialistic habits—which is not so much to criticize Connor as to
say that, like the rest of us, he inhabits, and is inhabited by, our
language and our culture.

But there is a more important point to be made in this context, and
it brings us back to the issues of repetition and onwardness in Beckett. The point is perhaps only a question: What are the limits of any
critique of origins, authority, or unity of being? And the answer may
only be, at best: We do not know. But this answer is not in-
significant, for it implies that it may well be a mistake to find in
Beckett any foreclosure of our vital ignorance in this matter. "The key
word in my plays," he once told an interviewer, "is 'perhaps.' "[23] So
far my argument has carried us in one direction. I have made the
case that in subjecting the Victorian trope of onwardness to an elaborate, multifaceted deconstruction Beckett sought, as he still seeks, to
preserve the absence at its center. In the process, he completed the
job that the modernists had begun in ridding plot of linear causality.
But Beckett only did half a job on the narrative tradition. If in the
work from *Godot* to *Happy Days* he obliterated plot, he did not obliterate character. This is the second most interesting thing about these
plays. In Ruby Cohn's words,

> One has to be blind not to distinguish Hamm from Dan Rooney; deaf not
> to know Mouth from M. Vladimir and Estragon are not identical
> twins. . . . On the rare occasions when Beckett speaks of his characters,
> he calls them "my people." Not symbols, or objects, or fictions, but
> people.[24]

Yet we *have* been curiously blind to this conventionality of Beckett's,
and to the deep down strangeness of it—that our leading exponent of
the disintegration of the self should have produced some of our most
memorable characters. The fact is finessed, overlooked, accommodated, and argued around, probably because it is difficult to integrate
with the "Beckett" that has been created by our collective discourse.

That Beckett should have contributed so richly to the art of characterization is not out of keeping with modernism, whose major
figures have given us unsurpassed examples of the art (the Duc and
Duchesse de Guermantes, the Baron de Charlus, Molly and Leopold
Bloom, Stephen Dedalus). If Beckett's characters appear on the verge
of extinction, going blind, confined to wheelchairs, sucked inexorably into the earth, their imperilment only sets off their vigor. And for
better or worse, it is more than likely a nostalgia for character among
even the most sophisticated of theatergoers that has given Pozzo,
Hamm, Krapp, and Winnie the secure place they occupy in the stage
repertoire. It is much the same frame of mind, I think, that leads
scholars of Joyce to celebrate Bloomsday.

It was not nostalgia that animated Beckett when, at the moment
he appeared to have abolished character from his prose fiction, he
reinstated it so brilliantly on the stage. It has frequently been noted
that when Beckett moves to a new genre or medium he appears to
revert to an earlier stage of historical development from that to which
he had brought the genre or medium in which he had been previously working. Thus one might argue that the characters in these
first plays are a consequence of such a reversion. But the argument
cannot account for the number of these characters—Estragon,
Hamm, Krapp, Maddy Rooney, Winnie—in play after play; in plays,
moreover, that consistently show the most radical departure from
tradition in the handling of other aspects of the medium—action,
decor. If one seeks to perfect the argument by pointing to the abandonment of character after *Happy Days* and by contending that this

theatrical austerity was where Beckett was headed—that his more recent work is a purer manifestation of what he has been trying all along to do—one makes *Godot, Endgame,* and *Krapp* somehow more primitive than *Footfalls* and *Rockaby.* Such an argument imposes a progressive teleology, a literalization of the trope of onwardness, on an oeuvre that, as I have argued, cannot support it.

I see no way around this: Beckett's "people" are characters, and they are as fully and legitimately Beckett's as anything he has created. The point introduces an important qualification to the argument I have been making, for character—a recognizable integrity of being maintained over time—is itself a kind of onwardness. And in case after case, the imminent extinction of the character intensifies our focus on its capacity to "carry on." The fact that during this same period, in texts like *The Unnamable* and *Texts for Nothing,* Beckett is writing prose fiction in which traditional characterization is subjected to the most ruthless disintegration cannot, any more than the teleological arguments, be taken to deny or diminish the importance of the characters in his plays. This would be to argue, as some have, that the prose is somehow closer to the real Beckett.[25] Such privileging of the prose fails to account for Beckett's continued productivity in theater and his extension to works in that medium of the same earnest care he devotes to his other work. More important, it slights the self-resistant nature of Beckett's art, the way, always, it pushes against itself. It is much more likely, then, that the theater and the prose took fire from each other and that his characters burn as brightly as they do because modes of disintegration were pursued with such determination in the fifties prose.

Of course, the plays can be, and have been, read as prose texts. And read closely, and analytically, these characters crumble into dust. Theodor Adorno, for example, reads *Endgame* as Beckett's abandonment of the last outpost of Western individualism. Beckett abandons it, he argues, "like an obsolete bunker": "*Endgame* insinuates that the individual's claim of autonomy and of being has become incredible. . . . The position of the absolute subject, once it has been cracked open as the appearance of an over-arching whole through which it first matures, cannot be maintained."[26] But Adorno's is a textual reading. As such, it is not wrong, but only half right. It fails to take into account what happens when the play is performed. And one of the things that happens is that the discontinuities riddle the parts of Clov and of Hamm are bound together by the force of individual performance. This happens time and again. And if the actors are good enough (whether they be Roger Blin and Jean Martin or Patrick Magee and Stephen Rea), the audience falls for it, as it should.

Bakhtin may or may not have been right when he wrote that "drama is by nature alien to genuine polyphony,"[27] but it would appear that theater's capacity to showcase a voice—or its tendency to make one voice dominate, as Bakhtin maintained was the case in Shakespeare[28]—may in fact have been part of what drew Beckett to the theater. Take what may be the most "polyphonic" role Beckett ever composed for the stage, that of Pozzo—

> (Lyrically.) The tears of the world are a constant quantity. For each one who begins to weep somewhere else another stops. The same is true of the laugh. (He laughs.) Let us not then speak ill of our generation, it is not any unhappier than its predecessors. (Pause.) Let us not speak well of it either. (Pause.) Let us not speak of it at all. (Pause. Judiciously.) It is true the population has increased. (Godot, 22)

Coming upon the different individual voices in this passage as one reads silently to oneself is not the same experience as listening to an actor bind them together from first to last, stamping them all with is own unavoidable voice and appearance. It is in fact the persistence of shape and sound on stage that brings out the discontinuities in these lines and makes them so funny. Walter Benjamin may have had this effect in mind when he wrote that "the character of the comic figure is not the scarecrow of the determinist; it is the beacon in whose beams the freedom of his actions becomes visible."[29] The point to stress here is that the unpredictable breaks that are at once the signs of this freedom and the cause of humor are not just any breaks; they are seen rather to belong to the character. This quality of "belonging" is what an actor enhances, and it must have been an important consideration for Beckett when he turned to the physicality of theater and what he has called its comparative "clarity."[30]

From the opening of En attendant Godot at the Théâtre de Babylone in 1953, critics have remarked on the way Beckett has consistently taken advantage of theater's physical presence—what Robbe-Grillet in a review of Godot's first run likened to Heidegger's description of

life on earth as a kind of raw "thereness."[31] Though Beckett seems
to have abandoned the experimentation with character he pursued
in the fifties, the theater remains a medium in which he has been
able, through the use of voice and image, to bring out similar kinds
of individually distinctive persistence. Through the agency of persistent physicality, he binds confusion over time. Anyone who has
heard Billie Whitelaw carry the lines of more recent plays such as *Not
I* or *Rockaby* has seen how Beckett designs his work to concentrate
our attention on that persistence. What I am arguing is powerfully
expressed in the image of P, the victim protagonist of Beckett's 1982
play *Catastrophe*, who, outlasting the canned applause that concludes
the play, seems to outlast the play itself. The same interest in the
persistence of character and voice (including its persistence beyond
the formal limits of art) is reflected in Beckett's cultivation over the
years of a select group of real people for his art—exceptional actors
whom he has not only directed but at times heard in his mind when
composing the parts they play. If, as Connor suggests, one consequence of the cultivation of this elite group has been to augment the
illusion of godlike author-ity in Beckett's own person (*Samuel Beckett*,
192–94), the roots of this practice and its continuation seem to lie in
Beckett's fascination with the persistence through discontinuity of
individually distinctive integrity.

As for the issue of personal author-ity, and more specifically that
of origin-ality, here too our discourse ought to acknowledge our collective ignorance. If there are myths that have controlled the way
we speak of authorship and originality and that deserve exposure,
there is still much regarding these two subjects that we do not yet
understand. One recurring aspect of current discourse about them is
a tendency to merge the issues of personal authorship and sociocultu-
ral authority. That a community can enforce a view of the world, can
misread a text to find in it what it wants, can make an acceptable
hero where it needs one, can convert complex and nuanced revisions
into naked repetitions, can subvert the subversive, normalize it, and
then draw its sting by venerating it—that a society can do all this,
painlessly and in ways that we subtly and not so subtly collaborate
with—is a slow death that must continually be brought to our attention, even if we can never fully escape from it. But such external,
culturally authorized and enforced impositions ought not to be confused with the force that brings any new text into existence. And if

there are myths of personal origin and authorship that abet the tyranny of cultural authority, the final returns on the subject of origins
and authoring are not yet in.

All of which is to say that Beckett's own persistence as writer and
director, his determination to have things his way, can be read as an
allegiance to his own distinctive productivity, which may (we don't
know) originate in himself, but which is always vigorously subversive. Nor is his author-itarianism the behavior of a stubborn, rigid old
man who would freeze his work by converting it into a set of naked
repetitions. As Connor himself points out, Beckett, even in directing
his work, is always altering it. An important example Connor introduces is Beckett's 1985 revision of *What Where* for German television
(Was Wo), which eliminated the megaphone and confined itself to
the faces of the actors *(Samuel Beckett, 200)*. Connor takes issue with
the essentialistic account of this transformation given by Martha
Fehsenfeld, who argues that Beckett was moving toward a truer rendering of his original idea—that it was meant to be a television play
all along. Connor's stress on Beckett the "freely-ranging" *bricoleur*,
engaged in a continual process of discovery, is in keeping with the
importance of continual self-resistance in creation that I have been
arguing here. More grist that Connor could have used for his argument is the Paris production of *Quoi òu* in April of the next year. This
version, directed by Pierre Chabert and also endorsed by Beckett,
replaced the inquisitor (Bam), as well as the megaphone, with a circular orange light; more striking, it dropped the mime element and
doubled the speed of performance. In the process, according to
Enoch Brater, it introduced an effect of farce that had been carefully
avoided in the German version.[32] The sequence of these productions
is powerful evidence that Beckett, in his translations and re-produc-
tions, as in the successive works of his oeuvre, is not going anywhere
in particular.

But what Connor fails to remark on in Fehsenfeld's report is, as
in all reports of Beckett at work, the anxiety of creation—the intense
concentration on doing the thing right. If Beckett's revisions are not
going anywhere in particular, they are nonetheless very much in
pursuit of what works. The other side of bricolage—its veiled aspect—is rejection: rejecting one thing after another until the rare right
thing turns up: "Then Sam said, 'keep his eyes closed the whole
time,' and that was the answer to it."[33]

For the 1988–89 Charles Eliot Norton lectures at Harvard, John Cage chose to read from a composition made up of 487 quotations, selected by chance and then disassembled and recombined with the assistance of a computer program based on the *I Ching*. Partway through the second lecture, a tape recorder in the auditorium suddenly began to make a racket that continued until it was found and turned off. Cage read steadily through the noise. Asked about it afterwards, he said that "the incident occurred just at a point when he had thought he would like some musical accompaniment."[34] This is a different frame of mind from that of the man who clutched Alan Schneider's arm during a London production of *Waiting for Godot* and whispered, "It's ahl wrahng! He's doing it ahl wrahng!"[35] Beckett's is a modernist ego. And for all his devotion to "failure," he manifests a desire for exacting artistic control that is in the same tradition of Paterian ascesis that ran through Joyce.

Beckett's allegiance to what goes by the name of Beckett is what lies behind his interventions against staging *Endgame* in a subway or having women play the parts of *Godot*.[36] These interventions are efforts to prevent the pastichification of Beckett, his dismemberment and redistribution into the bad infinity of postmodern endlessness. No doubt he makes mistakes and runs the risk of thwarting the bold but workable inventions of others, but going his own road Beckett seeks to continue writing his autograph, remaking his oeuvre in his own way. In so doing he lives the kind of persistence through difference that he has been recreating throughout his career, and that he has constructed for us so vividly in his dramatic characters and voices.

Foucault wrote at length, seconded eloquently by Deleuze, of the entirely external and relational nature of power, that power is a field existing *in* no place, always irreducibly "outside." Any notion of interiority that we may entertain of force arising from within is simply an illusion that "we must conjure up . . . in order to restore words and things to their constitutive exteriority."[37] If the reading I have proposed implies a Beckettian interior, it is not, I think, cause for alarm. One simply cannot know these things. But I am inclined to see the origins of individually distinctive persistence as lying outside language, in that terrain that Jacques Lacan acknowledged and at the same time strictly admonished his colleagues to post with the sign

"Don't touch."[38] If this is an accurate assessment of Beckett's thinking, then in this regard, too, he is in closer sympathy with his modernist masters than are many of his contemporaries. It suggests that he may not have outgrown his early enthusiasm for the sudden intrusions of involuntary memory, nor for the program that he articulated at the age of thirty-one in a letter to Axel Kaun:

As we cannot eliminate language all at once, we should at least leave nothing undone that might contribute to its falling into disrepute. To bore one hole after another in it, until what lurks behind it—be it something or nothing—begins to seep through; I cannot imagine a higher goal for a writer today.[39]

The Beckett who wrote this letter would appear to be much the same Beckett who, at the age of sixty-two, spoke of his obligation to find and bring back to life an *être assassiné*, killed before he was born, yet whom he had always felt buried inside him.[40]

It follows, then, that the kind of persistence I have been featuring in Beckett himself, as in his characters and voices, is quite a different kind of onwardness from that discussed in the first part of this essay, which, being a trope, was entirely a matter of language and therefore necessarily (and vitally) hollow at its core. Any view of Beckett that features primarily the Beckett of linguistic and tropological subversion fails to account for his intense earnestness—a quality that, perhaps more than any other, distinguishes him from his postmodern contemporaries.[41] This earnestness only becomes comprehensible, I believe, when one considers the other Beckett—the one that I have been holding up to view in the second half of this essay. But then both Becketts are inseparable components of the same late modernist, the complexity attended by the one serving only to sharpen the intent scrutiny of the other—its fascination for breath, for what pushes the words out into the air, sustaining them there in a voice we recognize, sustaining in the process Beckett's own unmistakable voice as it finds its way from one very different piece to another.

NOTES

1. To the student of categorical consciousness, Beckett reveals the semantic porousness of categories. Even those who might agree on a category for him more

often than not disagree on why he fits. Both Hugh Kenner and Irving Howe have called Beckett "the last modernist," but they assign him the label for strikingly different reasons; again for different reasons, David Lodge called Beckett "the first important postmodernist writer" and Ihab Hassan suggested the publication date of *Murphy* (1938) as a beginning date for postmodernism; while Marjorie Perloff locates Beckett in a still lengthening strain of modernism that began with Rimbaud. See Hugh Kenner, "Modernism and What Happened to It," *Essays in Criticism* 37 (April 1987): 97; Irving Howe, *The Decline of the New* (New York: Harcourt, 1970), 33; David Lodge, *The Modes of Modern Writing: Metaphor, Metonymy, and the Typology of Modern Literature* (Chicago: University of Chicago Press, 1977), 221; Ihab Hassan, *Paracriticisms: Seven Speculations of the Times* (Urbana: University of Illinois Press, 1975), 44; Marjorie Perloff, " 'The Space of a Door': Beckett and the Poetry of Absence," in *The Poetics of Indeterminacy: Rimbaud to Cage* (Evanston: Northwestern University Press, 1983), 200–47.

2. Michel Foucault, "What is an Author?" in *Language, Counter-Memory, Practice: Selected Essays and Interviews*, ed. Donald F. Bouchard, trans. Bouchard and Sherry Simon (Ithaca: Cornell University Press, 1977), 138, and "The Discourse on Language," in *The Archeology of Knowledge*, trans. A. M. Sheridan Smith (New York: Harper, 1972), 215; Herbert Blau, *The Eye of Prey: Subversions of the Postmodern, Theories of Contemporary Culture*, vol. 9 (Bloomington: Indiana University Press, 1987), 65–103; Steven Connor, *Samuel Beckett: Repetition, Theory and Text* (Oxford: Blackwell, 1988). See also Paul A. Bové, "Beckett's Dreadful Postmodern: The Deconstruction of Form in *Molloy*," in *De-Structing the Novel: Essays in Applied Postmodern Hermeneutics*, ed. Leonard Orr (Troy, N.Y.: Whitson, 1982), 185–221; Angela Moorjani, *Abysmal Games in the Novels of Samuel Beckett*, North Carolina Studies in the Romance Languages and Literatures, no. 219 (Chapel Hill: University of North Carolina Press, 1982); and Iain Wright, " 'What Matter Who's Speaking?': Beckett, the Authorial Subject and Contemporary Critical Theory," in *Comparative Criticism*, vol. 5, ed. E. S. Shaffer (Cambridge: Cambridge University Press, 1983), 59–86.

3. Fletcher's exact words are: "Like Matisse in the 1950s, Beckett stands dominant today as one of Modernism's great survivors, postmodernly modern to the last" (John Fletcher, "Modernism and Samuel Beckett," in *Facets of European Modernism*, ed. Janet Garton [Norwich: University of East Anglia, 1985], 216).

4. "A lonely gifted survivor, Beckett remains to remind us of the glories modernism once brought" (Howe, *Decline of the New*, 33). Howe's essay was originally published in 1967.

5. Alan Wilde, for example, uses the phrase "absolute irony" to group Beckett and others who have advanced to "the furthest perceptual thrust of the modernist movement" (Alan Wilde, *Horizons of Assent: Modernism, Postmodernism, and the Ironic Imagination* [Baltimore: Johns Hopkins University Press, 1981], 40). I should note here that the phrase "late modernist," which I apply to Beckett, is used with a quite different meaning by Wilde. Wilde associates late modernism with an "aesthetic of surfaces," which he elucidates in two chapters on Christopher Isherwood and Ivy Compton-Burnett (93–123). If there is a single aspect of Beckett that distinguishes my version of him from both Wilde's late modernism and numerous postmodernisms, it is his problematic, certainly indefinable, quality of depth, without the acknowledgment of which he is no longer read but rewritten.

6. Fredric Jameson, "Postmodernism, or the Cultural Logic of Late Capitalism," *The New Left Review* 146 (1984): 65.

7. See Matei Calinescu's assessment of kitsch in *The Faces of Modernity* (Bloomington: Indiana University Press, 1977), 225–62.

8. Lionel Trilling, "On the Teaching of Modern Literature," in *Beyond Culture* (New York: Viking, 1965), 3–30.

9. "A work can become modern only if it is first postmodern. Postmodernism thus understood is not modernism at its end but in the nascent state." See "Answering the Question: What is Postmodernism?" trans. Régis Durand, in Jean-François Lyotard, *The Postmodern Condition: A Report on Knowledge*, Theory and History of Literature, vol. 10 (Minneapolis: University of Minnesota Press, 1984), 79.

10. "If I go on long enough calling that my life I'll end up by believing it. It's the principle of advertising" (Samuel Beckett, *Three Novels* [New York: Grove, 1965], 53).

11. Connor, *Samuel Beckett*, 5–9 and passim. For "clothed," Deleuze uses, alternatively, "vetu," "masqué," "déguisé," and "travesti." Considering the concept involved, this series could go on forever. For the opposed concept, fittingly, only one term is used: "nu"; see Gilles Deleuze, *Différence et répétition* (Paris: Presses Universitaires de France, 1968), 36–39. The wording in my text slightly adapts both Connor and Deleuze for my own emphasis in the analysis that follows.

12. Samuel Beckett, *Happy Days* (New York: Grove, 1961), 36.

13. "They begin . . . by saluting play A as 'awful.' When play B comes along, that too is awful, not nearly as good as A. Play C is then dismissed as awful, worse than B, which though good was not a patch on A, which in the interval has become a masterpiece" (opinion of Alan Schneider as rendered by Beryl S. and John Fletcher in *A Student's Guide to the Plays of Samuel Beckett* [London: Faber, 1985], 89).

14. Perhaps the most widely cited description of *Godot*, this was first employed by Vivian Mercier in "The Uneventful Event," *Irish Times*, 18 February 1956.

15. Virginia Woolf, *To the Lighthouse* (New York: Harcourt, 1927), 55. In a series of deft strokes, Woolf plays Mr. Ramsey's expedition off against Scott's:

Who shall blame him, if, standing for a moment, he dwells upon fame, upon search parties, upon cairns raised by grateful followers over his bones? Finally, who shall blame the leader of the doomed expedition, if, having ventured to the uttermost, and used his strength wholly to the last ounce and fallen asleep not much caring if he wakes or not, he now perceives by some pricking in his toes that he lives, and does not on the whole object to live, but requires sympathy, and whisky, and someone to tell the story of his suffering to at once? Who shall blame him? (57)

16. James Joyce, *A Portrait of the Artist as a Young Man* (New York: Viking, 1956), 172.

17. Samuel Beckett, *Worstward Ho* (New York: Grove, 1983), 7. Commenting on *Worstward Ho* in the introduction to her *Beckett: Waiting for Godot* (London: Macmillan, 1978), Ruby Cohn touched on the resonance of Beckett's use of "on": " 'No' reverses to polyvalent 'on.' And that monosyllable—on—may serve as the watchword of Beckett's ever searching, ever exploring 'wordward ho' " (13).

18. For a fuller exposition of the complex directionality of Beckett's title, see Enoch Brater, "Voyelles, Cromlechs and the Special (W)rites of *Worstward Ho*," in *Beckett's Later Fiction and Drama: Texts for Company*, ed. James Acheson and Kateryna Arthur (London: Macmillan, 1987), 167–68.

19. Samuel Beckett, *Waiting for Godot* (New York: Grove, 1954), 15. As he does on occasion, Beckett winks at the reader in his stage directions: "Pozzo: *(Off)* On!" This binary joke is transformed and revived at the end of the play:

Vladimir: Pull on your trousers.

Estragon: What?

Vladimir: Pull on your trousers.

Estragon: You want me to pull off my trousers?

Vladimir: Pull ON your trousers. (60)

20. Productions have frequently, and rightly I think, suggested in their management of the decor that Winnie is not so much sinking as being engorged by a rising mound of earth. This is also a recollection and resistance of the drowning that concludes "The End" and that seems figuratively to conclude *Malone Dies:* not water but dry sand; not sinking but being pursued by the upward-moving earth. This reorientation of the vectors of force is given an additional twist by Winnie in her reflections: "Yes, the feeling more and more that if I were not held—*(gesture)*—in this way, I would simply float up into the blue. *(Pause.)* Don't you ever have that feeling, Willie, of being sucked up? *(Pause.)* Don't you have to cling on sometimes, Willie?" (33–34).

21. *The Collected Shorter Plays of Samuel Beckett* (New York: Grove, 1984), 60, 61, 63. A friendly critic admonishes that in Beckett's French version of *Krapp*, "Let me in" is rendered not in the imperative but in the past perfect *(passé composé):* "M'ont laissé entrer." "Let me in" could conceivably be spoken in performance as "They let me in," but should it necessarily? The question raises the important issue of how, or whether, Beckett's translations should be used to gloss the original. Note, for example, that the instruction preceding the line in English—"*(Pause. Low.)*"—becomes in French merely "*(Pause.).*" The English Krapp speaks with a different voice at this point; the French Krapp does not. I am inclined to see two different linguistic events here, performed by two different characters. The point is grist for the argument I have been making that Beckett's art works against itself—even as a self-translator he practices an art of subtle misremembrance. For more on Beckett's self-translation, see Brian T. Fitch, *Beckett and Babel: an Investigation into the Status of the Bilingual Work* (Toronto: University of Toronto Press, 1988).

22. As has often been pointed out, there is other internal evidence that *Krapp* was a vehicle of more than ordinary self-assessment for Beckett. Krapp was at one time an aspiring writer who actually wrote a novel, and his experience on "that memorable night at the end of the jetty" (*Shorter Plays*, 60) seems closely to render what may have been a similar revelation of Beckett's, roughly at the age of thirty-nine, on the Dun Laoghaire Pier just south of Dublin. It is tempting to see *Murphy* in Krapp's poorly selling novel (the French edition of *Murphy* sold extremely poorly in the late forties; Deirdre Bair, *Samuel Beckett: A Biography* [New York: Harcourt Brace, 1978], 490) and in Krapp's tapes the much more inward, autographical writing that Beckett began around the time of his revelation on the jetty, presuming that it occurred. On this last point, see Enoch Brater, *Why Beckett* (London: Thames and Hudson, 1989), 94.

23. Tom F. Driver, "Beckett by the Madeleine," *Columbia University Forum*, Summer 1961:23.

24. Ruby Cohn, *Just Play: Beckett's Theater* (Princeton: Princeton University Press, 1980), 13.

25. "For [Beckett] the 'important writing' always means prose" (Bair, *Samuel Beckett*, 562).

26. Theodor W. Adorno, "Trying to Understand *Endgame*," in *Modern Critical Interpretations: Endgame*, ed. Harold Bloom (New York: Chelsea House, 1988), 17. This essay was originally published in *New German Critique* 26 (Summer 1982).

27. Mikhail Bakhtin, *Problems of Dostoevsky's Poetics*, trans. R. W. Rotsel (Ann Arbor: Ardis, 1973), 28; see also 13–14.

28. Bert States refers to a "processing Consciousness" that dominates plays like *Endgame* and *Krapp's Last Tape*, though he finds it absent in *Waiting for Godot*. See *The Shape of Paradox: An Essay on "Waiting for Godot"* (Berkeley and Los Angeles: University of California Press, 1978), 11.

29. Walter Benjamin, "Fate and Character" in *Reflections*, trans. Edmund Jephcott (New York: Harcourt, 1978), 310. Mary McCarthy developed a similar critique of Bergsonian theory in her essay "Characters in Fiction" in *The Humanist in the Bathtub* (New York: Signet, 1964), 195–216.

30. Paul-Louis Mignon, "Le théâtre de A jusqu'a Z: Samuel Beckett," *L'Avant-scène du théâtre* 313 (15 June 1964): 8.

31. Alain Robbe-Grillet, "Samuel Beckett, or Presence on the Stage," reprinted in *For A New Novel*, trans. Richard Howard (New York: Grove, 1965), 111–25.

32. Enoch Brater's discussion of all three versions of *What Where* can be found in his *Beyond Minimalism: Beckett's Late Style in the Theater* (New York & Oxford: Oxford University Press, 1987), 152–64. For another view of the Paris production, see S. E. Gontarski, "*What Where* II: Revision as Re-creation," *The Review of Contemporary Fiction* 7 (Summer 1987): 120–23. Martha Fehsenfeld's richly detailed account of the making of *Was Wo* can be found in "Everything Out But the Faces: Beckett's Reshaping of *What Where* for Television," *Modern Drama* 29 (June 1986): 229–40.

33. Cameraman Jim Lewis, quoted in Fehsenfeld, "Everything Out," 236.

34. Mark Swed, "John Cage: A Rebel Sets Up in Ivied Halls," *Los Angeles Times*, 13 November 1988, Calendar section, p. 70.

35. Alan Schneider, "Waiting for Beckett: A Personal Chronicle," *Chelsea Review* 2 (September 1958): 8.

36. See Linda Ben-Zvi's shrewd conjectures regarding the importance of Beckett's gender assignments in "Women in *Godot*," *The Beckett Circle* 10 (December 1988): 7.

37. Gilles Deleuze, *Foucault*, trans. Seán Hand (Minneapolis: University of Minnesota Press, 1988), 43.

38. Jacques Lacan, "The Function and Field of Speech and Language in Psychoanalysis," in *Ecrits: A Selection*, trans. Alan Sheridan (New York: Norton, 1977), 57.

39. "German Letter of 1937," trans. Martin Esslin, in Samuel Beckett, *Disjecta: Miscellaneous Writings and a Dramatic Fragment*, ed. Ruby Cohn (London: Calder, 1983), 171–72.

40. "J'ai toujours eu la sensation qu'il y avait en moi un être assassiné. Assassiné avant ma naissance. Il me fallait retrouver cet être assassiné. Tenter de lui redonner vie . . ." (Charles Juliet, *Rencontre avec Samuel Beckett* [Paris: Editions Fata Morgana, 1986], 14.

41. As time passes and we gain in historical perspective, Beckett's earnestness (his modernist center of gravity) stands out with increasing insistence. Since writing this

essay, I have read Breon Mitchell's "Samuel Beckett and the Postmodernist Controversy," a piece that reinforces mine on this and other points. Mitchell writes that "there is something in the deep seriousness of Beckett's attitude toward art that looks suspiciously modernist. The least that can be said is that he does not fit in comfortably with the playful self-reflexivity of many of his present-day colleagues" (*Exploring Postmodernism,* ed. Matei Calinescu and Douwe Fokkema [Amsterdam and Philadelphia: J. Benjamins, 1987], 114).

Beckett, Shakespeare, and
the Making of Theory

CHARLES R. LYONS

Both the theater and criticism depend upon the production of the
new and the reappropriation of the old. Each generation demands its
own dramatic innovation and, as well, readdresses those classic texts
that it finds particularly apt or useful by subjecting them to new
modes of production and revisionist critical analysis. Because of the
ways in which we divide up areas of study, we usually discuss the
respective permutations of playwriting, performance, and critical discourse as discrete phenomena with individual histories. Of course,
none of us would quarrel with the fact that these activities function
interdependently, because production and criticism obviously follow
original acts of writing and attempt to negotiate special relationships
between texts and the spectators or readers who consume them.
However, when we speak or write about these activities, we usually
work within the separate vocabularies of dramatic literature, theater
history, and aesthetic theory. This habit of emphasizing the generic
and rhetorical differences with which we characterize playwriting,
performance, and criticism suppresses our recognition of the dynamics of their interaction and the subtle connections and covert reci-
procities that inform their combined histories.

The nexus of theory, writing, and performance provides the general subject of this essay. In particular, I would like to use this occasion to pose some questions about certain relationships between Samuel Beckett's texts and several of the movements in aesthetic theory and criticism that provide the theoretical scene with which they interact. Critical theory usually demonstrates its most telling revisionist positions in its response to Shakespeare. As I discuss the work of Samuel Beckett in the context of theory, I often point therefore toward essays on Shakespeare to identify significant transitions in critical strategy.[1] I discuss New Criticism's rejection of Bradleian mimesis as the theoretical context in which Beckett's writing began, and I posit certain relationships between the critical emphasis on linguistic image and the self-conscious antinaturalism of avant-garde playwriting. As well, I talk about the apt fit between the analytic strategies of existential phenomenology and Beckett's early dramatic writing; and I relate the problematics of the subject in the later plays to the questioning of the subject in poststructural discourse. In Beckett's radical dramatic simplification, the presence of the speaking/ listening figure, the necessary and yet circumscribed actor, forces us to deal with the function of *character* in a revised mimesis. The paradox of human presence in texts that contend with the very notion of subjectivity enacts the dilemmas of dramatic criticism. In a very simple sense, I relate Beckett's writing to sequential shifts in emphases that foreground the consciousness of the writer, the processes of reading and interpreting both new writing and the classics, and, at the present moment, the perception of the text as contingent upon its cultural moment. Because this topic exceeds the scope of a single essay, my remarks here function as a prolegomenon to the project of seeing the dynamics of the relationship between Beckett's writing and the aesthetic ideologies that form the theoretical arena in which they play.

In this discussion, I assume the following important exchanges— some of which, I realize, are not self-evident, but which, I trust, will become clearer as my discussion proceeds: (1) new forms of dramatic writing and performance often provide models of perception that criticism re-represents and appropriates within the methodologies that direct its own argument; (2) new modes of both writing and performance encourage theatrical and scholarly reinterpretations of the classics that appropriate the analytic structures that have developed in response to avant garde texts but become more fully articulated and valued in application to texts that are established in the canon; (3) certain modes of experimental playwriting extend and develop the critical strategies in which they are discussed in a dialogic relationship that informs both the continuation of new writing and the development of theory.

I recognize certain inherent difficulties in seeing these interactions within the clear sequential scheme of a history. First of all, each of these activities is subject to conflicting influences and sometimes responds to antithetical stimuli simultaneously. For example, in the early 1960s important productions at the newly retitled Royal Shakespeare Company used selected visual techniques of the epic theater—especially an elegant spareness of scene in combination with well-wrought properties that invoked the materialism of the objective world. At the same time, the company used this simplified aesthetic to develop self-consciously Beckettian images of the isolated subject. Peter Brook, Peter Hall, and John Bury, for example, responded to the visual stimuli of the productions of the Berliner Ensemble that came to London in the late 1950s and reacted as well to the growing interest in both Brechtian and Beckettian dramaturgy stimulated by and reflected in the publication of Martin Esslin's critical biography, *Brecht: A Choice of Evils*, in 1959, and *The Theatre of the Absurd* in 1961. And, of course, the influence of Jan Kott's conflation of *King Lear* and *Endgame* on Brook's production of the Shakespearean tragedy has become emblematized in theater history. While the absurd and the epic seemed to mark antithetical directions in the contemporary theater, Shakespearean production assimilated aspects of each as the Royal Shakespeare Company marked out its aesthetic course in the 1960s and 1970s.

The activities of writing, performance, and criticism respond in different rhythms to changing tastes and ideologies.[2] At specific moments, any one of the phenomena may appear more prominent and work to incorporate others. For example, the absurd's use of comedy to represent human suffering with some seriousness played into the ongoing critical reappraisal of comedy in both performance and criticism, which was illustrated in the emphasis on the darker aspects of Shakespeare's romantic comedy in both scholarship and production. Whereas one aspect of the reassessment of comedy as a serious aesthetic phenomenon focused on the existential project of seeing the self in relationship to an absurd world, another positioned comedy within the dynamics of society by incorporating the ideas of comic structure articulated earlier by the Cambridge Anthropologists, who traced an evolutionary scheme between ritual and comedy. These theories foregrounded the comic function of displaying and overcoming the threat of death. Criticism became interested in the balance between comic structure, with its emphasis on social unity and the accommodation of self to society, and the presence of images of the finite, mutable, and disjunctive. Comedies or tragicomedies that foregrounded the problematic began to receive the most critical attention, and in Shakespeare studies and performance, even *Twelfth Night* metamorphosed from a happy comedy to a melancholy one.[3] While the new emphasis on the painful in comedy precedes the international attention paid to Beckett, *Waiting for Godot* soon became the signal text for marking tragicomedy as the quintessential modern form.[4]

Northrop Frye's *Anatomy of Criticism* gave individual status to irony as the genre that mediates between tragedy and comedy and represents a world without heroes; Beckett's bleak environments that hold clownlike performers were seen to fit closely into Frye's new category, which extended from the irony of satire to the edge of tragedy. The new attention paid to *Troilus and Cressida* in both the theater and criticism positioned this problem play as the most modern of Shakespeare's texts in its equivocal softening of the edges between comedy and tragedy. The reassessment of this structural hybrid made generic purity as a viable aesthetic ideal seem quaint and old-fashioned.[5] The revaluation of *Troilus and Cressida* corresponds to the valuation of *Godot*. We need to think more closely about the ways in which the ironies, equivocations, and dislocations exposed in the texts and displayed in performances of *Godot, Endgame*, and *Troilus and Cressida* influenced the foregrounded ironies and subversions of the comic in the darkening of Shakespearean romantic comedy in the theater and criticism in the 1960s and 1970s.

In the past fifteen years, two emphases in theory have extended our sense of the seriousness of comedy and corrected the more naive theatrical and critical application of the ideas of the Cambridge Anthropologists.[6] Bakhtin's notion of carnivalization—the balance between order and disorder, orthodoxy and subversion—provides a conceptual structure in which the playfulness of comedy assumes purposefulness. As well, Victor Turner's sophisticated juxtaposition of structure and antistructure and the perspective of the liminal has given critics and theater practitioners a new and currently vital anthropology that invests comedic action with social significance.[7] Consequently, Beckett's comic and ironic tropes play with a field in which playfulness is seen as functional; and their seriousness, in turn, becomes part of the material that theory addresses to demonstrate the function of comic writing.

Looking in another direction, it is possible to see Brecht's subversive revision of orthodox history as an aesthetic anticipation of certain ideas in Foucauldian historiography. Brecht performed a theatrical archaeology that exposed the mechanisms of political dominance and gave the oppressed a voice. Brecht's drama also anticipates the kind of revisionist history that marks the new historical and feminist criticism of Shakespeare. The intervening phenomenon of structuralist aesthetics insures that these newer arguments identify the patterns of dominance and submission as voicings of a culture rather than as the playwright's intentional exposure of political realities. In some clear sense, however, Brechtian dramaturgy provides an explicit model for these later discussions of the implicit social critique that may function within a dramatic text and its performance.[8] The new historicism and related arguments in feminist criticism identify the processes in which texts can voice critiques of the ideologies that dominate their cultural moment. In a sense, these critical arguments identify voices within both canonized and uncanonized texts that have been stilled by the continuing authority of those ideologies.

The same phenomenon occurs in playwriting. Churchill's *Top Girls* and *Cloud Nine*, Shange's *Colored Girls*, and August Wilson's *Ma Rainey's Black Bottom* (to identify only a few) display figures whose oppression critiques authority and whose newly articulate voices speak against the status quo. No one would argue against the firm Brechtian foundation of this kind of playwriting. The politicalization of the text accomplished by the new historicism and feminist theory renews the energy generated by the enthusiasm for radical political drama in the culture of the 1960s and early 1970s. The political voice of the 1980s finds the representation of the marginalized and oppressed in new playwriting and, most particularly, in the "early modern" drama of the Renaissance.[9] Criticism articulates this political sensibility through and against the elaborate screens of deconstructionism, "correcting" the formalism of poststructuralism with a Foucauldian vision of history. In these arguments, performance becomes important because it constitutes the activity of those who occupy the periphery of society and who refract and articulate the structures of the dominant center from the perspective of that marginalization.

At a less visible point of interaction, Jean-Pierre Vernant's identification of the archaic heroes of classic tragedy as vehicles for the discussion of contemporary political issues posits a structural relationship between the dramatization of history and fifth-century politics that could not have been articulated as clearly before the radical practices of Brecht had been assimilated into both dramatic convention and critical argument. Brecht's clarification of the political value of the figure drawn from history gives a particular resonance to Vernant's theoretical arguments. Vernant posits a model of aesthetic familiarization and defamiliarization as a means of defining the political function of fifth-century tragedy.[10] He notes that the citizen spectators would identify with the chorus, as members of the polis, in a special way because many of them had participated as amateur performers in the choruses of earlier festival events; and yet the deliberately archaic verse form of the choral odes themselves would distance this language as removed from the speech of the present. The professional cadre of actors performing characters drawn from the archaic past of this culture would be seen as distant, remote; and yet they would speak in a language that more closely appropriated the speech of fifth-century Athens. As the significant issues of the polis were explicated in the crises of this tragic drama, the response of the civic audience was stimulated by an aesthetic practice in which the familiar was made strange and the strange was made familiar. While Vernant does not refer specifically to Brechtian theory, his argument takes place in the context of widespread familiarity with the function of *Verfremdung* both in theory and theatrical practice. And the understanding of alienation or estrangement, as a significant function in twentieth-century theater, informs the argument.

I mention the possible assimilation of Brechtian dramaturgy and its obvious analogues for two reasons: First of all, the theatricalization of a specialized view of history in Brechtian drama relates to the politicalization of classic texts in literary theory and, therefore, illustrates my claim for the interaction of playwriting and the revisionist criticism of established texts in the canon. Second, Beckett's dramaturgy has been defined as antithetical to Brechtian political theater even though Beckett's first produced play, *Waiting for Godot*, uses images of authority and oppression to limit the parameters of behavior and *Endgame* focuses almost exclusively on a relationship that could be profitably discussed in terms of the Hegelian/Marxian lordship/bondage paradigm.[11] The apparent invulnerability of Beckett's texts to political interpretation is probably not sufficiently explained by their solipsism or Beckett's own refusal to lead a political life, but may well derive from the fact that *Waiting for Godot* entered the public world at a time when its interpretative problems could best be explained within the terminology of existentialism. Could there have been any clearer way of addressing Beckett's texts in the 1960s than seeing them as related to the existential search for self-definition in which the human figure, alienated from any sense of community, isolated in an environment that is virtually empty of significance as place, is limited to an exploration of the processes of consciousness in his or her attempt to forge an operative image of the self?

Within the limited range of the kind of action allowed the Beckettian figure, the existential interpretation of Beckett's protagonists, which places them in a world in which only they can author or authorize their action, presents a vision of the world that is very much like the universe projected by Cedric Whitman in his revisionist interpretation, *Sophocles: A Study of Heroic Humanism*. Consider for example:

There is no divine interference in the play; "Apollo knows the future, but does not create it." The only difference between human and divine knowledge is that the latter is not limited by time, and therefore may see all things as finished. . . . In the *Oedipus*, however, time has no special function, except as the road upon which the mind travels in order to find out what is timelessly true: . . . But what really functions is the mind of man, and its success reveals its failure. The failure has been emphasized, in terms of human nothingness, the folly of human wisdom, the gap between man and the gods, the emptiness of human good fortune. . . . the essential interest lies in the strength of Oedipus, the keenness of human wisdom which can find out its own secret, the function of a divine necessity within man which makes a standard of its own and holds the standard to be worth more than empty good fortune.[12]

Martin Esslin's essay on Beckett in *The Theatre of the Absurd*, subtitled "The Search for Self," discusses an exchange between Vladimir and Estragon that builds on the image of "all the dead voices" in a discussion that evokes a similar world:

> These rustling, murmuring voices of the past are the voices we hear in the three novels of his trilogy; they are the voices that explore the mysteries of being and the self to the limits of anguish and suffering. Vladimir and Estragon are trying to escape hearing them. The long silence that follows their evocation is broken by Vladimir, *"in anguish,"* with the cry "Say anything at all!" after which the two relapse into their wait for Godot.
>
> The hope of salvation may be merely an evasion of the suffering and anguish that spring from facing the reality of the human condition. There is here a truly astonishing parallel between the Existentialist philosophy of Jean-Paul Sartre and the creative intuition of Beckett, who has never consciously expressed Existentialist views. If, for Beckett, as for Sartre, man has the duty of facing the human condition as recognition that at the root of our being there is nothingness, liberty, and the need of constantly creating ourself in a succession of choices, then Godot might well become an image of what Sartre calls "bad faith"—"The first act of bad faith consists in evading what one cannot evade, in evading what one *is*."[13]

In relation to my assertions about the interaction among writing, criticism, and performance, several things need to be said about these two gracefully written passages of criticism, the former published in 1951 and the second in 1961. Whitman's reading of the Sophoclean texts precedes both the publication and performance of Beckett's play. Here the potential contemporary model may be the dramas of Sartre. However, both interpretations build upon the practice of reading texts through the dominant or, in the critic's frame of reference, the most vitally current ideology. Whitman's radical reinterpretation of the Sophoclean text aggressively counters the history of its interpretation and remains a provocative anomaly that has been only partially assimilated by scholarship. Esslin's interpretation of *Waiting for Godot*, on the other hand, forms a base for the scholarship that has built up around the texts of Samuel Beckett. Whitman's study attempts to reify the classic text. Esslin's study attempts to ground the radically new within a complex but identifiable philosophic position as he posits the analogies between the self-consciousness of Sartre and the intuitive aesthetic perception of Beckett. Each of these three texts—one dramatic and two critical—works within the dominant intellectual paradigm of postwar Europe that was soon to be revised by structuralism. But while Beckett's later plays were produced in that context, *Godot* became a public artifact when the arguments of existential phenomenology provided the intellectual context for their interpretation.

The repetition of paradigmatic situations and verbal tropes in Beckett's texts gives their voice a certain affinity to the reconstituted image of the subject in Georges Poulet's discussions of Racine.[14] Poulet's critical strategy, based upon existential phenomenology, builds an image of an implicit subjectivity within an author's oeuvre that encloses the texts. The narrow focus of Beckett's writing, its pattern of writing and rewriting the figure of the aging character grappling with the surrounding space and some narrative of the past, seems to provide a model for the intricately organized unity and the transcendent image of subjectivity that the Geneva School put forward as the project of imaginative writing. As well, the progressive deletion of referential detail in Beckett's texts, the increasing diminution of corroborative images of place and situation, the consequent emphasis on the presence of the speaking figure—all these phenomena encourage readers to think of the texts as the representation of the single consciousness isolated from anything except the images that revolve within its limits. The dramatized figure's oscillating engagement and disengagement in the processes of perceiving and ascertaining the possibilities and limitations of a bleak environment make Beckett's drama appear to theatricalize the project of existential phenomenology.

One of the phenomena that mark the relationship of theory and text at a given moment is what I would call their shared representational function. When I use the term *representation*, I am not talking about the practice of realism but rather about the aesthetic and the critical text as the enactment of a perception contingent upon its own situation in time and place. One of the ways in which we experience new writing is to envision it as a form of perception, a schema in which some aspect of the world is reconfigured in an aperçu tied in some way to the present moment both in content and in mode of representation.[15] And when criticism addresses a specific text or hypothesizes about imaginative literature more generally, the critical essay itself displays a perception of the world—or, at least, a segment of that world—either directly or indirectly. The material in the text the essay addresses allows the critic's conceptualization of reality to assume a particular shape. Lukács's Marxian analysis of Scott performs a representation of the world just as Poulet's phenomenological study of Racine or Ernst Jones's psychoanalytic reading of *Hamlet* builds particularized images of the human psyche engaged in mediating between internal and external realities. Even as inclusive a system as Northrop Frye's theory of myths takes on the project of positioning literature as the civilized resolution of humankind's alienation from the natural world.[16]

Edward Said's essay "The Text, the World, the Critic" describes critical discourse in terms of "its dialectic of engagement in time and the senses, . . ." He writes:

> Just as it is all too often true that texts are thought of as monolithic objects of the past, to which criticism is a despondent appendage in the present, then the very conception of criticism symbolizes being outdated, being dated *from* the past rather than *by* the present. . . . if we assume instead that texts make up what Foucault calls archival facts, the archive being defined as the text's social discursive presence in the world, then criticism, too, is another aspect of that present. In other words, one should prefer to say that rather than being defined by the silent past, commanded by it to speak in the present, criticism, no less than any other text, is the present in the course of its articulation, struggles for definition, attempts at overcoming.[17]

Said's essay speaks to our present awareness of the discursive situation of criticism, an awareness that, in itself, enacts the same self-reflexity that marks contemporary fiction and drama.[18]

The provocative title of Jan Kott's *Shakespeare Our Contemporary*, which I mentioned earlier, admits the revisionist process of Shakespearean criticism and exemplifies Said's notion that "criticism . . . is the present in the course of its articulation."[19] Kott's attempt to read *King Lear* through Beckett's *Endgame*, in an essay that was challenging in the early 1960s, now seems so inextricably tied to the early attempts to deal with *Godot* and *Endgame* existentially that it has become as specifically "dated" as the interpretations of Dowden or Bradley or Carolyn Spurgeon, even if we honor it as significant archivally.[20] The material on Beckett in *Shakespeare Our Contemporary*, like Martin Esslin's early work on Beckett, does not, however, seem as dated as the conceit of reading Shakespeare through Beckett. Is that because we have experienced the contingent relationship between Beckett and existentialism as part of our own history? Do the newer studies of *King Lear* that assimilate the distance that Shakespeare studies has traveled since the early 1960s have more immediate vitality for us at this point? Kott's essay clearly illustrates the tendency in revisionist criticism to read the classic text as if it were organized within the same aesthetic conventions and implicit ideologies as those the critic sees in the contemporary text. *Shakespeare Our Contemporary* relates to Beckettian drama, self-consciously, as clearly as A. C. Bradley's *Shakespearean Tragedy* relates to nineteenth-century realism unself-consciously.

Bradley's detailed analyses of the tragedies describe them as masterfully perceptive case histories of human behavior, which, in their vividness, sometimes break through and distort the formal structure that attempts to contain them. Bradley's energetic writing acts out a belief in the correlation between dramatic representation and the psychological phenomena of human action, a correlation that relates it to the naturalistic project of Ibsen's playwriting. At the end of the century, both new drama and criticism assumed the possibility of holding the mirror up to nature, and playwriting and scholarship maintained a sure confidence that the aesthetic text and the corresponding critical essay could replicate and explicate an instance of human behavior—as an object in the world. Both Ibsen's plays and Bradley's lectures enact the belief that behavior can be displayed in the progressive revelation of signifying details that manifest behavior directly and reveal its motives indirectly. Reader and spectator can, therefore, interpret these significant details and assign them significance and veracity according to received notions of psychology. While the absence of self-consciousness from *Shakespearean Tragedy* would have restrained Bradley from identifying his collection of lectures on *Shakespeare Our Contemporary*, his commentaries do, of course, reconstitute these "Renaissance" plays as "modern"—that is, related to the new realism—by identifying their dependence on a nineteenth-century idea of ethos and motive.

The New Critical revolution's displacement of the primacy of *character* and *action* in the critical lexicon and redirection of attention to issues of language was analogous to the movement away from con-

ventional processes of representation in the theater's rejection of realism. In the avant-garde drama of the early twentieth century, the
representation of human behavior as an objective presence dissolved
into the anamorphic transformations of expressionism, the conflicting planes of cubism, and the irreconcilable fragments of theatrical surrealism. *Character* seemed almost to disappear from the
lexicon apart from the exercises of the neo-Aristotelians. Criticism
exercised similar strategies in atemporal analyses of strata of meaning
that were seen to operate simultaneously, and this kind of analysis
emphasized spatial rather than narrative or sequential principles of
organization. As playwriting foregrounded the techniques of theatrical production and the moment of performance, critical texts exam-
ined the operation of the language of the literary text in minute detail;
and these explications frequently isolated dramatic language from the
context of the speaker as an agent within the scene as dramatic situation. The assumption that one could hold the mirror up to nature
became a "naive idea" in relationship to the greater sophistication of
the New Criticism and the new art that privileged process over mimesis. However, both the antirealistic art and New Criticism were themselves imitative of ideologies of relativism and fragmentation. The description of tiers of meaning in William Empson's *Seven Types of Ambiguity* (1930) or Ingarten's *Das literarische Kunstwerk* (1931) reflects the
assumption that various mediations of what is observed can function
simultaneously. Theorists like Ingarten and Empson diffuse the single-
point perspective of Bradleian mimesis in their demand that we read
texts vertically rather than horizontally, that we replace an interest in
narrative sequence with our awareness of an intricate network of sub-
structural verbal processes that organize the text as poem.[21]

The representation of temporal process, explored in Proust by both
Poulet and Beckett, exercises nonlinear paradigms and simultaneity
and also confounds conventional narrative sequence as an organizing
principle. The "complexity" of Shakespearean language made these
dramatic texts fertile ground for the excavations of New Criticism,
but this methodology assumed that the plays would be experienced
in reading, not performance. Bradley's interest in character assumed
as well that the plays would be read as novels. Bakhtin asserted the
supremacy of the nineteenth-century novel and claimed that within
the new realism drama was itself "novelized."[22] New Criticism does
not demand "novelistic" reading, since it does not foreground narra-

tive, but, on the contrary, treats dramatic poetry more as lyric. The dissolution of linear sequence in the avant-garde playwriting of the early twentieth century aligns with the foregrounding of structure displayed spatially in criticism. Both criticism and playwriting at this point identified the clarification of narrative movement as reactionary.

While the radically diminished plot of Beckett's first produced play surprised its audiences, *Waiting for Godot* continued the rejection of narrative schemes of organization in the earlier avant garde. The nonlinearity of *Waiting for Godot*, the absence of conventional plot, and the infinite deferral of the resolving appearance of the title figure capped the experimental theater's rejection of the "novelistic" drama of the late nineteenth and early twentieth centuries and the parallel novelization of Shakespeare in criticism. The success of *Godot* in the theater was analogous to the notoriety achieved in the literary world by the publication of L. C. Knights's essay titled "How Many Children Had Lady Macbeth?" some twenty years earlier. This provocative article defined the rejection of Bradleian mimesis by the younger critics who would set the course of Shakespearean criticism in the following quarter century. Knights's paper ridicules the character-oriented criticism of Bradley and emphasizes the need to deal with the Shakespeare text as poetry. Knights even quotes G. Wilson Knight's assertion that we should perceive each of the Shakespearean plays as "an expanded metaphor."[23]

Critics have identified the innovation in Beckett in the same terms as those in which New Criticism has asked us to read Shakespeare. Consider, for example, the following citation from an essay written by Martin Esslin in 1976:

In plays like *Not I, That Time,* and *Footfalls,* it is by no means essential that the audience in the theatre should be able to decode the complex story lines and intellectual puzzles they enshrine. On the contrary, what the audience should experience and take home with them after their brief exposure to these *dramatic metaphors* [italics mine] is precisely the *overall impact* of a single over-whelmingly powerful image, composed of the startling visual element; the strange murmur of subdued voices in a dim half-light; the strange and powerful *rhythms* of both light and voices; the magical effect of the poetic phrasing and the richness of the images the language carries along on its relentless flow.

It is by making his images *unforgettable* through the startling novelty of their visual impact and the density of a multitude of linguistic, visual, and dramatic elements deployed at one and the same time at *a multitude of levels* [italics mine], that Beckett reaches his audience.[24]

Esslin's reading of these plays foregrounds their innovation as the theatrical rejection of the complexities of "novelistic" narrative. While Esslin addresses the complexities of language, his interpretation frees that language from its narrative base and suggests that we respond to an all-inclusive visualized image. Beckett's own reading of Proust, which develops a notion of the simultaneity of past and present in the textual moment, New Criticism's sense of the dramatic text as "expanded metaphor," and phenomenological studies of the Geneva School reconfigure the text as the manifestation of a singular but expansive moment of consciousness that embodies the processes of time without moving sequentially through an Aristotelian chronology. These readings assume a transaction between the consciousness of the author and the imagination of the reader or spectator; and that transaction absorbs narrative data and then suppresses it in the reconfiguration of the *moment* communicated.

Both criticism and drama in the last fifty years have put increased pressure on the responsibilities of reading; and the shift of the significant *subject* from author to text to reader responds to the demands made on the reader to intervene actively in order to complete the text. While New Criticism and phenomenologically oriented criticism sustain the idea of the author as subject even while they emphasize the processes of reading, the theoretical exercises of the past twenty years have diminished the image of the writer/subject.

Roland Barthes's essay "The Death of the Author," first published in 1968, has become an emblem in the history of critical theory that rivals the facetiously titled "How Many Children Had Lady Macbeth?" which preceded it by thirty-five years. While this essay itself has achieved seminal status, Barthes's argument confirms critical practices that precede it. Wayne Booth's notion of the implied author had already differentiated the actual persona of the author from both the consciousness that structures the text and the narrator who determines what material is communicated to the reader. Booth's arguments in *The Rhetoric of Fiction* established a sense of the

implied author as an aesthetic function that positions the n
and, while the idea of this fictional persona is established
author himself as a "second self," Booth's choice of the adjective
implied incorporated the work of the reader and prepared the way for
Iser's notion of reading.[25] And by this time, the historical persona of
the author had already been displaced in phenomenologically oriented criticism by a consciousness created not only by the individual
text but by the sum of texts that constitute an oeuvre in Poulet's
sense. The dynamics of a text, in Poulet's terms, are realized by the
complicity of two imaginations: the idiosyncratic consciousness created by the constellation of images that form a text, or an oeuvre, and
the consciousness established in reading in a process of "transubjec-
tivity." Poulet's reading does include the critical formation of an originating subject, but his configuration of a psychic biography remains
independent of an actual biography even though it is dependent on
a kind of documentation in essays, letters, and nonaesthetic writing
of all kinds, as well as literary works. The relationship between this
psychic biography and the author's history in any conventional sense
of that term is irrelevant. While Poulet's readings maintain the image
of the originating consciousness, their emphasis on the reader's mediation of the individual images that constitute the material of that
consciousness anticipates the shift in attention from the authorial
subject to the consciousness of the reader.[26]

One of the particular objectives of this essay is to demonstrate that
Beckett's texts enact the assumptions that dominate literary and aesthetic theory in the last two decades. Consider, for example, the title
of Wolfgang Iser's chapter on the trilogy in *The Implied Reader*: "Subjectivity as the Autogenous Cancellation of Its Own Manifestations."[27] With its sequentially tentative predications of narrator, the
trilogy—*Molloy, Malone Dies*, and *The Unnamable*—provides Iser with
substantial material for his propositions concerning the nature of
reading itself. That is, the dynamics of the relationship of the implied
narrators of the trilogy to the texts they "produce" is itself mimetic
of the relationship that Iser poses between reader and text. He details
the processes of configuring and reconfiguring the relationship of
speaker, fictional world, and narrative in a series of speculations
that self-consciously bridge the indeterminacies that mark a text. Iser
states:

It is only through inevitable omissions that a story gains its dynamism. Thus whenever the flow is interrupted and we are led off in unexpected directions, the opportunity is given to us to bring into play our own faculty for establishing connections—for filling in the gaps left by the text itself.[28]

Iser poses a notion of a reader whose participation in the *realization* of the text contributes to the formation of its "virtual dimension." Because of the potentiality for different configurations that form the tissue for the bridging of the gaps, the text remains inexhaustible. That inexhaustibility forces the reader to make decisions and, in the case of writing as fragmented as Beckett's, to be self-consciously aware of his or her own capacity for providing interconnective material.[29]

The reader or spectator is the subject in question in Iser's theoretical description of the communicative function of the novel. And, with facility, Iser concludes his individual analysis with a discussion of a play, *Fin de partie* or *Endgame*, as the definitive indeterminate text. This dramatic text exercises repetitive gestures, statements, and responses that suggest the possibility that the interaction of Hamm and Clov fulfills the rules of established game that the two figures have played previously and may play again. However, the text also offers clues that this version of the game may be different and may move toward some kind of closure—that within the terms of the fiction, Hamm may be moving toward a death. The inability of the reader or spectator to determine what the final moments of this play mean forces them to recognize that their interpretation is hypothetical, speculative, subjective. As Iser states:

If the rules of the *Endgame* have to be projected onto it by the spectator, then clearly the text itself cannot establish that any one of the possibilities is the correct one. And if one does draw up a consistent code to apply to the whole game, it can only be at the expense of all other levels of the text; and when the spectator turns his attention to those levels excluded by the 'code' he seems to be fixed on, he has no alternative but to reject his own meaning projections. Thus *Endgame* compels its spectator to reject the 'meanings' it stimulates, and in this way conveys something of the 'unendingness' of the end and the nature of the fictions which we are continually fabricating in order to finish off the end or to close the gaps in our experiences.[30]

Iser's rhetorical strategy here is to focus on the hypothetical experience of a performance of *Endgame* as a model for the spectator's attempt to free himself from entrapment in the fictions that shape his own experience. The essay ends, therefore, with an idea of the text as mimetic of the spectator's action, not as the expression or manifestation of a physical process experienced by the author. Both Brecht's and Beckett's dramatic texts resist closure; that is, they demand mediation by the spectator or reader in order to constitute wholes. Brecht's texts operate by negation to provoke their audiences to focus on alternate behaviors; Beckett's texts require their audiences to formulate hypothetical connections that emphasize the arbitrariness of the very minimal images of character and narrative they provoke. In different ways, the plays of Brecht and Beckett require active intervention on the part of those who read or witness them. The model of spectator they assume approximates the kind of involvement with the text that recent criticism both demands and valorizes.

The emphasis on the processes of reading in criticism has produced highly complicated theories of narrative organization, and the novel has become the privileged literary form in recent years. While the emphasis on language in Shakespeare studies from 1930 through the 1960s built images of atemporal texts that bound complexity to the idea of conceptual unity, recent study of prose fiction foregrounds the complexities of sequence. The emergence of narratology provides one motive for the shift away from Shakespeare's texts as the material with which theory articulates its most telling positions. The temporal expansiveness possible in the novel allows for the new interest in the problematics of sequence. Gérard Genette's *Narrative Discourse: An Essay in Method* builds an elegant refraction of Proust's *A la Recherche du temps perdu* that, like Barthes's *S/Z*, requires a detailed marking of the relationship of segment to segment in the progression of the text.[31] At the same time, in a fascinating coincidence, Beckett's work for the theater begins to take the shape of performed narratives; and the formal distinctions between his prose fiction and drama recede.[32] While the repetition of the narrative in the sequence from *Not I* to *Rockaby* allows the spectator to process the difficult sequencing of images and events these recitations present, the kind of detailed critical manipulation of a text that works like Genette's model cannot occur in the theater except in simplified approximation. The practices of narratology do not yield much in a single reading either but, rather, constitute strategies in which to accomplish a series of rereadings.

While Iser's discussion of *Endgame* provides provocative ways in which to think about its performances, in general, the nonmimetic strategies that have dominated theory since the advent of New Criticism have posed specific problems in dramatic criticism, especially when we attempt to deal with the text as it is voiced in the theater at the moment of performance.[33] For example, it is difficult to accomplish the New Critical processing of a play called for by G. Wilson Knight, realigning corresponding metaphors, when one's attention is focused on actors speaking in a direct, line-by-line progression through the text.[34] Correspondingly, when the words of a text are distributed among the disparate personalities of several actors, it is difficult for us to follow the direction of the phenomenologist and reunify this dispersion into the voice of the single consciousness. Because actors appropriate the task of speaking the words we would *normally* read, their speech impedes the subvocalization that would let us speak the paradoxical "I" that conflates writer and reader in Poulet's transubjective union.[35] The structuralist would deny the existence of that subjective voice and focus on the text in performance as the compound of a series of cultural systems or codes, verbal and nonverbal. From this perspective, the spectators' engagement with the performance, as with the ritual, would preclude their consciousness of the hidden significance of the organizational principles enacted. In the structuralist's terms, the experience of performance is aesthetic; the critical search for the implicit substructure is a scientific process. The text itself may be vulnerable to a structural analysis, but performance provides an inappropriate condition for that activity; and performance, as well, is subject to the operation of its own systems of categorization and cultural codes. Theatrical performance—in which the image of the playwright as an individual creative subject is fractured by the extratextual intervention of director, designers, and actors—might seem the quintessential poststructuralist activity. Here the sense of the dramatic text as an arbitrary collection of the traces of disparate voices should be evident. However, in the immediate event of theatrical production, the unity provided by the presence of the actor/character tends to mask the collision of readings that precedes the performance.[36]

Part of the movement that presently counters the status of deconstructionism as a dominant critical movement calls for a return to mimetic criticism. Consider, for example, A. D. Nuttall's *A New Mimesis: Shakespeare and the Representation of Reality* (1983), David Bevington's *Action is Eloquence: Shakespeare's Language of Gesture* (1984), and Michael Goldman's *Acting and Action in Shakespearean Tragedy* (1985). While these critical studies, with varying degrees of self-consciousness, address the limitations of poststructuralism as an instrument with which to address the Shakespearean text in performance, each fails to be sufficiently willing to practice the kind of skepticism toward interpretation that seems necessary at this moment, and each study tends to enclose its readings within a notion of the coherence and unity of both character and text. That is, from the perspective of the 1980s, the new mimetic criticism seems insufficiently responsive to the dangers of circumscribing these texts within a unified, univocal, enclosing *meaning*. While the humanistic New Criticism revealed the complexity of language, interpretation consistently grounded that idea of multivalence in the description of a unified text that embodied the meaning that the critic assigned to it. The impact of poststructuralism on Shakespeare studies in the 1980s makes us see the benefits of being skeptical about interpretation. However, the reaction to poststructuralism that takes the form of "a new mimesis" threatens, once again, to enclose the Shakespearean text—and subsequently others—within a reductive unity. However, the desire to return to mimetic theory in criticism, well marked in the recent works of Goldman and Bevington, enacts the very dilemma I identify in working with theories that do not address the convention of human presence in space and time—the presentation of the dramatic text in performance. Beckett's writing for the theater, which exploits and disintegrates the presence of the human figure and its contingency, performs the paradox in the simultaneity of its mimetic and antimimetic functions.

For two reasons, my discussion reaches back in reference to the shift from Bradleian mimesis to phenomenological emphasis on the subject of the reader. First of all, Samuel Beckett's writing began at that moment when both literature and literary theory self-consciously rejected the strictures of realism and the idea of character.[37] Second, Beckett's dramatic writing displays the theatrical crisis caused by the disintegration of the presence of character as a viable image. In other essays on Beckett I have used Robbe-Grillet's early marking of Beckett's paradoxical interest in the image of human presence in dramatic performance. The point made by the novelist/filmmaker is apt for this discussion as well. Recall that Robbe-Grillet writes:

> The condition of man, says Heidegger, is to be *there*. The theatre probably reproduces this situation more naturally than any of the other ways of representing reality. The essential thing about a character in a play is that he is "on the scene": *there*.[38]

Robbe-Grillet isolates instances in the early Beckett plays in which dramatic figures attempt to question and to evaluate their own presence as images of character. At this point in Beckett's writing, it is possible for us to identify the playwright's dependence on the physical presence of the actor and, simultaneously, the processes in which a dramatic text refuses to assign the meaning "character" to that presence in a Bradleian use of that concept.

In the search for plausibility, both old and new mimetic analyses of character tend to build a unified image of character that obscures a text's presentation of fragmentation and disjunction. Dramatic texts, since fifth-century Athens, have worked to undermine the relentlessly concrete presence of the actor with texts that question the unity or intrinsic wholeness of character. In performance the actor's presence imposes a unity on the dramatic language assigned to him or to her. However, it is undeniable that the presence of the human figure in time and space resists the attempts of dramatic language (either in the text itself or in critical explication) to displace it or dissolve its centrality. The desire to maintain the manifest presence of the subject and the equally strong desire to dislocate it inform Beckett's drama as well as the controversies of theory. Beckett's later works, in particular, use the stage to perform what we call the crisis of the subject in critical discourse. That is, these plays build an image of the dramatic figure that both stimulates audiences to perceive its metonymic, fragmented presence as *character* and simultaneously undercuts the possibility of believing in the presence of *character* in any conventional sense. Because of their dependence on the human presence of the actor as the principal object in the theatrical space, these plays seem to call out for a consideration of character/subject in a way that poststructural analysis cannot address; and yet, Beckett's presentation of a subject whose presence is not palpable to itself apart from its own fluctuating processes of conjecture subverts the presence of the dramatic figure as character. To enclose the texts of any Beckett drama within a mimetic frame that pictures them as the representation of behavior is to ignore the aesthetic function that questions the possibility of representation and the possibility of the presence of a subject as anything but a speculation. In this sense, Beckett's plays perform the project that Michel Foucault details in a posthumously published interview:

> What I refused was precisely that you first of all set up a theory of the subject—as could be done in phenomenology and existentialism—and that, beginning from the theory of the subject, you come to pose the question of knowing, for example, how such and such a form of knowledge was possible. What I wanted to know was how the subject constituted himself, in such and such a determined form, as a mad subject or a normal subject, through a certain number of practices which were games of truth. . . . [39]

Foucault defines the processes of self-formation as clearly speculative, as dependent on socially determined forms and models, as exercises that proceed according to the rules of "games of truth," a phrase that details the significance and yet the arbitrariness of form.

In a performance of Samuel Beckett's *Not I* the presence of the actor/character is reduced to the image of an illuminated mouth that speaks a barely comprehensible text. If we assume that the third person narrative that the mouth speaks is self-referential—and that judgment is, in itself, an intervention—we must attend to that segment of the text that claims it is spoken involuntarily and not heard as language but merely as inchoate sound, *buzzing*. To extrapolate a conventional *character* to enclose that isolated physical sign demands the self-conscious intervention of the spectator. In Enoch Brater's 1986 collection of essays on Beckett, Thomas Whitaker argues with my claim that the *character* in *Not I* exists as an image generated in the spectator's imagination to be questioned and confounded by the performance. In the discussion of *Not I* that Whitaker questions, I propose that "the text lists biographical details and records incidents in the peculiar life of a character, but the only real characterization of Mouth is the one created in the spectator's imagination by implication." Whitaker counters this assertion by invoking the audience response to Jessica Tandy's performances as the evidence of the play's mimetic power: "Audiences quite rightly found Jessica Tandy's rendering of that old woman's blighted, bitter, and yearning life—articulated only through the hysterically detached medium of her mouth—to be a present experience both poignant and searing."[40] This mimetic reading of *Not I* occludes the phenomenon of its performance that dislocates text from consciousness. This separation of text from conscious awareness forces the audience to address both the prior pain of the biography the narration suggests, and the equally painful dislocation of narrative from consciousness that the performance enacts. When, in the same collection of essays, Keir Elam cites this passage from my book on Beckett more fully, he builds a hypothetical description of the spectator's work in witnessing a performance of *Not I* that I would like to appropriate here:

> This seems a promising line of attack, that is, to shift attention from the biographical consistency or otherwise of the dramatic "I" to the effects of the very I/not I dialectic on the audience's perceptions and speculations. It is a shift from a "negative" rhetoric to the rhetoric of negation. The problem then is no longer to solve a teasing enigma but to chart the play's (albeit enigmatic) ways of informing and disinforming, of stimulating and perplexing the spectator. This, indeed, might be the first communicational force of the title: an invitation of warning to the audience to take responsibility for its own projections and constructions as if to say that the one thinking and suffering present is inevitably "you."[41]

Not I constitutes a theatrical/textual crux that exemplifies the concerns of Beckett's dramatic writing and the serious questioning of the subject in critical theory. *Not I* performs both the problematizing of the notion *subject* and the resistance of "liberal humanism" to that project. That is, the complicity of performed text and spectator's response encompasses both the impulse to formulate a subject and the recognition that the subject isn't there in any form other than speculation.

The text of *Not I* displaces the image of the conscious subject engaged in the "game of truth" to some fictional moment prior to the dramatic action and displays both the self-constituting and self-denying functions of its narrative as the detritus of this fictional *earlier* moment. We recognize that this prior moment is itself empty, available to the figure of Mouth only as compulsively voiced sound. The image of the prior experience of the figure in which we place Mouth's consciousness of the narrative as narrative is an extrapolation, an invention stimulated by the performance but never acknowledged by it.[42] The past of this dramatic figure has no presence apart from the construct we sustain to position the experience we witness.

The theatrical energy manifest in *Not I*'s questioning of the subject, within the presentation of theatrical performance that both exploits and subverts the presence of the human actor, provides a paradigm of character and the questioning of character that (1) foregrounds drama's need for the human actor and the problematic practices of discussing dramatic language outside of the context of fictions of speech; (2) exposes the reductiveness of mimetic arguments that would ground dramatic speech as the work of some "inner coherence" on the part of the actor or the character; and (3) reveals the need to assimilate both the recognition of *character* as a dramatic function and the problematics of assigning *subject* to character as anything other than an aesthetic field in which language asserts itself as speculation.

Questioning the authenticity and stability of the text has been the logical accompaniment to the dissolving figure of the author in critical discourse. To a large degree, this activity has taken the form of recognizing the degree of editorial and printer intervention in the process of establishing texts, particularly Shakespeare's. The recognition of the contingent relationship between text and historical moment also informs our perception of the instability of texts and the fact that any interpretation reconstitutes them as a different text; in the language of Edward Said, whom I quoted earlier, we recognize that "criticism, no less than any other text, is the present in the course of its articulation." This process of reconfiguring the text in successive readings, each tied to its moment, destabilizes the idea of a fixed text whatever the state of the relationship between edition and origin. In the theater, the intervention of many agents in performance and the assimilation of performance conventions into our thinking about the written text further complicate our discussions. The problems of authenticity and stability concern Beckett studies despite the fact we study clearly *authorized* texts. For example, is *the* text of *Godot* the French "original" or the English "translation"? Should the text we consider critically incorporate the revisions that Beckett has made in production? Those of us who have had the opportunity to study Beckett manuscripts are aware of the persistence and care of Beckettian revision; at what point do we make the arbitrary decision that, because published, a Beckett text is finished, complete? To what degree do we inscribe the rhythms of actors that Beckett has directed into our own reading of the texts of these plays? To what degree are these texts objects in the world external to our sense of authorial privilege? The crisis at the American Repertory Theatre's 1984 production of *Endgame*, which focused on JoAnne Akalaitis's directorial interventions and relatively minor textual changes, demonstrated that Beckett's works exist in a peculiar limbo—they are like classic texts that have become the material for aesthetic reinterpretation in performance in a world different from that in which they originated, and yet they are still partially protected by authorial declaration and academic desire to preserve the "integrity" of the conditions of their origin.

Our recognition of the *instability* of the text, as I have noted, coincides with the difficulties we encounter with the image of the *subject* of the writer. For a time, it became a convention of criticism to discuss the developments of modernism as the increasing appropriation of the objective world into the mediations of the subjective. Erich Kahler's *The Inward Turn of Narrative*, for example, deals with the progressive transformation of objective reality into subjective reconfigurations as a history.[43] Northrop Frye's revision of the idea of subjectivity recognizes the power that structuralism and poststructuralism have given language to displace the primacy of the subjective. In *The Great Code*, Frye responds to explorations of continental criticism in a concise gloss to the problematics of the term *subject*:

> This sense of being confined to an objective order, and feeling a constraint in being so confined, has been enshrined in the language for a long time. The bigger the objective world becomes, the smaller in range and significance the subjective world seems. . . . The word "subject" in English means the observer of the objective, and it also has the political meaning of an individual subordinated to the authority of his society or its ruler, as in "British subject." It is not really possible, however, to separate the two meanings. The "subject" is subjected to the objective world, and not only subjected but almost crushed under it, like Atlas.[44]

The paradoxical delight and oppressiveness of language, in terms of both sound and attenuating conceptual reference, dominates Beckett's plays. Beckett's writing proposes the subject simply as a container, a ground, a human scene in which to enclose the language; and as such a container, the explicit or implicit *I* is merely a hypothesis—both to the voice that speaks and to the ears that listen. The language of a play like *Not I* evacuates the conventional relationship between language and character, and yet the "overwhelmingly powerful image," to use Martin Esslin's phrase, seduces us to conjure up a *character* even as we recognize that this mimetic conceit is our own intervention.

As the power of the subject in aesthetic theory concedes its authority to "cultural history" through the agency of language, the contingent relationship between text and historical moment moves to the foreground. Stephen Greenblatt's opening chapter of *Shakespearean Negotiations* is titled "The Circulation of Social Energy"; and he builds an elusive but provocative notion of the theater as the site of a series of exchanges among "culturally demarcated" zones. Robert Weimann, in his earlier use of the term *appropriation*, discusses the same process in more Marxian terms:

> If, as Marx quoted, "art" is "one of the special modes of production," then surely Shakespeare's theater and his society were interrelated in the sense that the Elizabethan stage, even when it reflected the tensions and compromises of sixteenth-century England, was also a potent force that helped to create the specific character and transitional nature of that society. Thus, the playgoers did not determine the nature of the plays, for although the latter certainly responded to the assumptions and expectations of the spectators, the audience itself was shaped and educated by the quality of what it viewed. Indeed, the sensibilities and receptivity of the audience and the consciousness and artistry of the drama were so mutually influential that a new historical synthesis seems conceivable only through an increased awareness of the dialectics of this interdependence.[45]

The work of both Greenblatt and Weimann demonstrates the distance that theory has traversed from ahistorical modes of phenomenology and the analysis of imagery. The ideological paradigms of existential phenomenology and the formalism of New Criticism gave

us the theoretical tropes with which to address Beckett's drama originally. And, at this point, it is easy to see that Beckett's writing,
coextensively with this kind of criticism, reconfigured the image of
theatrical representation in a nonmimetic mode that foregrounded
the disjunctive, the fragmented, and the atemporal while, as Iser
suggests, isolating the "traditional expectation" of meaning as "de-
fensive."[46] The indeterminacies figured in Beckett's plays, and their
insistence on the experience of the moment—the diminution of reference to any other place and time and event—demand careful attention, precise readings, and scrupulous attention to the details of performance. These texts share the emphasis on readership in recent
critical theory by demanding the kind of reading these strategies
value. The problematic speaker or listener who occupies the stage in
Beckett's later drama celebrates the mimetic power of human presence in the theater at the same time that he or she problematizes the
idea of the subject as dynamically as the discourse of poststructuralism.

As I remarked at the beginning, the objectives of this essay have
been more extensive than its occasion permits. Its purpose, however,
has been to suggest that the theoretical context in which Beckett
wrote and in which Beckett's writing plays a role constitutes a complicated nexus, an intersection of ideas, conventions, and speculations
about which we need to continue to think and converse. At this
stage, Beckett's writing has been less vulnerable to the claim of historical contingencies than Shakespeare's texts. As I suggest above,
this may be because we recognize that a principal contingency in
Beckett's writing is the prevalence of the notion of the isolated, alienated subject. In the next stage of our work with these texts, we will
probably attend to the power of the few objects that constitute the
minimal physical detritus that occupies the Beckettian scene and focus more intently on the conceptual debris that informs the language
that revolves in the dramatized consciousness. Here our project will
be to identify both the material things and the voiced predications as
cultural artifacts that demonstrate the interactions between the text
and the moment of its origin.

NOTES

1. The present *scene* of critical theory, particularly within Shakespeare studies,
provides an interesting context for speculating about Beckett's texts, as I hope this
essay demonstrates. In the 1960s and 1970s, writing on Shakespeare ceased to be the

field in which transitions in theory were most clearly marked. When attention of those interested in theory shifted to Paris and interest in the authorial subject declined, it became problematic to address *the* dominant subject in literature. In the late 1970s and the 1980s, Shakespeare studies took up the project of assimilating the strategies of French criticism. *Shakespeare and the Question of Theory,* ed. Patricia Parker and Geoffrey Hartman (New York: Methuen, 1985), illustrates the double path of that project: the shift in interest of Shakespeare or Renaissance specialists and the interest in Shakespeare manifested by those whose primary work applies theory to other writers.

2. The theater has exercised a practical awareness of the subjectivity of interpretation and its relationship to the immediate moment since the 1960s. Because directors have functioned more as coauthors than as interpreters, the theater has been free from the constraints of authorial intention for a longer period of time than has criticism. Performance anticipates theory in other areas as well. John Cage's work with the Merce Cunningham Company forced the spectator to participate in aesthetic play that prefigured the decentering aspects of poststructural theory.

3. See, for example, John Dover Wilson, *Shakespeare's Happy Comedies* (Evanston: Northwestern University Press, 1963), 183.

4. See, for example, Wylie's Sypher's essay "The Meanings of Comedy," as well as Meredith's "An Essay on Comedy" and Bergson's "Laughter," in Sypher's *Comedy* (Garden City, N.J.: Doubleday, 1956), 193–255.

5. John Styan, *The Dark Comedy* (Cambridge: Cambridge University Press, 1962); Kark S. Guthke, *Modern Tragicomedy: An Investigation into the Nature of the Genre* (New York: Random House, 1966).

6. Note, for example, Robert Weimann's dismissal of the ahistoricism of Francis Fergusson's concept of "ritual expectancy" (in Fergusson's discussion of *Hamlet* in *The Idea of a Theater*) in Weimann's *Shakespeare and the Popular Tradition in the Theater,* ed. Robert Schwartz (Baltimore: Johns Hopkins University Press, 1978), xx.

7. See M. M. Bakhtin, *Rabelais and his World* (Cambridge: Harvard University Press, 1968); Victor Turner, *Dramas, Fields, and Metaphors* (Ithaca: Cornell University Press, 1974), and *From Ritual to Theatre: The Human Seriousness of Play* (New York: PAJ Publications, 1982). In discussing the *freedom* that accompanies leisure, Turner notes the "freedom to play . . . with ideas, with fantasies, with words (from Rabelais to Joyce and Samuel Beckett) . . ." (37).

8. In his discussion of naturalism and convention, Robert Weimann refers to the well-known debate between Brecht and Lukács; see *Shakespeare and the Popular Tradition in the Theater,* ed. Robert Schwartz (Baltimore: Johns Hopkins University Press, 1978), 249–51. Stephen Greenblatt uses Brecht's "alienation effect" to amplify his description of the processes of "emptying out" the official position in "Shakespeare and the Exorcists," in his *Shakespearean Negotiations* (Berkeley and Los Angeles: University of California Press, 1988), 126.

9. The identification of Renaissance texts as early modern follows the historical scheme of seeing the emergence of modern state systems within an economy dominated by Europe as the beginning of the "modern" era in the sixteenth century. The basic argument is found in I. Wallerstein, *The Modern World-System* (New York: Academic Press, 1974). See also Jürgen Habermas, *Communication and the Evolution of Society* (Boston: Beacon Press, 1979).

10. Jean-Pierre Vernant, "Le moment historique de la tragedie," in *Mythe et tragedie en grèce ancienne*, by Vernant and Pierre Vidal-Naquet (Paris: Francois Maspero, 1972), 13–14.

11. I discuss *Endgame* as a political drama in a chapter in the forthcoming *Irish Writing: Exile and Subversion*, ed. Paul Hyland and Neil Hammells, in the Insights Series, Macmillan and St. Martins Press.

12. Cedric H. Whitman, *Sophocles: A Study of Heroic Humanism* (Cambridge, Mass.: Harvard University Press, 1951), p. 140–41.

13. Martin Esslin, *The Theatre of the Absurd* (New York: Doubleday, Anchor, 1961), 39–40.

14. Georges Poulet, *Studies in Human Time*, trans. Elliott Coleman (Baltimore: Johns Hopkins University Press, 1965).

15. I use *schema* in a sense close to Gombrich's notion of the relationship between schema and correction, the process in which the individual artist "corrects" the forms in which cognitive perception addresses the real through the illusory. See Gombrich's *Art and Illusion: A Study in the Psychology of Pictorial Representation* (Princeton: Princeton University Press, 1960), 3–30. For an interesting discussion of Gombrich's unhappiness with the literary appropriation of his idea of convention, see Murray Krieger, "An E. H. Gombrich Retrospective: The Ambiguities of Representation and Illusion," in his *Words about Words about Words* (Baltimore: Johns Hopkins University Press, 1988), 172–203.

16. Northrop Frye makes this point most clearly in a series of lectures he wrote for the CBC, published as *The Educated Imagination* (Bloomington: Indiana University Press, 1964).

17. Edward Said, "The Text, the World, the Critic," in *Textual Strategies: Perspectives in Post-structuralist Criticism*, ed. Josué V. Harari (Ithaca: Cornell University Press, 1979), 185.

18. Consider, as well, Kenneth Burke's essay "Terministic Screens," in *Language as Symbolic Action: Essays on Life, Literature, and Method*, ed. Kenneth Burke (Berkeley and Los Angeles: University of California Press, 1968), 44–62.

19. Displacing the *authority* of the text shares in this process. This phenomenon has at least two facets: first of all, it distances the subject/author from the text as archival document by identifying specific processes of intervention (see, for example, Stephen Orgel, "The Authentic Shakespeare," *Representations* 21 [Winter 1988]: 1–25); second, it identifies tropes of historical contingency that serve to position political paradigms that serve the critic's articulation of the present through the reified text (see Stephen Greenblatt, *Shakespearean Negotiations* [Berkeley and Los Angeles: University of California Press, 1988]).

20. Consider the following statement from Martin Esslin's introduction to the Anchor edition of *Shakespeare Our Contemporary* (Garden City, N.Y.: Doubleday, 1966):

> One of the finest performances within living memory was, so the director himself assures us, inspired by Kott's chapter " 'King Lear,' or Endgame," which Brook had read shortly after the French edition of the book appeared in 1962. In that production a play which had been regarded as unactable for many generations came to life with tremendous impact, and as a highly contemporary statement of the human condition. And this is because it was presented not as a fairy tale of a particularly stubborn story-book king, but as an image of aging and death, the waning of

powers, the slipping away of man's hold on his environment: a great ritual poem on evanescence and mortality, on man's loneliness in a storm-tossed universe. (xxi)

21. Even while Frye discusses texts in terms of their "moving body of imagery," his scheme ultimately encloses them within a graphic-oriented scheme as moments or segments within his inclusive circle.

22. M. M. Bakhtin, *The Dialogic Imagination*, ed. Michael Holquist, trans. Caryl Emerson and Michael Holquist (Austin: University of Texas Press, 1981), 5. In 1916 James Joyce argued for the opposite process in his support of the vitality of the "dramatic form" in which the image of authorial presence "refines itself out of existence." Here is Joyce's famous image of the writer as an invisible and indifferent God, "within or behind or beyond or above" his creation, "paring his fingernails" (*A Portrait of the Artist as a Young Man* [New York: Viking, 1956], 217).

23. L. C. Knights, "How Many Children Had Lady Macbeth?" reprinted in *Explorations* (New York: New York University Press, 1964), 33. Knights's 1933 essay cites the first edition of G. Wilson Knight, *The Wheel of Fire* (Oxford: Oxford University Press, 1930), 16. In this essay, which attacks Bradley's mimetic reading of *Macbeth*, Knights counters the notion of dramatic as defined both by Bradley and by William Archer, the critic and translator who promoted the plays of Ibsen so aggressively in England. Knights was among those young Cambridge students who supported the poetry of T. S. Eliot; and he claims here that *Macbeth* "has greater affinity with *The Waste Land* than with *The Doll's House*" (33). Knights's point supports my assertion that Bradley's criticism relates to the naturalistic drama of his moment. At this point in my argument I would also point out that Knights's criticism shares a similar contingency in that he wants us to read Shakespeare as if these texts were written by Eliot.

24. Martin Esslin, *Mediations: Essays on Brecht, Beckett, and the Media* (Baton Rouge: Louisiana State University Press, 1980), 123–24.

25. See both Wayne C. Booth, *The Rhetoric of Fiction* (Chicago: University of Chicago Press, 1961), 74, and Wolfgang Iser's discussion of Booth in *The Implied Reader: Patterns of Communication in Prose Fiction from Bunyan to Beckett* (Baltimore: Johns Hopkins University Press, 1974), 103.

26. In *Narrative Discourse: An Essay in Method*, trans. Jane E. Lewin (Ithaca: Cornell University Press, 1980), Gérard Genette brilliantly explicates various narrative schemes that organize Proust's *A la recherche du temps perdu*. Here, again, Proust's texts provide the material for a highly complicated analysis of reading that focuses on issues of temporality. Proust seems to form the ground for modernist notions of structure and the processes of reading.

27. Iser, *The Implied Reader*, 164–78.

28. Iser, *The Implied Reader*, 280.

29. Consider the following from Wolfgang Iser, *The Act of Reading: A Theory of Aesthetic Response* (Baltimore: Johns Hopkins University Press, 1978), discussing the phenomenon in which Beckett's language negates its own statement:

> By this use of language the reader is forced continually to cancel the meanings he has formed, and through this negation he is made to observe the projective nature of all the meanings which the text has impelled him to produce. . . . The primary negations of the Beckett text give language background, and so the formulated text has a kind of unformulated double. This "double" we shall call negativity. . . . (225–26)

30. Iser, *The Act of Reading,* 273.

31. See Genette, *Narrative Discourse,* which was originally published in French in 1972.

32. I discuss the differences and analogies between Beckett's later fiction and drama in "Male or Female Voice: The Significance of the Gender of the Speaker in Beckett's Late Fiction and Drama," in *Women in Beckett: Performance and Critical Perspectives,* ed. Linda Ben-Zvi (Urbana: University of Illinois Press, 1990).

33. See Charles R. Lyons, "Character and Theatrical Space," in *Themes in Drama,* vol. 9; *The Theatrical Space,* ed. James Redmond (Cambridge: Cambridge University Press, 1987); and my introduction to *Critical Essays on Henrik Ibsen* (Boston: G. K. Hall, 1987), 1–23.

34. G. Wilson Knight, *The Wheel of Fire* (Oxford: Oxford University Press, 1930; 4th ed., London: Methuen, 1946; 5th ed., New York: Meridian, 1957), 1–16.

35. Consider the following statement from Georges Poulet, from "Criticism and Interiority," in *The Languages of Criticism and the Sciences of Man* [later published as *The Structuralist Controversy*], ed. Richard Macksey and Eugenio Donata (Baltimore: Johns Hopkins University Press, 1972):

Reading implies something resembling the apperception I have of myself, the action by which I grasp straightway what I think as being thought by a subject (who, in this case, is not I). Whatever sort of alienation I may endure, reading does not interrupt my activity as subject. Reading, then, is the act in which the subjective principle which I call *I,* is modified in such a way that I no longer have the right, strictly speaking to consider it as my *I.* I am on loan to another, and this other thinks, feels, suffers, and acts within me. (60)

36. The rehearsal process more than the performance should provide data for the poststructuralist project—both because the rehearsals manifest a collision of readings and because they perform the text playfully, as a speculation, a trial, an experiment, without the constraints of an official performance. That is, in rehearsal the work of the actors may be self-consciously speculative, proceeding from trial to trial, interjecting commentary into repetition, without the need to provide a sequence that adds up to anything other than the experiment. In performance, the unity provided by the continuity of the presence of the actor/character tends to obscure the collision of readings that precedes the performance. I suspect that this difference provides the reason why many of us interested in theoretical issues find ourselves more comfortable attending rehearsals than witnessing conventional performances that seem to enclose texts with a false hermeneutical unity. While his assumptions about theory differ, his perception of the problematic nature of closed, artificially unified performances of the Shakespearean text, as opposed to the playful alternative, suggests that John Russell Brown (*Free Shakespeare* [London: Heinemann, 1974]) shares my enthusiasm for the greater openness of the rehearsal process in which actors may voice dissent and offer readings that counter the overriding concept of the director.

37. Beckett's monograph *Proust,* which was first published in 1931, shares the antimimetic bias of L. C. Knights, G. Wilson Knight, and others who attacked Bradleian mimesis. See *Proust* (New York: Grove Press, n.d.). Two passages from that study relate to this immediate discussion. In the first, Beckett contrasts the techniques of Proust and Dostoyevsky. He claims that the Russian novelist "states his characters

without explaining them. It may be objected that Proust does little else but explain his characters. But his explanations are experimental and not demonstrative. He explains them in order that they may appear as they are—inexplicable. He explains them away" (66–67). In discussing Proustian subjectivity and the function of time, Beckett claims that the personality of the subject is continually modified and "can only be apprehended as a retrospective hypothesis." Note the metaphor here: "The individual is the seat of a constant process of decantation . . ." (4).

38. Alain Robbe-Grillet, "Samuel Beckett or 'Presence' in the Theatre," in *Samuel Beckett: A Collection of Critical Essays*, ed. Martin Esslin (Englewood Cliffs, N.J.: Prentice-Hall, 1965), 108.

39. Michel Foucault, "The Ethic of Care for the Self as a Practice of Freedom," interview, trans. J. D. Gauthier, S.J., in *The Final Foucault*, ed. James Bernauer and David Rasmussen (Cambridge, Mass.: MIT Press, 1988), 10.

40. Thomas Whitaker, "'Wham Bam, Thank You Sam': The Presence of Beckett," in *Beckett at 80 / Beckett in Context*, ed. Enoch Brater (New York: Oxford University Press, 1986), 210.

41. Keir Elam, "*Not I*: Beckett's Mouth and the Ars(e) Rhetorica," in *Beckett at 80 /Beckett in Context*, 131–32.

42. Imagine a performance of *Not I* that would project a cinematic visualization of the old woman's narrative behind the image of the grotesquely isolated organ mouthing its words. Giving that *past* the authority of visualization would flesh out the equivocality of subject and sentimentalize the performance. For information concerning the first performances of *Not I* in New York, Paris, and London (including the adaptation for BBC television), see Enoch Brater, *Beyond Minimalism: Beckett's Late Style in the Theater* (Oxford: Oxford University Press, 1987).

43. Erich Kahler, *The Inward Turn of Narrative*, trans. Richard and Clara Winston (Princeton: Princeton University Press, 1973); originally published in German, 1970.

44. Northrop Frye, *The Great Code: The Bible and Literature* (New York: Harcourt Brace Jovanovich, 1982), 21.

45. Weimann, *Shakespeare and the Popular Tradition*, xii.

46. Iser, *The Act of Reading*, 223.

Harold Pinter/Politics

Benedict Nightingale

Ten or twenty years ago Harold Pinter was the very last British dramatist one would have expected to find publicly crusading against nuclear weapons, state torture, America's domination of the lands to her south, and other actual or supposed ills. The idea that this activism might extend to his plays would have been even more unthinkable.

True, a few alert critics, notably Martin Esslin and Ruby Cohn, detected political resonances in his work, especially his early work; but they knew that these were resonances and reverberations only. Pinter's primary emphasis was the embattled individual in his or her personal relationships. More than any of his British contemporaries, he seemed concerned with the primary drives and needs: for a place to sleep, belong, and be secure; for status and attention; for influence and power; for emotional and sexual bonds and attachments. At a time when most British playwrights felt some responsibility to address public issues, and many were content to see their characters in their social and political roles alone, Pinter concentrated his attention on the human animal in its most intimate dealings. He seemed the most private of writers—and, as would-be interviewer after would-be interviewer was pained to discover, the most private of men as well.

What a reversal there has been! It now seems that there is scarcely
a liberal or radical cause that Harold Pinter does not espouse, and
espouse loudly. He is an active supporter of Amnesty International,
the Campaign for Nuclear Disarmament, Arts for Nicaragua, the Index on Censorship, and International PEN. Indeed, it was in behalf
of the last of these organizations that he went to Turkey with Arthur
Miller in 1985, a visit whose principal events the American dramatist
was memorably, and suggestively, to describe in the *Observer*.[1]

The two men became convinced that human rights were being
systematically abused in that country. They heard stories of mass
arrests, beatings, and torture. By the time they arrived at the American embassy for a dinner in Miller's honor, they were finding it
difficult to observe diplomatic niceties. It was Miller who made a
short speech calmly questioning U.S. support for a military dictatorship, but it was Pinter who became the center of one verbal fracas
after another. In the end he reportedly told the ambassador that
diversity of opinion was difficult "if you've got an electric wire
hooked to your genitals," was angrily informed that his remark was
a breach of hospitality, concluded he was being thrown out, and left.
Back in London a few days later, Pinter and Miller discovered that
their parting press conference had been retroactively "banned" and
that an investigation was to be held into their entire trip.

That Turkish trip was a significant one, both for Pinter himself
and for those interested in his personal and professional evolution.
It still provides the most vivid illustration of the indignant, vociferous, and demonstrative man he became, and has remained, in the
1980s. It clearly reinforced his own growing political skepticism and
sense of alienation, particularly in relation to the United States. And
it led eventually to the composition of the short play *Mountain Language*. But neither the visit nor the events in Pinter's political life
immediately preceding and following it should be seen as precisely
representing an "awakening." It would be better to talk of a reawakening after what Pinter himself has called a longish period of "sleep-
walking."[2]

It would, after all, be difficult for a Jewish boy to grow up in the
east London of the 1930s and 1940s without developing a political
consciousness. "The sense of the Gestapo was very, very strong in
London, in England," he said recently. "We knew about them as
children . . . we knew the German force was a very, very strong

one."[3] And he has several times told interviewers of the resurgence of violent anti-Semitism in the East End itself with the reappearance of the English fascists after the war. He had a number of physical fights. Others he managed to avoid, with displays of the kind of verbal legerdemain his characters were frequently to employ in his plays.[4]

By 1948 the eighteen-year-old Pinter was prepared to risk imprisonment for the sake of his political convictions. He refused military service, announcing at various tribunals and trials that he regarded himself as a conscientious objector, not because he was a pacifist, but because he disapproved of the emergence of McCarthyism in America and of the growing rift between Britain and her former ally, Soviet Russia. Why, he asked himself, should he be party to "the tragic forces of starting the Cold War almost before the last war had finished"?[5] As he said in an interview in 1980, "I've always had a deeply embedded suspicion of political structures, of governments, and the way people are used by them. I was determined not to be used in that way."[6]

These feelings may have helped shape the plays he wrote in the late 1950s—more of this in a moment—but their longer-term effect was quite different. That suspicion, that determination not to be used, led to withdrawal, not protest or implied protest. Pinter the man had by now lapsed into what he recently called a "detached contempt" for politics and politicians, a belief that any political engagement was futile. And Pinter the writer, in his own words, "simply continued investigations into other areas."[7] When the magazine *Encounter* asked British people involved in the arts what they thought of their country's entry to the Common Market, his reply was the most succinct: "I have no interest in the matter and do not care what happens."[8] Explaining this statement in 1967, he declared that politicians left him variously irritated, indignant, indifferent, bored, and confused. "Generally I try to get on with what I can do and leave it at that," he said. "I don't think I've got any kind of social function that's of any value, and politically there's no question of my getting involved because the issues are by no means simple." He did, however, admit that although political structures did not alarm him personally, they caused "a great deal of suffering to millions of people"—and added the following, often quoted words:

I'll tell you what I really think about politicians. The other night I watched some politicians talking about Vietnam. I wanted very much to burst through the screen with a flame-thrower and burn their eyes out and their balls off and then inquire from them how they would assess this action from a political point of view.[9]

The impression one gets from what Pinter said during this "sleep-walking" period, and from what he has added since then, is that his political feelings were still alive, and that he was to some extent still conscious of them; but that a combination of ennui and helplessness had driven them underground, where they remained dormant until 1973. The overthrow of President Allende, in Pinter's opinion at the behest of the United States, told him "that I couldn't sit back and not take responsibility for my actions and thoughts, and act upon them." It was necessary, in his words, to "make a bit of a nuisance of myself."[10] And that is what he began to do—though not with evident impact either on the public at large or on his own work until the 1980s.

As early as 1974 he joined the campaign for the release of Vladimir Bukovsky, telling the *Times* that the dissident Russian had been imprisoned "effectively for criticising the Soviet government's use of psychiatric hospitals for political prisoners,"[11] and he has never hesitated to attack abuses of human rights in the Eastern bloc. But increasingly he has taken the view that the West emphasizes communist injustices in order to distract its citizens from wrongs nearer home, and has come to regard it as his duty to fight those supposed wrongs. Indeed, his suspicions of the United States in particular now appear to have few bounds. In 1984 he told a *Times* interviewer that the Americans were preparing to wage a limited nuclear war in Europe, and that civilization as a whole would be "very lucky to get to the end of this century."[12] Since then he has taken more and more interest in what he describes as the "dungeons" of South and Central America, accusing the United States of supporting repression and torture in El Salvador, Chile, and elsewhere. Recently he paid a visit to Nicaragua, met President Ortega, was deeply impressed by Ortega's social achievements, and left the country enraged by American attempts to destabilize what he had become convinced was the only decent regime in that part of the world.[13]

His opinion of Britain under Margaret Thatcher's Conservative government is not exactly high, either. In 1984 he told an interviewer that the country had become the compliant victim of U.S. military ambition, "as much a satellite of America as Czechoslovakia is of Russia,"[14] and more recently he has inveighed against what he sees as an increase in police power, official secrecy, and state censorship. He has publicly expressed anxiety about the future of broadcasting, the free press, and the arts generally in Britain, and in 1988 he acted on his fears. He and his wife, the historian Antonia Fraser, invited to their house several other prominent writers, including David Hare, Margaret Drabble, and Salman Rushdie, and organized a sort of literary think tank, the June Twentieth Group, dedicated to countering conservative ideas. They were much mocked in some newspapers as champagne radicals; but then, as Pinter told the BBC, "derision and mockery are staple weapons of the British establishment and always have been—and I must say I find that kind of complacent malice and self-congratulatory spite beneath contempt."[15]

It has indeed been an astonishing turnabout. The hermit Pinter is now enough of a public irritant to have become the butt of conservative columnists and leader-writers, and seems, if anything, to relish the fray. Now he is decrying poverty and homelessness in London; now he is attacking a government law prohibiting municipalities from giving sympathetic publicity or financial support to homosexual organizations. As he told the BBC in late 1988, "The homosexual is an alien force, someone to be feared and therefore to be rejected and repressed."[16] And who was it leading a delegation to Downing Street to demand action in defense of Salman Rushdie after Rushdie had been threatened with death by Iran in early 1989 for his book *The Satanic Verses*? By then the answer was almost inevitable: Harold Pinter.

He has carried his libertarian message to universities and international conferences and public meetings—and, to a much more limited extent, also to the place that won him the status and authority to become an effective campaigner in the first place: the stage. The year 1983 saw the first production of *One for the Road*, a short play involving a gloating apparatchik and the family he is in the process of destroying: a man who has been brutally tortured; his wife, who has been repeatedly raped; and their small son, who ends up murdered, presumably for committing the only offense anyone mentions, spitting and kicking at some unnamed dictator's military personnel.

Two years later, in 1985, *Harpers* published Pinter's dramatic fragment *Precisely*, which embodied his feelings about nuclear weapons.
This showed one bureaucrat complacently assuring another that just
twenty million people would be killed in a future war, and the two
of them agreeing that those who claimed the final count would be
much higher were communist subversives and "bastards" who
should be shot, or (better) hung, or drawn and quartered.

> A: I want to see the colour of their entrails.
> B: Same colour as the Red Flag, old boy.[17]

And in 1989 the National Theatre produced Pinter's *Mountain Language*, a play that derived from his discovery in Turkey three years
earlier of "the real plight of the Kurds, which is quite simply that
they're not allowed to exist and certainly not allowed to speak their
language."[18]

What one would call the main plot, if the play didn't run some
seventeen minutes only, involves an old woman and her prisoner
son. First, her thumb is half bitten off by a police dog. Then she's
denied the right to speak to the young man in the only tongue she
understands, and has to sit silently while he's taken away for a beating offstage. Finally, she proves unable to take advantage of a sudden, arbitrary reversal of government linguistic policy. Though she's
now permitted to speak as she wishes, she has lost the power to
speak at all. These events are intercut into a subplot involving a
young woman who offers her sexual favors to some unseen bureaucrat in hopes of helping her husband, whom she (and we) have just
seen hooded and half-collapsed at the end of a corridor in the prison
camp where the play is set.

At the time this chapter was written, in mid-1989, these were
Harold Pinter's only new dramatic works since *A Kind of Alaska* in
1982. During the same period he has directed Donald Freed's *Circe
and Bravo* for London's Hampstead Theatre. He has appeared occasionally as an actor in his own work, playing Goldberg in *The Birthday
Party* for BBC-TV and Deeley in his own American stage production
of *Old Times*. He has made film adaptations of other people's work,
and seems likely to continue doing so. His latest screenplays, again
at the time of this writing, are based on Fred Uhlman's *Reunion*,
Elizabeth Bowen's *The Heat of the Day*, and Margaret Atwood's *The*

Handmaid's Tale, all novels with political connotations, the last of them about a Christian fundamentalist regime in America. But his own theatrical output has dwindled to a trickle, and may well dry up altogether. "I'm no longer interested in myself as a playwright," he informed the BBC in 1985.[19] "I don't think I'll be writing plays much more." "I understand your interest in me as a playwright," he repeated to the *New York Times* in 1988, "but I'm more interested in myself as a citizen."[20]

The obvious retort is: Are the roles of playwright and citizen incompatible? The example of Bernard Shaw, above all, is there to remind us that they need not be. *One for the Road, Mountain Language,* and the shard *Precisely* would seem themselves to emphasize the point. Indeed, they show a closer, or at least a clearer, link between the onstage and the offstage Pinter than was ever apparent before he took to writing directly on political subjects. What the citizen-playwright is telling us is not merely that the most terrible abuses of human rights are occurring, but that we're fooling ourselves if we believe they could never occur in his own country, England. Indeed, there is much in all three plays to suggest that we are watching people who could be British trapped in situations that could occur in a Britain of the not-very-distant future.

In *Precisely*, bureaucrat *A* is addressed as Stephen and bureaucrat *B* as Roger. They use phrases like "old boy" and "bloody cheek" and see their opponents' estimate of the total number of victims of nuclear war, between forty and seventy million, as "almost the entire population"—which in Britain it clearly would be. The characters of *One for the Road* are called Nicolas, Victor, Gila, and Nicky, names that singly might be found in some other European country, but collectively suggest an English location, especially when some of the language they use is taken into account. The torturer's sentimental reference to nature, trees, "a nice blue sky," and "blossom" would seem to evoke Kent or the Cotswolds more than Central America, the Middle East, or the Mediterranean. His cricket slang—"I open the batting," "you're on a losing wicket"—obviously has a similar but stronger effect.

Mountain Language may have derived from Pinter's experience of Turkey and his knowledge of the Kurds, but the production of the play he himself directed at the National Theatre suggested a location far nearer home. The women forlornly waiting outside the prison wore the kind of cardigans and raincoats you would find in any town or village from Dover to Belfast, and the uniforms of the soldiery were recognizably British too. The name of the wife of the hooded internee was Sarah Johnson, her husband was called Charley, and the bureaucrat with whom she offered to have sex was Joseph Bokes. A reference to Babycham, a perry very popular in Britain, and such distinctive argot as "Lady Duck Muck" added to the impression that the "mountain language" being banned might be Welsh or Gaelic, and that the prison itself might be in Northern Ireland or in one of the more desolate mainland shires.

That is not of course the whole truth. The prevalence of English names could after all be regarded as a convenience, the kind of liberty a translator might take when adapting a foreign play for an English audience. It would be pretty literal-minded to conclude that their use meant that Pinter's "political" plays had no relevance to any other country or countries. Indeed, it's evident that both *Mountain Language* and *One for the Road*, which he wrote immediately after an angry conversation with some young Turkish women he regarded as remarkably complacent about events in their country, are supposed to be comprehensive in their scope.[21] They are meant to evoke Turkey and all or any of the ninety countries that Amnesty International believes practice torture—and a potential and to some extent even an actual Britain.

Pinter himself made the point explicitly when he spoke about *Mountain Language* to the BBC in 1988. He agreed that the play concerned the Turks and their treatment of the Kurds. He went on to say that the Basques, the Estonians, the Irish, and the Welsh had all seen their languages banned at one time or another. He added that the abuses he was showing were "serious facts throughout the world, which most people prefer understandably to ignore, to pretend don't exist." He went on: "The people who have been through these appalling deprivations and awful assaults, they're exactly the same as you and me. If they're 3,000 miles away, people say, why don't you look at England? Well, we are looking at England. In other words, do not ask for whom the bell tolls, it tolls for thee." In his opinion, he concluded, the play was "very, very close to home."[22]

It would seem, then, that the concerned citizen and the committed playwright are not merely compatible: the playwright has become an extension, almost an instrument, of the citizen—and, in Pinter's own view, not the most important extension or instrument. That does, however, raise some interesting and troubling questions for those of us who admire his past accomplishments as a dramatist. What, if anything, can we say about the quality of his new "political" work—and, indeed, how "new" is it? It is one thing to integrate the roles of playwright and citizen. It is quite another to reconcile the role of the citizen and the role of what, while recognizing the difficulty of defining those adjectives, one might call the good playwright or the effective playwright.

Pinter himself has gone to some pains to suggest a link—indeed, a consistency of feeling and attitude—between his recent work and his first plays. What some of his original critics "dismissed as absurd rubbish," he has said, actually embodied a "political metaphor."[23]

To some extent this seems a revisionist view. In his earlier public statements, such as they were, he tended to disclaim any moral intention, let alone one so specific, and to avoid interpreting his work in any way at all, let alone one so relatively limited. "I'm not committed as a writer in the usual sense of the term, either religiously or politically," an interviewer quoted him as saying in 1961. "And I'm not conscious of any particular social function. I write because I want to write. I don't see any placards on myself, and I don't carry any banners. Ultimately, I distrust any definitive labels."[24] He actually walked out of Peter Brook's *US*, explaining later that he disliked being subjected to propaganda, detested "soapboxes," and thought the play was presumptuous in its apparent desire to shock and ineffective in its attempt to inspire opposition to the Vietnam War. "It's impossible," he concluded, "to make a major theatrical statement about such a matter when television and the press have made everything so clear."[25]

The conclusion a critic could reasonably have drawn from Pinter's comments about his own writing during this period was that his function as a dramatist was to "find" interesting characters, give them their freedom, and edit their words and deeds into a play with all the impersonality he could muster. "I've got an idea of what *might* happen," he explained in 1967. "Sometimes I'm absolutely right, but on many occasions I've been proved wrong by what actually does happen."[26] And the function of individual members of an audience was to listen, ponder, and come up with their own interpretations if they wished, always confessing to an educated uncertainty when, as was often the case, the evidence seemed incomplete or ambiguous.

Did it follow, then, that there could never be any consensus about at least part of a play's thrust or meaning, and that such a consensus could never receive Pinter's imprimatur? If you read parts of the letter he wrote to the director Peter Wood back in 1958, you might indeed conclude that he took this somewhat extreme view at that time. "Where is the comment, the slant, the explanatory note?" he asked Wood, who wanted to clarify his production of *The Birthday Party*. "In the play. Everything to do with the play is in the play." And he went on: "Meaning begins in the words, in action, continues in your head and ends nowhere. There is no end to meaning. Meaning which is resolved, parceled, labeled and ready for export is dead, impertinent—and meaningless."[27]

Yet there are contradictions here, as Pinter himself recognized at more than one point in the same letter. The play "dictated itself," yet he wrote it "with intent, maliciously, purposefully, in command of growth." And though his opinion of his protagonist, Stanley Webber, was not "the point of the play," he nevertheless did hold an opinion about him and his predicament. Indeed, he went so far as to offer an interpretation of *The Birthday Party* as a whole:

> The hierarchy, the Establishment, the arbiters, the socio-religious monsters arrive to effect alteration and censure upon a member of the club who has discarded responsibility . . . towards himself and others . . . he collapses under the weight of their accusation—an accusation compounded of the shitstained strictures of centuries of "tradition."[28]

Nor was this the only occasion on which the younger Pinter emphasized his early work's social and political aspects. In an interview he gave the BBC as long ago as 1960, he talked of the false security of the main characters of both *The Birthday Party* and *The Room*, and of the intruders who came to upset it: "This thing, of people arriving at the door, has been happening in Europe in the last 20 years. Not only the last 20, the last two to three hundred."[29] Again, he recalled in 1984 that "the political metaphor" of *The Dumb Waiter* was "very clear to the actors and director of the first production in 1960," even if it was missed by critics at the time.[30] Yet again, he told the *New York Times* in 1988 that the original idea of two men invading

Stanley's home in *The Birthday Party* "came from my knowledge of the Gestapo."[31]

So one cannot quite accuse Pinter of post-hoc rationalization when he says, as he has done recently, that his early plays "seemed to have to do with authoritarian structures of one kind or another,"[32] or "dealt with the individual at the mercy of an authoritarian system,"[33] or "were political plays [that] were talking about society as I understood it at the time in certain manifestations,"[34] or took "an extremely critical look at authoritarian postures . . . power used to undermine if not destroy the individual or the questioning voice or the voice which simply went away from the mainstream and refused to become part of an easily recognisable set of standards and social values."[35] Nor can one altogether accuse him of revisionism when he claims, as he did in 1988, that "one of the most important" lines he's ever written is the one delivered by Petey to the waxen Stanley as he is taken away to some unmentioned and probably unmentionable fate at the end of *The Birthday Party*—"Stan, don't let them tell you what to do"—and adds that he himself has "lived that line all my damn life, never more than now."[36] On the other hand, looking at his comments overall, one may reasonably wonder whether Pinter isn't now offering us a less complete and balanced view of his early plays than he would have done before he committed himself so thoroughly to politics. What he's giving us, in short, is a post-hoc *emphasis*.

Perhaps this hardly matters. After all, a dramatist surrenders control of his plays with their performance or publication. And as Pinter himself implied in the letter to Peter Wood, his own explanations, interpretations, and conclusions are no more than that: his own. The important thing is what audiences and readers make of his plays; and even without his prodding, they should be able to see their political implications. Indeed, some of them did so even in the relatively early days, notwithstanding Pinter's own belief that he was regarded as a cross between N. F. Simpson and Ionesco. As early as 1962 Ruby Cohn suggested there was a connection between his work and that of the Angry Young Englishmen of his generation. "Pinter's anger, like theirs, is directed vitriolically against the System," she wrote; his plays were "bitter dramas of dehumanization"; "the religion and society which have traditionally structured human morality are, in Pinter's plays, the immoral agents which destroy the individual."[37] In 1963 James T. Boulton actually complained that *The Birthday Party*

over-obviously evoked specific organizations "such as the IRA."[38]
And in 1970, about the time Pinter was writing *Landscape* and *Silence*,
Martin Esslin was able to argue that basic political problems lurked
within his plays' private worlds. "The use and abuse of power, the
fight for living space, cruelty, terror," he explained. "Only very
superficial observers could overlook this social, this political side of
the playwright."[39]

It is indeed difficult to overlook the contrasting reactions to
authority of the two assassins in *The Dumb Waiter*—Ben's unerring
need to obey, Gus's impulse to question and challenge—and the
contrasting results of those reactions. In effect, one is offered a
worm's-eye-view of power: invisible, inscrutable, unaccountable, arbitrary, brutal, absolute. Again, one can hardly overlook some of the
things said by the intruders, Goldberg and McCann, in *The Birthday
Party*. Now their conversation consists of officialese—"certain elements might well approximate in points of procedure to some of
your other activities"; now it turns into inquisition—"You betray our
land"; "We can sterilise you"; "Stick a needle in his eye"; and so on.
They and their sinister colleague or chief, Monty, might almost be
working from the police headquarters of *One for the Road* and preparing Stanley for an even more unsettling reception there. Certainly,
they know how to dominate and disorient; to terrify, brainwash, and
destroy.

It is even more difficult to overlook the thrust of the play Pinter
wrote in 1958 but did not allow to be performed until 1980, *The
Hothouse*. It is, after all, set in a government-run asylum. The men
in charge are an insecure, blustering incompetent, a sly and malicious
opportunist, and an icily ambitious bureaucrat. Their "patients" are
known by their allocated numbers only, and, may, it seems, be raped
or killed without complaints from outside or inside. "It's supposed
to be a mental home, but I don't think it is," Pinter recently told the
BBC. "It's a home for political dissidents."[40] That was a somewhat
anachronistic claim, since the play was written before the West had
become aware of the misuse of psychiatry in Soviet Russia; but there
is little if anything in the text to contradict it.

Esslin did not, however, seem to be referring only to the early
plays when he wrote about "this social, this political side" of Harold
Pinter. His suggestion was that the concerns of the so-called "sleep-
walking" period were less exclusively private than they might at

first appear. And certainly Roote, Gibbs, and Lush, the men at the center of *The Hothouse*, have more than a little in common with Mick, Davies, Ruth, Anna, Spooner, and several other characters Pinter created both before and after 1970. They want people or places, or both, under their control, in their power. They know, many of them, how to manipulate situations to their advantage; they maneuvre, some of them, with great flair and cunning. Mick, Ruth, and Spooner have an instinct for politics, even if the politics they practice are of the living room, bedroom, or attic. As Pinter himself pointed out in 1988, "How power is used, how you terrorise someone, how you subjugate someone, has always been alive in my work."[41]

There is, of course, a danger of stretching the word *political* so far beyond its obvious sense that it becomes meaningless. After all, not every play involving acquisitive people and their shifting relationships can usefully be described with such a term. Yet in Pinter's case one does often feel that characters are bringing more than private skills to their highly private worlds. Their goals may be domestic merely; their methods are more broadly pertinent. Consider the guile with which Mick, having failed to frighten away the tramp Davies in *The Caretaker*, wins the slavish allegiance of the old man, allows him to alienate his true friend Aston, lures him into making a damaging admission, and then rejects him. It's a plot that a Renaissance courtier and a modern government executive would find equally instructive.

There are Pinter plays, then, that are obviously political because they deal, explicitly or implicitly, literally or metaphorically, with the structures and substructures that exercise control over the individual; and there are Pinter plays, occasionally the same ones, that may perhaps be called political, since they anatomize individual yet exemplary power struggles. And it might, I suppose, be argued that there is yet another variety of Pinter political play, close to the first category but broader in its implications. Such work doesn't necessarily involve authoritarian structures. It does, however, have something to say or suggest about the outer worlds in which the characters lead their embattled lives.

In an interesting recent article for *Theatre Journal*, for instance, Graham Woodroffe discusses one particular play in relation to the racial tensions in the changing Britain of the 1950s. Indeed, he actually titles his essay "Taking Care of the 'Coloureds': The Political

Metaphor of Harold Pinter's *The Caretaker.*" In it, he notes Davies's
anger at the "Greeks, Poles and Blacks, all them aliens" who have
failed to acknowledge his superiority. He notes the old man's distaste
for the new Commonwealth residents, a family of Indians, who live
next door to Aston and Mick's house. And he notes how evasive
Davies himself becomes when he's questioned about his own ethnic
background. "On the one hand he espouses the kind of racist attitudes that accompanied the call for immigration controls," writes
Woodroffe, "but on the other hand he is the indignant victim of racial
prejudice."[42]

As is often the case with distinct and limited interpretations of
Pinter's work, Woodroffe does somewhat labor the unobvious. The
water leaking through Aston's roof into his bucket metaphorically
suggests an "anxiety about the flow of immigrants into the country";
the smile exchanged at one important point by Aston and Mick hints
at the complicity of Labour and Conservative parties, tacitly colluding
in the exclusion of unwanted intruders from abroad. But Woodroffe's
approach is refreshing in that it emphasizes, to a degree rare in Pinter
scholarship, that by no means all the plays occur in a social vacuum.
On the contrary, there are those that leave one with a strong and
somewhat discomfitting sense of the environment beyond the rooms
in which they are characteristically set.

The Caretaker is a good example, with its junk shops and cheap
cafés and public toilets and rainy streets, not to mention the asylum
where Aston was given electric shock treatment. So is *The Homecoming*, with its constant evocations of an urban underworld: a violent
confrontation involving a pimp and a prostitute under an arch near
the docks; a near-rape on a bombed site near Wormwood Scrubs
prison; sexual encounters to come in the Soho flat where the female
protagonist, Ruth, can expect to "get old . . . very quickly." In this
sordid city even the local swimming-baths are "just like a urinal, a
filthy urinal." The impression cumulatively left by *The Room, Night
School, A Night Out*, the revue sketches *The Black and White* and *Last
To Go*, and the recent radio plays *Family Voices* and *Victoria Station* is
also of a seedy and dilapidated London, a place where lonely people
slump in milk bars or stand at coffee stalls or sit in gaunt terrace
houses watching the all-night buses trundle from the unfashionable
south or east to the desolate north or west.

Max, Lenny, and Joey in *The Homecoming*, Mick and Aston in *The*

Caretaker, Rose and Bert in *The Room*, and Wally and Solto in *Night School* seem inseparable from this world. They belong to it as much as cockroaches to a decaying tenement. At all events, one certainly feels that there's a strong link between the individual and his or her environment—and yet one also feels that the nature of that link is shadowy. One cannot say, as one can (for instance) of Edward Bond's *Saved*, that the cultural and economic deprivation the characters have endured in London has shaped their attitudes, feelings, and behavior. One knows nothing about how or why Davies became a tramp beyond his eccentric claim that one day he found his wife's underwear in a saucepan, walked off, and (presumably) kept walking. There is not the strong sense of socioeconomic determinism you find in Bond, Howard Brenton, David Hare, Trevor Griffiths, Barrie Keeffe, Nigel Williams, Stephen Poliakoff, and John McGrath, among many other contemporary British playwrights.

Indeed, one might almost argue that there's a reverse determinism in Pinter. Nature seems more influential than nurture. The world is what it is because people are what they ineluctably are. We can, no doubt, say that Ruth and Lenny were to some extent formed by the sinister and dangerous subworld of hustling, pornography, and sex-for-sale that they appear to have inherited. But don't we feel still more strongly that there's something deep in their glands and bowels, some innate and unalterable need, that makes them glad to perpetuate it? Indeed, doesn't one feel that it was just such animal instincts that first created this shabby, sleazy London, this visceral "home" for the returning Ruth? Other dramatists may owe philosophic allegiance to Marx: Pinter's approach would seem to have more in common with Konrad Lorenz.

Seen from this point of view, then, some of the plays Pinter wrote before *One for the Road* are "political" partly because they tacitly invite us to speculate about the relationship of individuals to their society, and partly, and more important, because they present a striking and disturbing picture of the raw material with which politicians must deal. That is to say, they look at the human animal in a way, and perhaps at a level, alien to most "political" dramatists. That is also (of course) to say that they are much more than "political."

But no one can seriously claim that the great majority of Pinter's plays can be adequately discussed in terms of their political resonances and implications only. If *The Caretaker* did not involve a great deal more than tensions during a period of racial change in Britain, it would scarcely be revived as often and internationally as it now is. Again, *The Birthday Party* would surely lose, not gain, in texture and interest if it more clearly concerned a dissident and representatives of some "political" establishment.

As it is, Pinter seems at pains to make both Stanley's alleged sins and his persecutors' accusations as wide-ranging as possible. Indeed, his Goldberg tends to emphasize the private, leaving more public complaints to McCann: "When did you last have a bath?," "Where's your old mum?," "You verminate the sheet of your birth." Given the nature and abundance of the play's references to parents and children, one might as or more plausibly argue that the play's subject is the cruelty of growing up, being forced finally to cut the umbilical cord, and having to face the adult world. Hence the contrast between Stanley as he is at first, untidy, irresponsible, churlishly dependent on the possessive Meg, and the Stanley of the end, scrubbed, shaved, and transformed into a pin-striped, bowler-hatted zombie, ready for the office or the grave. As Martin Esslin puts it, the play may be seen as a metaphor for the process of "expulsion from the warm, cosy world of childhood."[43]

Yet Esslin is the first to acknowledge that this, too, is an excessively precise interpretation. Perhaps *The Birthday Party* is better seen as involving everyone's repressed guilts and unspoken fears, everyone's dim suspicion that one day his past may catch up with him and punishment be exacted for what he has done or is thought by someone, somewhere, to have done. It defines an insecurity the more unsettling for involving nothing specific. Though it is by no means his best play, there is about it that sense of mystery that, surely, goes far toward explaining the hold Harold Pinter has long maintained over our imaginations; that feeling that people aren't quite saying what they mean or meaning what they say; that peculiar combination of intensity of emotion and social obfuscation, animal instinct, and inscrutability of motive. To define most of the dramatist's work closely is to limit it. To insist strongly on its "political" relevance is to diminish it.

Conversely, a Pinter play that is to be seen solely or mainly in one way, or interpreted on a single level only, is likely to be an inferior Pinter play. That is not just a personal opinion. It was in effect Pinter's own view when he revealed to an interviewer back in 1967 that there was a play, called *The Hothouse*, that he had withheld from production. "It was heavily satirical and it was quite useless," he said.

> The characters were so purely cardboard. I was intentionally—for the only time, I think—trying to make a point, an explicit point, that these were nasty people and I disapproved of them. And therefore they didn't begin to live. Whereas in other plays of mine every single character, even a bastard like Goldberg, I care for.[44]

If that is even remotely a fair assessment of *The Hothouse*—and it is hard altogether to refute—what are we to make of his recent "political" plays? *Precisely* can perhaps be discounted, since it is only a sketch, delivered by Pinter in place of an acceptance speech when he received the Elmer Holmes Bobst Award in Arts and Letters at New York University in late 1984. But it is pretty evident he does not "care for" the interrogator Nicolas in *One for the Road* or the salacious, bullying sergeant of *Mountain Language*. The former may perhaps be conceived with a kind of appalled empathy, since Pinter has acknowledged that he too has "violent" feelings and firmly believes that the play's audiences saw something of themselves in the character: "Think of the joy of having absolute power."[45] On the other hand, he was clearly signaling that both Nicolas and the Sergeant are "nasty people" of whom he "disapproves." And he was, it would seem, "trying to make a point, an explicit point" about them and their kind.

The new Pinter would, however, probably quarrel with this conclusion. On several occasions he has suggested that both *One for the Road* and *Mountain Language* were composed in much the same unplanned way as his earlier work. He started with a character or image and "let rip and [didn't] think."[46] After his confrontation with those complacent Turkish women, he went home and, still in a state of "rage,"[47] launched immediately into *One for the Road*, finishing it in three days. "I wanted to see how detestable [Nicolas] could be," he recalled later. "I think by the end I found him detestable enough."[48] *Mountain Language*, too, he has described as an intuitive exploration of images troubling his mind: "They shocked me into life and into the act of writing." And it, too, "went like a bomb" when he eventually composed it in 1988.[49]

Yet that play's genesis was suggestively different from *One for the Road*. Pinter actually began it three years earlier, after his trip with Miller to Turkey, but found it impossible to continue. As explained to the BBC at about that time, he thought of writing about a mother forbidden to speak to her imprisoned son, but "my annoyance and revulsion was so strong I knew there was no play to be written."[50] "I knew what I felt, which was a sense of outrage," he said in a public forum in 1984. "There was no real life in it, I would have done better just to speak . . . about it."[51]

In this same interview he went further, radically questioning "political" drama and his own talent for it: "The problem with writing a play from a particular point of view is that the play is written before you've written it, and therefore is in a certain sense dead." And he amplified this thought for the BBC in 1985:

> One of the joys of writing is in fact not knowing how the thing is going to turn out; but when I know perfectly well what I think about something, as I do in these cases of nuclear weapons and torture, I therefore know what's going to happen in the play. It's as if I'd already written the play. The play has come to its conclusion before I've written it.[52]

Again, his example was the then-unfinished *Mountain Language*, a piece he clearly thought even more "useless" than *The Hothouse*.

One detects in Pinter's recent utterances a great and understandable need to believe in his recent work while keeping faith with his artistic principles; and the strain sometimes shows. His new plays are "political": well, so were his old ones. His new plays have something intellectually and emotionally preplanned about them: nevertheless, they "dictate" themselves and, he hopes, have an authentic life of their own.

Again, his new plays have, he has insisted, no specific didactic aim. When he wrote *One for the Road*, he "wasn't thinking then of my audience."[53] *Mountain Language* is not an "ideological piece of work, it's simply a series of short, sharp, brutal encounters" about which spectators must "make up their own minds."[54] Nevertheless, he clearly wants to instruct. He wants to face his audience with uncomfortable truths, and he wants to draw their attention to abuses "which most people prefer understandably to ignore and pretend don't exist."[55] He wants those leaving *One for the Road* to feel that "this is an accurate state of affairs that exists all over the world. I will at least contribute to Amnesty International. I will investigate and find out what's going on in the world."[56]

But Pinter's contradictions, if such they be, obviously matter less than the questions they raise. Has he in fact found a way of injecting firsthand life and energy into politically constructive drama? Or is *Mountain Language* as "dead" as he feared it would be before he decided to disinter and refashion it in 1988—and does *One for the Road* smell somewhat of the dramatic charnel house too? What are the qualities of what, to repeat, are the only remotely substantial plays Pinter has written since 1982?

The similarities between the two are obvious enough. In each, state power seems as whimsical as it is oppressive, unscrupulous, and irresistible. A brutalized man is released while his wife remains under arrest, and his seven-year-old son is killed; in every case the action is without explanation. One day people may be "badly punished" for speaking their language, and the next the prohibition is lifted, again without apparent cause. In each play, both torture and sexual exploitation seem commonplace. In each, any unsolicited reference by the victims to family relationships of their own is absolutely taboo. Nicolas gets openly angry once only, when the abused Gila refers to her father. In *Mountain Language*, the reason the old woman's son is beaten is that he remarks that, like his prison guard, he has a wife and three children. These people are not permitted to share the bonds of humanity. Their status is that of "shitbags," an insult directed at them in each play.

In each, the persecutors themselves combine a contemptuous sadism with anti-intellectualism and a certain religiosity. Nicolas disingenuously apologizes to the battered Victor ("You're a man of the highest intelligence") for the damage his men have done to his "lovely house" with its "lots of books." The sergeant in *Mountain Language* calls Sarah Johnson "a fucking intellectual" and, when his commander reminds him that her buttocks wobble, says that "intellectual arses wobble the best." Nicolas describes himself as "a religious man," twice declares that "the voice of God speaks through me," calls his troops "soldiers of God," and defines his job as to "keep the world clean for God." No such claim is explicit in *Mountain Language*; yet the sergeant, as crude a character as Pinter has ever created, can still point out that people who have committed no crime may not be "without sin." The "socio-religious monsters," as Pinter called them in his letter to Wood, are clearly still alive and capable of destruction.

Again, those monsters are still fulfilling what one might call their zoological imperatives. They are only too eager to deprive others of their loved ones, security, freedom of movement, self-respect, and sanity. The old mother, like Stanley in *The Birthday Party* and Lamb in *The Hothouse*, ends up in a kind of catatonic stupor. But now the assault goes further. Life itself is at risk—and so, less drastically, is something of particular importance to Pinter: language. Throughout his oeuvre people have used words simultaneously as camouflage and weapons, disorienting and dominating their victims from behind their private smokescreens. Now speech itself has also become an object of attack. In both plays it is clearly dangerous to volunteer any but the most carefully considered words, and in *Mountain Language* a whole word-system has been proscribed, stolen. As if to emphasize the iniquity of this, the soldiers' language is brusque, cold, and cliché-ridden when it is not coarse and insulting. Again and again we get such words as "not permitted," "outlawed," "military decree," and, no less than eight times in the course of the play's seventeen minutes, "forbidden." Clearly we are meant to contrast these loveless repetitions with the loving ones the prisoner's mother thinks aloud, presumably in her mountain language: "When you come home there will be such a welcome for you. Everyone is waiting for you. They're all waiting for you. They're all waiting to see you."

That, no doubt, is a gain; but it is difficult to ignore the artistic loss that's surely also apparent in *One for the Road* and *Mountain Language*—of characterization, for a start. If the not-uninteresting Roote of *The Hothouse* is, by Pinter's admission, made of "cardboard," the principal characters of both these plays must consist of see-through paper. Their place and purpose in the moral scheme are what's important about them, and in each case that is entirely obvious. They are set and stuck, foredoomed to play the roles of vices and victims in homilies about political oppression. It could certainly be argued that Nicolas is rather more complex than, say, the sergeant with his cruel sneers, his combination of grandiloquence and foul-mouthed slang, his musings about death and nature and madness, his wild laughter and heavy drinking. But all this seems externally and even rather melodramatically conceived, a luridly impressionistic case study of a torturer rather than the torturer himself. In spite of (or perhaps partly because of) those exaggerated invocations of a punitive God, one is not left with the impression that Pinter has done what would be genuinely enlightening: that is, felt his way into the psychopathology of a modern monster. There are even times when one wonders if Nicolas's artistic ancestry is not the caricatured SS officer of the B-movies.

Not all these criticisms—judging by the play's mostly warm reception in England in particular—will command general consent. They can anyway hardly be "proved." But when Nicolas says to his tattered, bruised quarry, "I've heard so much about you, I'm terribly pleased to meet you," it is surely all too easy to hear the echo of the kind of Nazi sadist who informs his quivering victim, "I zink ve are going to get to know each other very, very well." This is not altogether a facetious comparison. What has given so many of Pinter's plays much of their distinctiveness is, again, their characters' tendency to express themselves on more than one level at once. A speech about the complexities of a one-way street system in *No Man's Land* is also a warning to an intruder that he may be venturing into an emotional situation he cannot handle. Mick's bizarre description of the London bus system in *The Caretaker* carries a rather similar message for Davies. But with Nicolas the verbal ruse is too transparent; oblique threat has become obvious, formulaic sarcasm.

That dramatizes what is surely the central problem with both *One for the Road* and *Mountain Language*. Pinter's originality has to do with his rich use of subtext, with suggestiveness and that mystery of which I spoke before. If there is violence in his plays, and there often is, it is generally to be found beneath the words and behind the actions, adding to the tension and sense of danger. The description of his work that he himself offered and then withdrew some years ago, that its subject was "the weasel under the cocktail cabinet," is actually very apposite.[57] But in these two plays the terror is up front, on the surface, and, perhaps as a result, curiously banal. The characters and situations are what they seem, and that is that.

Pinter's own answer to these objections might be roughly the same as his riposte to a critic who worried about his lack of "perspective": neither perspective nor subtext matter much to someone who is being tortured. Aesthetic qualms must cede to moral urgency. But that raises, and perhaps begs, several questions. Are these objections aesthetic only? Isn't one of the merits of Pinter's best work that it promotes a kind of creative paranoia in the spectator? If people are in emotional disguise, warily circling each other, maneuvering, plotting, then wisdom is to learn to sniff out what is really happening. The experience of a good Pinter play is a lesson in ontological self-defense. But with *Mountain Language* and *One for the Road* there is little if any work for the spectator to do, little if anything for him or her to discover. The weasel has, so to speak, been taken out of the cabinet, stuffed by a taxidermist, and put on public view.

Actually, a rather similar analogy was made by Pinter himself when he recalled his meeting with the Turkish women who provoked him into writing *One for the Road*. "[They] saw reality in a totally different way," he said.

> They saw a table which had a very striking tablecloth on it and vases of flowers on it, striking and beautiful and worth preserving. They didn't look under the table at any time and find what the people who are being tortured find: mess, pain, humiliation, vomit, excrement, blood.[58]

What has made so much of his past work so disturbing is its implicit invitation to us to sniff out the blood beneath the tablecloth. What makes his new work so much cruder is that the blood, excrement, and vomit are under our noses, in our faces. At its best, his past work took up permanence resident in the mind, troubling it, haunting it, maybe reshaping its opinions, *including* its political ones. His new plays take direct aim at the stomach and rely on short-term shock.

But Pinter would doubtless argue that crudeness and shock may actually be constructive, partly because they bring home that the world's political wrongs need immediate attention and not leisurely contemplation, and partly because they prevent people from doing what they're all too inclined to do: avoid unpleasant facts. The question, however, is whether they do indeed accomplish these ends. Pinter himself has observed that many members of his audiences, precisely the people he most needed to reach, walked out of the New York production of *One for the Road*, rather as he himself had walked out of *US*.[59] As he might have remembered, it is a human instinct, if not a very praiseworthy one, to wince away when being bludgeoned with cruel and ugly truths. Such spectators, if they are worth reaching at all, may need approaching with more of that guile, that subtlety Pinter once inimitably possessed.

But there were and are hardier spectators, both for *One for the Road* and for *Mountain Language*. What has been the impact of the plays on them? Each must naturally speak for him- or herself; and it must be admitted that some have been extremely enthusiastic. That has especially been the case in England, where more than a few critics have come to expect a sociopolitical slant to the drama and are even inclined to attack as "irrelevant" dramatists who fail to offer it. *One for the Road* won a major award there. And the influential Michael Billington of *The Guardian*, for example, found *Mountain Language* "masterly"—"It distils the daily barbarism of military societies with painterly precision."[60]

But even if that claim is true, it raises yet another worrying question. As we've seen, Pinter wishes to evoke "military societies" in the plural, with perhaps some emphasis on a putative Britain of the future. But generality can also betoken vagueness, a matter of some concern when the subject is as real and pressing as that of his "political" work. One wonders if it is possible to universalize the topical at all. Certainly, it is difficult to do so without dissipating point and impact. A play can easily end up by being about everywhere, and therefore about nowhere at which we are able to direct our feelings of outrage. That is surely the case with both *One for the Road* and *Mountain Language*. Both tell us that terrible oppression exists, but they lack not only the informativeness but also the front-line authority of, say, a TV program, a newspaper article, or even a stage documentary chronicling particular yet characteristic examples of injustice. Kenneth Brown's *The Brig*, dated though it now may be, surely tells us more about what it is like to be in a military jail than does *Mountain Language*. The film *Midnight Express* is even more limited in scope, a case study of prison life, specifically involving Turkey. But Pinter's "political" plays, derived though they both are from that country, tell us less about Turkish prisons without telling us more about violence, victimization, and the abuse of power in any other country or countries.

How useful can these plays then be? What can they achieve beyond reminding us that appalling things continue to happen in our world—and giving the cognoscenti an interesting insight into the mind of a major dramatist as it has evolved over the years? What change can they bring about? The answer is "not a lot," as Pinter himself has ruefully acknowledged. "Not very much, no," he replied when he was asked that very question about *One for the Road.* "I don't think it has a great effect, no."[61] We might also parenthetically remember what we've noted before, that his work as a whole implicitly suggests that his pessimism is deep-rooted. If human beings themselves are innately fearful and acquisitive, what hope is there of changing their society or their political systems for the better? There is, perhaps, a curious contradiction in Pinter writing "political" plays at all.

At all events, it seems possible to conclude that Pinter has abandoned a kind of play he wrote uniquely well for a kind of play lesser dramatists continue to do better; he has, so to speak, assiduously rowed his way into the narrows and shallows; and all with no great likelihood of political usefulness. Yet what else could he do, given a "reawakening" that is clearly as passionate as it is principled? How could such a firsthand work as he now writes not be "political," given the images of political horror that are crowding his head? How could he not be true to emotions that are, for better or worse, manifestly central to his life?

NOTES

1. *Observer* (London), 21 July 1985.
2. Public interview with Benedict Nightingale at the Institute of Contemporary Arts, London, in 1984.
3. Television interview with Anna Ford, BBC, 1988.
4. In an often-quoted section of an interview with Lawrence Bensky ("Harold Pinter," in *Writers at Work: The Paris Review Interviews,* 3d ser. [New York: Viking, 1967; London: Secker & Warburg, 1968]), Pinter spoke of men persistently lurking with broken milk bottles under a railway arch on the way to a Jewish club he frequented: "The best way was to talk to them, you know, sort of 'Are you alright?' Yes, I'm alright,' 'Well, that's alright then.' And all the time keep walking towards the lights of the main road." See this interview as reprinted in *Pinter: A Collection of Critical Essays,* ed. Arthur Ganz (Englewood Cliffs, N.J.: Prentice-Hall, 1972), 29.
5. Ford interview.
6. Interview with Miriam Gross, *Observer* (London), 5 October 1980.
7. Interview with Nicholas Hern, published as an introduction to Pinter's *One for the Road* (London: Methuen, 1984).

8. Quoted in Martin Esslin, *The Peopled Wound: The Work of Harold Pinter* (Garden City, N.Y.: Anchor, 1970), 25.

9. Bensky interview.

10. Interview with Michael Dean, BBC-TV, 1985.

11. Letter to the *Times* (London), 22 March 1974.

12. Interview with Bryan Appleyard, *Times* (London), 16 March 1984.

13. Ford interview.

14. Nightingale interview. See also Appleyard interview and an interview with Sue Summers in the *Independent* (London) on 18 October 1988.

15. Ford interview.

16. Ibid.

17. *Harpers*, May 1985.

18. Ford interview.

19. Dean interview.

20. Interview with Mel Gussow, *New York Times*, 6 December 1988.

21. Pinter has described the inception of *One for the Road* in his interviews with Hern, Nightingale, and Dean.

22. Ford interview.

23. Hern interview.

24. Harold Pinter, "Writing for Myself," *Twentieth Century Magazine*, 168 (February 1961), 172–75.

25. Bensky interview.

26. Ibid.

27. Letter to Peter Wood, 30 March 1958, published in *Drama*, Winter 1981, and republished in *Harold Pinter:* The Birthday Party, The Caretaker, *and* The Homecoming: A Casebook, ed. Michael Scott (London: Macmillan, 1986), 79–82.

28. Ibid.

29. Interview with John Sherwood, BBC European Service, March 1960.

30. Hern interview.

31. Gussow interview.

32. Dean interview.

33. Ibid.

34. Ibid.

35. Ford interview.

36. Gussow interview.

37. Ruby Cohn, "The World of Harold Pinter," *Tulane Drama Review* 6, 3 (March 1962). Reprinted in *Pinter: A Collection of Critical Essays*, 78–92.

38. James T. Boulton, "Harold Pinter: *The Caretaker* and Other Plays," *Modern Drama* 6 (September 1963). Reprinted in *Pinter: A Collection of Critical Essays*, 93–104.

39. For an elaboration of this point, see Martin Esslin, "Language and Silence," in *Pinter: A Collection of Critical Essays*, 34–59.

40. Ford interview.

41. Gussow interview.

42. Graham Woodroffe, "Taking Care of the 'Coloureds': The Political Metaphor of Harold Pinter's *The Caretaker*," *Theatre Journal*, December 1988, 498–508.

43. Esslin, *The Peopled Wound*, 84.

44. Bensky interview.
45. Hern interview.
46. Ford interview.
47. Hern interview.
48. Dean interview.
49. Ford interview.
50. Dean interview.
51. Nightingale interview.
52. Dean interview.
53. Hern interview.
54. Ford interview.
55. Ibid.
56. Nightingale interview.
56. See Pinter's speech, made in Hamburg, on being awarded the 1970 German Shakespeare Prize, reprinted as an introduction to *The Complete Works of Harold Pinter*, vol 4. (London: Methuen; New York: Grove, 1981).
57. Nightingale interview.
58. Dean interview.
59. Hern interview.
60. Review by Michael Billington, *Guardian* (London), 22 October 1988.
61. Nightingale interview.

Peter Barnes and the Problem of Goodness

BERNARD F. DUKORE

I know and love the good, yet, ah! the worst pursue.
　　　　　—Petrarch, *Sonnet* 225 (ca. 1327)

The good want power, but to weep barren tears.
The powerful goodness want: worse need for them.
　　　　　—Percy Bysshe Shelley, *Prometheus Unbound* (1819)

I love my fellow creatures—I do all the good I can—
Yet everybody says I'm such a disagreeable man!
And I can't think why!
　　　　　—W. S. Gilbert, *Princess Ida* (1884)

A good man nowadays is hard to find.
　　　　　—Eddie Green, *A Good Man Is Hard To Find* (1927)

Terrible is the temptation of goodness.
　　　　　—Bertolt Brecht, *The Caucasian Chalk Circle* (1944/45)

"To Martin," reads the dedication of Peter Barnes's 1978 play *Laughter!* The unsurnamed dedicatee is Martin Esslin, who eleven years earlier helped to promote Barnes's career as a dramatist. In 1967, Esslin was a member of the playreading subcommittee of the British Arts Council, which awarded bursaries to selected playwrights who submitted scripts. One day, another member of the subcommittee,

Stuart Burge, then director of the Nottingham Playhouse, handed
him a script. "This man's a bloody genius!" said Burge of its author.
"You're right," Esslin confirmed after reading it, "he *is* a bloody
genius!" "I'll produce it in Nottingham," promised Burge. "I'll translate it into German," Esslin vowed. The script was *The Ruling Class*,
for which Barnes was awarded a bursary; a Nottingham production
followed (6 November 1968), which transferred to London (26 February 1969) and won the prestigious John Whiting Award (1968) as well
as the *Evening Standard* Award (1969, shared with Edward Bond for
Narrow Road to the Deep North). A German translation soon sparked
numerous productions.

"To Martin," I too can say, since in the mid-1970s he urged me to
purchase a copy of Barnes's *The Bewitched*. Although I had seen and
enjoyed the one-act plays *Leonardo's Last Supper* and *Noonday Demons*
in 1969, it was *The Bewitched*, which I read one rainy day in London,
that persuaded me of Barnes's stature, led me to read everything he
had published, and made me want to write about him.[1] In this area,
as in so many, I am glad to follow Esslin's lead.

By the time Barnes made his initial impact in the theater, absurdism was no longer avant-garde; as an influential dramatic force, it
had peaked. Literally, he arrived after the absurd. How or even
whether absurdist drama can treat morality or goodness is question-
able—which is not the case with such modern nonabsurdist drama
as that of Bertolt Brecht, who influenced Barnes. In fact, Brecht is
another dramatist for whom Esslin helped to lead the way: his *Brecht:
A Choice of Evils* (1959) is the first book-length study in English of
Brecht's plays.

"There is no creativity," says Barnes in the introduction to his
Collected Plays, "only discovery. If I return again and again to the
same themes, like a child to the fire, it is because they are essential
and I still owe them something."[2] Notwithstanding this disclaimer,
one theme to which he returns with great creativity is the problem
of goodness, the ramifications of which he explores with the variety
that derives not from reiteration but from what he calls discovery.
Appropriate to his varying treatments of the theme, the diverse epigraphs that head this essay also befit his style, which includes allusions to classical and contemporary, poetic and pop.

Today, as in Petrarch's time, Barnes believes, people who love the
good find themselves in pursuit of what is quite different. To Brecht,

goodness, not evil, is a natural human urge—a theme of *The Caucasian Chalk Circle*. As Brecht also says in his short poem "The Mask of Evil," about a Japanese carved mask of an evil demon: "Sympathetically I observe / The swollen veins of the forehead, indicating / What a strain it is to be evil."[3] To strain to be evil, to strive to avoid natural temptations toward goodness, is necessary for survival. Like Brecht, Barnes perceives goodness to be a temptation, but unlike Brecht he also emphasizes that evil is a lure—perhaps more seductive, since its rewards are often more immediate and more materially gratifying.

The germ of *The Ruling Class*, he discloses, was his desire to write about a good human being. "A good man nowadays is hard to find," goes a line in a popular song, but its title, which lacks the adverb, recognizes that the difficulty is not a modern phenomenon. Thinking about what constitutes a good man, says Barnes, "by a sort of process of elimination I got to Jesus Christ. I didn't want to do a play about Jesus Christ, but I wondered what would happen to him if he were here today in modern times." He concluded that "he would be in an insane asylum, that he would be considered mad. So then I got to the idea, what about a man who believes himself to be Jesus Christ and is insane."[4] He echoes Dostoyevsky, who in 1868, a century before the first performance of *The Ruling Class*, was attempting to write a novel whose main idea, he said, was "to portray a positively good man. There is nothing more difficult in the world, and this is especially true today." The "only one positively good figure" ever to have existed has been Jesus Christ.[5] Dostoyevsky's novel takes its title from the way its characters consider its protagonist, which is also how those in Barnes's play regard his "The Idiot."

"You are talking directly to God," Jack, the fourteenth earl of Gurney, tells his relatives, who "*all look up at him in horror.*" He is, he adds with explanatory details, "the Creator and ruler of the Universe, . . . Yaweh, Shangri-Ti and El, the First Immovable Mover, . . . the one True God, the God of Love, the Naz!" (22). Even before this revelation, following which the bishop faints, the words of the earl, who calls himself the God of Love, shock everyone. "If the Bishop doesn't mind," Jack proposes, "I think we should pray." "Pray?" Sir Charles incredulously asks. When Jack innocently infers that they must surely pray for love and understanding, Lady Claire looks at her husband and responds ironically: "Every night. Without success." Jack catches the solicitor trying to slip away. "I'm Methodist," is his excuse. "I'm sure you're still a Christian," says Jack, and pleads, "Come, for me." The solicitor responds not to religion but to the peerage: "Yes, my lord" (21).

According to the diagnosis of Jack's psychiatrist, Dr. Herder, he suffers "from delusions of *grandeur*. In reality he's an Earl, an English aristocrat, a peer of the realm, a member of the ruling class. Naturally, he's come to believe there's only one person grander than that—the Lord God Almighty Himself" (24). How does he know he is God? "When I pray to Him," he explains, "I find I'm talking to myself" (26).

Is there any harm in the delusion of J. C., as he is called? "The Gospel Dispensation promised only salvation for the soul," he says, "my new Dispensation of Love gives it to the *body* as well." Thus, almost everything one sees, touches, and feels glorifies his love. Such actions and assertions as *"(Mimes putting on a hat.)* The top hat is my mitre and the walking stick my rod. *(Twirls imaginary stick.)"* disconcert onstage and offstage audiences, thereby preventing at least the former from attending to his idea of "the unity of Universal Love" (25–26). Why does Tucker remain a servant even though J. C.'s father had bequeathed him £20,000? "Out of love," suggests Jack. "Rot," Sir Charles responds (27)."Pomp and riches, pride and property will have to be lopped off," declares J. C. "All men are brothers. Love makes all equal. The mighty must bow down before the pricks of the louse-ridden rogues." Fraternally, he leaves with Tucker, urging his uncle and aunt, "Enjoy yourselves whilst I'm gone. Relax. Have sex." Responding to J. C.'s last injunction, Lady Claire prompts her husband, "Well, you heard what he said, Charles." But he reacts to J. C.'s earlier declarations: *"(trembling with rage)* I did . . . bowing before rogues . . . destroying property . . . all men equal . . . *(Pointing after* Earl.) My God, Claire, he's not only *mad*, he's *Bolshie!"* (28–29). Notions of love pass him by. To Charles, who considers the class system and property to constitute goodness, the implications of J. C.'s doctrine are seditious.

The universal inclusiveness of this doctrine further disorients onstage and offstage audiences. All is one in this deity's all-embracing mind. Will he join Tucker in a drink? "Not during Yom Kippur." A few moments later, in a wacky transformation of Matthew's comparison of the kingdom of heaven to a mustard seed (13:31–32), he decrees, "Love cannot doubt nor faith the mustard seed" (30). Soon, he *"puts his hands together, Indian style,"* intones "Pax et benedíctio" and "Dóminus vobíscum," then sings and dances "The Varsity Drag," from the Broadway and Hollywood musical *Good News* (33–34).

When Jack merely speaks idiotically, he bothers no one, perhaps because the listeners consider meaningless or absurd speech his norm and accordingly ignore it as a frill. When he expresses love of his fellow creatures, however, they think him deranged, perhaps because such sentiments deviate from the norm. When Mrs. Piggot-Jones and Mrs. Treadwell ask him to open the church festivities, he inquires about his role: "Do I charm bracelets, swing lead, break wind, pass water?" "No, you make a speech," the latter replies. "On what text, Mother Superior?" he asks. Ignoring the title, Mrs. Piggot-Jones answers: "We leave that to the speaker. It can be any topic of general interest. Hanging, Immigration, the Stranglehold of the Unions. Anything . . ." "So long as it isn't political," Mrs. Treadwell interrupts helpfully. Although his reaction, "Nat-ur-ally," is what they expect, they are appalled when he suddenly calls England "a fly-blown speck in the North Sea, a country of cosmic unimportance," and proclaims, "You can't kick the natives in the back streets of Calcutta any more." At his decision not to employ parables, as he mistakenly did at Galilee, but to declare plainly, "God is love," Mrs. Treadwell is *"frightened."* He reminds the women of his commandment to "love one another as I loved you," to which Mrs. Piggot-Jones exclaims, as if he were the devil incarnate, *"(retreating)* Stay back! My husband is a Master of Hounds!" Moments later, *"Their nerve breaks. They turn and plunge for the door, but are frozen in mid-flight as they see* [J. C.'s huge] *cross for the first time."* Shrieking *"cries of fear the two women rush Up Stage Centre"* and out the door (35–37). To them, his words of love and equality proclaim a social revolutionary Antichrist.

In striking contrast, the second half of the play has J. C. become Jack; the God of Love turns into Jack the Ripper. In similarly striking contrast, widespread approval greets Jack, who unlike J. C. conforms to the norms of society in general and of his class in particular. Upon asserting that nowadays "You're MOCKED in the Strand if you speak of patriotism and the old Queen. Discipline's gone. They're sapping the foundations of our society with their adultery and fornication! [. . .] The barbarians are waiting outside with their chaos, anarchy,

homosexuality and worse!," Truscott, the Master in Lunacy, certifies
his sanity. As Dr. Herder observes, "the Earl's behaviour just happened to coincide with his idea of sanity" (87–89). So does it match
that of the others in his class, as Barnes emphasizes by Mrs. Piggot-
Jones's and Mrs. Treadwell's approbation of the changed Jack, who
though homicidally insane in act 2 employs phrases of conventional
morality.

> *Earl of Gurney:* Tucker, why are those table legs uncovered? Stark naked
> wooden legs in mixed company—it's not decent. Curved
> and fluted, too. Don't you agree, Mrs. Treadwell?
>
> *Mrs. Treadwell:* Well, I do think young girls nowadays show too much.
> After all, the main purpose of legs isn't seduction.

"Let's have no talk of bestial orgasms, erotic tongueings," he commands. "I find the whole subject distressing," Mrs. Piggot-Jones
concurs. "I can't understand why the good Lord chose such a disgusting way of reproducing human-beings." To his pronouncement
that "the Hangman holds society together. He is the symbol of the
Great Chastiser. He built this world on punishment and fear," Mrs.
Treadwell and Mrs. Piggot-Jones *"nod vigorously."* With fear snuffed
out, says Jack, echoing first Shakespeare's *Troilus and Cressida*, then
a well-known joke by Mrs. Patrick Campbell, "see what discords
follow. Sons strike their doddering dads, young girls show their bos-
oms and ankles and say rude things about the Queen. Anything goes
and they do it openly in the streets and frighten the horses."[6] As a
remedy, he would return fear by reinstating the death penalty. With
an executioner, who keeps "the forelock-touching ranks in order,"
one knows that God is "in his heaven, all's right with the world," an
echo of Browning's "Pippa Passes." When the women agree, Jack
concludes, "that's only to be expected. Breeding speaks to breeding."
Mrs. Piggot-Jones, *"flushing with pleasure,"* is delighted that this
meeting "is so different from our last visit" (92–94). As Claire explains, what really captivates them is his manner, which has "just the
right blend of God-given arrogance and condescension" (96).

     In act 1, these two women find J. C.'s sermons of goodness not
tempting but terrible, and his injunctions to love one's fellow creatures detestable. In act 2, they find Jack's abhorrence of sexuality
and repudiation of love, as well as his advocacy of using violence and

fear to keep the lower classes in order—or, inverting the Petrarchian and Gilbertian epigraphs, the pursuit of the worst and the hatred of one's fellow creatures—comforting.

To the powerful, who lack Shelleyan visions of the good, Jack's sentiments in act 2 express goodness. No longer an advocate of love, he perverts the Sermon on the Mount. "If thy hand offends thee, cut it off," he states as he frames the butler for murder. Because his manner accords with the social norm, Inspector Brockett, a lackey of Jack's class, praises him: "My lord, I'd just like to say what a pleasure it's been meeting you.[. . .]You've shown me what 'noblesse oblige' really means" (107–8). Even Sir Charles is impressed: "This time you behaved like a Gurney should" (112). Barnes emphasizes that Jack's repudiation of true goodness and his embrace of his class's values is not aberrant. While he plans to pass measures in the House of Lords to reinstate the death penalty, his cousin Dinsdale aims to do the same in the House of Commons. Moreover, the statements of the other lords resemble Jack's: "For thirteen years there has been no flogging, and there has been a steadily rising volume of crime, lawlessness and thuggery" and "In order to protect the public the criminal must be treated as an animal." At the end of the play, Jack rejects his previous sentiments: "*God the Son* wants nothing only to give freely in love and gentleness. It's loathsome, a foul perversion of life! And must be rooted out. *God the Father* demands, orders, controls, crushes. We must follow Him, my noble Lords." Distorting Shakespeare's *Henry V*, he calls upon everyone to "Follow your spirit; and upon this charge / Cry, God for Jack, England and Saint George." *"He's one of us at last!"* exclaims Sir Charles, following which everyone sings the hymn derived from Ecclesiasticus 44:1–3: "Let us now praise famous men / And our fathers that begat us. / Such as did there rule in their kingdoms / Men renowned for their power" (117–18).

As Barnes noted when he began to consider the subject, the man who preaches goodness and love can function only in an insane asylum. To flourish socially, the dramatist concluded, he must renounce such beliefs. In society as we know it, *The Ruling Class* reflects, goodness has no place. The problem of goodness is central to Barnesonian drama. Furthermore, the antithesis of J. C. and Jack— that is, of the moral visions they represent—also informs may of Barnes's plays.

Leonardo's Last Supper is set in sixteenth-century Italy. Lasca, the head of the family of morticians who prepare Leonardo da Vinci's corpse for burial, explicitly equates God's "goodness" with his own financial "profit" (127). His wife calls accusing someone of witchcraft, thereby ensuring that person's death, her "Christian duty" (129). What were their "good years"? Leonardo asks them; "1494," they respond, "the plague year," since it was good for business (141). Apart from his usual work that year, Lasca made a great deal of money when he "bottled shit," the smell of which, at the time, was considered a means to ward off the plague. "Lasca's Excremental Goodness," it was called (142). The dawn of the modern age, the play dramatizes, was truly modern: money-making by any means, including murder, is the age's preoccupation; goodness is perverted into profit; and one of the purported manifestations of goodness is excrement.

The title *Noonday Demons* may derive from the Ninety-first Psalm, which says that God will shield whoever trusts in him from "the pestilence that walketh in darkness" and "the destruction that wasteth at noonday." Traditionally, demonic powers are highest at noon. Early in the play, the Tempter tells Eusebius, a hermit saint, that none of his privations—which include a daily diet of muddy water and seven black olives, sleeping while standing against a wall, and living enchained inside a cave—will accomplish the slightest good: *"The story's always the same, isn't it? virtue defeated, justice sold, shame lost, equality loathed, innocence despised, guilt condoned, evil advanced"* (161). The Tempter is not a separate character but a facet of Eusebius, who speaks to himself in a different voice, using modern, not archaic, language. "I agulten thee Lord, forgivest Thou me," says Eusebius, for example; the devil comments, *"That hi-fi mumbo-jumbo won't do you no good"* (156–57). Whereas J. C. and Jack are aspects of the same character, the latter subduing the former, Saint Eusebius and the devil, who also reside in the same person, hold a dialogue with each other.

But can a hermit be a good person? To put the question differently, can a hermit accomplish goodness, which is not hermetic but social? Putting Eusebius to a social test, Barnes introduces a rival hermit, Pior, into the cave, which he too claims as his own. Their social actions, which are really asocial actions, include ritualistic verbal abuse, efforts at exorcism by hurling bowlfuls of water at each other, invocations of God's curses, and battle, beating each other with chains, crying, "Kill, kill, kill for Jesus!" and "Kill, kill, kill for Christ!" (179). Despite their protestations of holiness, their self-styled goodness lacks socially beneficial consequences. Although they claim to know and love the good, they pursue the̅ worst when given the opportunity to demonstrate their actual values.

In the world of *The Bewitched* (1974), the values of Jack are triumphant, those of J. C. a memory. Here, in late seventeenth-century Spain, are what Jack would consider the good old days, when blasphemy (as he prescribes in parodying "Dry Bones") is punished by breaking the offender's bones on the wheel and when flogging, bludgeoning, torture, and execution are routine penalties. The very notion of goodness is alien to the play's characters. "In a world of tawdry values and vanishing ideals," one aristocrat muses, without intending irony, "I sometimes think money's the only decent thing left" (207–8). Priests, says one of them, "hunt, dice, dance and lie; so greed and lechery flourish" (219). But fear, torture, and murder also abound—all in the name of Christ. As this same priest states, "'Tis our [human] nature t' inflict pain. But cruelty cannot run free[;] like crude ore 't must be refined in the service o' Jesus Christ" (236).

"There is no God," cries the childless King Carlos II of Spain before the end of the first act, prompting *"Thunder, a streak of lightning and a great voice."* "YES THERE IS," booms God's voice. "I've prayed t' you. Where's my son?" asks Carlos, prompting *"Another streak of lightning."* God's voice *"wearily"* answers, "NO SON—ONLY LIGHTNING" (252–53). As the last speech implies, there is no son for the monarch and there is no savior, no God of love, no exemplar of goodness, for mankind; instead, there is only lightning, used by the God of wrath to scourge humanity.

To Ivan the Terrible, title character of "Tsar," the first of two one-act plays that comprise *Laughter!*, Christ's "hands nailed flat casn't strike me" when he does evil (344). "Man's not good," declares Ivan. "He's a two-eyed, two-balled dawish freak [whose] seared soul's more foul than his sinsoiled carcass" (345). Not love but "hatred's this world's fulcrum" and "power's sucked into this magnetized centre, where I stand" (354). Appropriately, his son declares, "F' love o' Christ I hate" (357). The values of Jack dominate Ivan the Terrible's realm, from which those of J. C. are absent.

In "Auschwitz," the second one-act play of *Laughter!*, as in *The Bewitched*, the values of Jack also dominate. Except for a short, expressionistic sequence in the concentration camp for which it is named, "Auschwitz" is set in Hitler's Germany. Is goodness possible in this social context? Taking the inversion of ethics as a given under the Nazi regime, Barnes indicts those, in the audience as well as on stage, who substitute smug self-satisfaction for actions that demonstrate goodness. Because of the conflict between Gottleb, a quintessential Nazi, and the civil servants who administer Auschwitz, and also because of the engaging jokes of the clerks, which help them to bear their miserable lot, spectators and readers tend initially to accept the latter as good people.

Can one condemn a person who quips about privation, for instance, Else, who remarks, "Coming to work this morning, I stopped to pull in my belt. Some idiot asked me what I was doing. I said, 'Having breakfast'" (370)? Can one censure a man who jests about his very survival, for example, Stroop, who agrees with all his superiors say and, when asked if he disagrees with anything, replies "Unemployment. I'm near retirement. You can't please everyone, so I find it best to keep pleasing my superiors" (371)? To Barnes, one must reprove them. "Comedy is itself the enemy," states the character named Author in a prefatory scene. "Laughter only confuses and corrupts everything we try to say. It cures nothing but our consciences and so ends up by making the nightmare worse. A sense of humour's no remedy for evil." Softening hatred, laughter is an "excuse to change nothing, for nothing needs changing when it's all a joke" (343). Barnes would have the clerks try to change, not bear, their society. As he says elsewhere, human beings have "creative energy for good and evil.[. . .] But the radiant light lies shattered by fear, helplessness and the wicked triviality of day to day living."[7]

"This is war," the office chief Cranach tells Gottleb. In it, the play reveals, not Gottleb but reality is what he and the other functionaries consider the enemy. "We no longer believe in a secure sentence structure," he says. Because "neutral symbols've become the safest means of communication," he endorses their use to record deaths. Besides, they are "more concise and less emotive." Actually, they are unemotive, with the result that, as Stroop says, death "isn't any of our business" (379).

These civil servants use bureaucratese to hide reality, thereby disengaging their emotions and ethics from what they do. Thus, they become as guilty as, if not more guilty than, the Nazi Gottleb, who

Miltonically adopts evil as his good. Ironically, it is Gottleb who forces these supposedly good people to confront the truths they evade. When they cite file numbers for building specifications, he calls the buildings "extermination facilities [. . .] in Auschwitz [. . .] for the complete liquidation of all Jews in Europe." "We don't know that," they protest. They "don't know that," he charges, only because they know "enough to know [they] don't want to know that" and lack the imagination to see the dead human beings "roasted" behind the roman and arabic numerals that record their murder. "Even if you read of six million dead, your imagination wouldn't frighten you, because it wouldn't make you see a single dead man" (401–2). He forces them to confront the reality of genocide, visualized when upstage filing cabinets part to reveal expressionistically the sights and sounds of Auschwitz; but by ritualistically chanting the neutral roman and arabic numerals, the functionaries succeed again in concealing reality, visualized when the filing cabinets close.

Smugly congratulating themselves on having defeated their Nazi antagonist, they claim, in Else's words that belie the reality spectators have witnessed and readers read, "We may not be much, but we're better than Gottleb. This time it didn't end with the worst in human nature triumphant, meanness exalted, goodness mocked." Calling themselves "ordinary people [. . .] like them, you, me, us," they march to the front of the stage "to sing at the audience," whom they implicate as "the Brotherhood of Man," from the Broadway and Hollywood musical How to Succeed in Business without Really Trying (409). To claim kinship with one's fellow creatures, as they do, or Gilbertianly to profess to love them and protest that they do all the good they can, is insufficient. Such people cannot imagine why anyone, including the author of Laughter!, finds them disagreeable. As Barnes dramatizes, goodness is inseparable from a social context. To be good, one must do good.

This is a major theme of Red Noses, winner of the Laurence Olivier Award as best drama of 1985. Red Noses suggests a basis of actions that might achieve goodness. "Goodness is the real danger, not corruption," warns Pope Clement VI. "Guard against the corruption of goodness," he admonishes Fathers Flote and Toulon, an echo of the Brechtian epigraph, since, the pope continues, no one "knows what will result from one wild act of goodness. Charity makes destitution permanent. To give everything you possess to a beggar is to kill a consumer and put a hundred men out of work." The abandonment of goodness is "a small price to pay to remove the terrible necessity of choice from mankind."[8]

In *Red Noses*, set in France during the Black Death, leaders of different groups disagree on what goodness is. To the pope, as the quotation indicates, goodness is maintaining the status quo. The gold merchants and feudal lords agree. To Scarron, leader of the Black Ravens, goodness is the opposite of the status quo, which he hates and would ruthlessly overturn to create a socialistic society. "Plague time heralds a new dawn sun rising in the West"—an indication that when the world is "born again," even the direction of the sunrise will change (16). To Grez, head of the Flagellants, goodness can be earned from God by penitential self-scourging. Initially, Father Flote, the protagonist, believes goodness lies in using laughter to distract the plague-stricken from their miseries so they might die happily. To this end, he founds a brotherhood of Red Noses, which the pope blesses because "there's liberation in the plague," "restraints, customs and laws of centuries buckle, old moulds crack," and Flote might provide "holy oil" to lubricate the Church's road in this difficult time (51).

Forsaking the pain offered by the Flagellants and the hate-filled struggle required by the Black Ravens, the populace eagerly accepts the laughter offered by the Red Noses, who as the pope commands, "dazzle 'em and take what's left of their minds off the harsh facts of existence" (51). To Grez's complaint, "They attract multitudes of men, we can't attract flies," Scarron explains: "The people suffer enough, they've no need to watch your suffering." A follower of the Ravens agrees, "We've had too much of misery," but upon hearing a trumpet's *"merry 'toot-toot,' followed by a drumroll and laughter of a crowd,"* he abandons them for the Noses: "Suffering and revolution is too hard. We want dolphins and dancing mice" (69–70). Putting aside their rivalry, Grez and Scarron make common cause to kill their chief opponents, the Red Noses.

Since "Master Pestilence needs no help from us," Flote persuades both them and his own followers not to fight each other but instead "appeal to Heaven. Let Heaven decide." With the announcement that the plague is over, Flote exclaims, "It's the sign! God's sign we asked for" and commands, "Blow trumpets for a new age, new world, light, birth." Rather than fight among themselves, "all forms of rebellion must come together" to achieve a good world. Agreeing to do so, the erstwhile rivals dance and sing, "Join together" (78–80).

However, their decision is too late. With the plague's end, the status quo returns. Church and state unite to crush the Flagellants and Ravens. When the pope orders the Noses to continue to divert people's attention from despotic social reality, they refuse. Their old style of humor, Flote perceives, is no longer funny, since those in power "feed us lies, crush the light, sweep the stars from the heavens," since "inequality's in, naming rich and poor, mine and thine," and since "power rules and men manifest all their deeds in oppression." That type of comedy "was a way of evading truth, avoiding responsibility. Our mirth was used to divert attention whilst the strong ones slunk back to their thrones and palaces" (103–4). Clement VI has them killed.

Although he orders no monuments built to them, although he wants them forgotten by the sands of time, he recognizes that "to be nameless and have lived, showing how men should live, is a true remembrance. The Canaanite woman helping Jesus lives more happily without a name than Salome with one. Better the nameless good Samaritan than Herod, these poor clowns than Pope Clement VI." The explicit link of the Red Noses with the Canaanite woman and Samaritan man provides an implicit recognition of the goodness of Flote's final position, which unites laughter with social revolution. While Flote thought he had failed, "no man fails completely who shows us glory" (106). In an epilogue *sub specie aeternitatis*, the voices of Flote and his clowns, en route to God, emphasize this view. "Every jest should be a small revolution," says Flote, and all the Noses sing a reprise of their song of union with the Flagellants and Ravens, "Join together" (108–9).

As Shelley wrote, the good want power, the powerful goodness; and as Green composed, a good man is hard to find. Whereas the notion of portraying a good person was the genesis of *The Ruling Class*, Barnes's first major play, the idea of dramatizing what happens when a good man obtains power is the genesis of his new dramatic work, *Sunsets and Glories*.[9] Such terms as *good* and *goodness* recur more frequently in *Sunsets and Glories* than they do in any of his other plays. Instead of taking his main source from recent history, as he did in *The Ruling Class*,[10] he takes it from the end of the thirteenth century, about fifty years before *Red Noses*. The mainspring of *Sunsets and Glories* is Peter de Morrone, who became Pope Celestine V, the only person in history to abdicate from the papacy.

Shortly before his death, Pope Nicholas IV bemoans his lack of accomplishments: "No monster me, sadly no saint either. [. . .] I did not change the world into something greener. I had the power to, but it was the power that stopped me greening. [. . .] Goodness drained from me when I became supreme Pontiff" (prologue). As a result of factions among the cardinals, each unwilling to let another snap up papal revenues, they have been unable to decide upon his successor. Recognizing that God, not they, can choose the next pope, the cardinals, one by one, fall into an inspirational trance and chant the name Peter de Morrone, whom one of them derides as "a peasant, untutored in worldly affairs with no experience of ruling. He's a man of wondrous sanctity and goodness, but . . . ," and in mid-sentence he falls to his knees and takes up the chant (1.1).

Will Morrone, a hermit-priest, who with a companion, Father Sala, resides atop a high, cold mountain and who, like the fourteenth earl of Gurney, rests on an immense crucifix, accept the papacy? The offer, he fears, may be a satanic temptation. The college of cardinals, explains Cardinal Gaetani, chose him because his "goodness" can save the Church, which increasingly powerful nation-states threaten. "We must become one community under God's Anointed, not a hundred different warring States." Singing (to the tune of "Show Me the Way to Go Home"), "Lord, I am tired and I am old. It's snowing and my feet are cold," Morrone prays for divine guidance. A voice that begins as an echo turns to a response, suggesting that God speaks through it. "Can I go down, mix with the mass of men, not be of this world but in it?" asks Morrone. "In it—up to your neck," replies the echo. "Why me?" he asks. "Because you're there, goosehead," replies the echo—the answer recalling George Leigh Mallory's reason for climbing Mount Everest: "because it's there" (1.2).

To influence Celestine V, the name Morrone takes as pope, Neapolitan King Charles II presses him to remain in Naples. The cardinals urge him to go to Rome since he "cannot rule without the organisation created for ruling" and since, parodying Browning's "Pippa Passes," as *The Ruling Class* did, "the Pope's in Rome, all's right with the world" (1.3). Understanding that all is not right with the world, he elects to stay.

Swept away by Celestine's "goodness," Cardinal Gaetani foregoes fornication with his whores, whom he nevertheless pays. One of them is wary of generosity: "I've found nothing ever comes free. All free gifts have strings, so I always pay for them—it's cheaper." Her payment is advice: since "the consolations of the carnal are fixed and short," he is right not to copulate; however, "power is better than your best copulating." His motives are more complex: "I didn't indulge for practical as well as spiritual reasons. The Holy Father is a saint. But he'll be destroyed 'less I can protect him. To do that, I must stand by him but he'll not allow it if I stink of lust" (1.4).

Overwhelmed by the demands of office, Celestine signs secular grants and creates new cardinals desired by Charles II for his political ends, approves religious dispensations dictated by Sala for his friends, and inks documents drafted by self-serving cardinals. Is this the result of giving power to a good man? If so, the play might end here. It does not. Celestine recognizes he needs good men close to him. The sexually abstemious Gaetani advises him that if he gives prelates, scholars, princes, and kings "a free hand, it will end in your pocket. This world is covered with daggers. Let me help, and be your true friend, Holy Father" (1.5). With "a good man on the throne of the world," as one cardinal puts it, rival factions unite to perpetuate the system that rewards the rich and powerful, and Charles II's queen urges him to stop Gaetani's influence (1.6).

Celestine wrestles with practical issues of papal power. Gaetani urges him to institute a new accountancy system to enforce taxes. "Our clerics extort monies for private gain. Eliminate individual corruption in the Church and your reign will be blessed." "What has Christ's Church to do with monies and taxes?" asks Celestine. "Everything, Your Holiness," says Gaetani. While Celestine comically resolves a dispute between foolish kings, Gaetani warns him that he paid for peace with his dignity and image, which are consequential, for "the mask is more important than the face." "No," maintains Celestine, "it's more important to *be* than to appear" (1.7).

Overcome with doubts of his worthiness, Celestine also questions the Church's effectiveness in doing God's will:

Christ was poor, we are rich. Christ was meek and low, we are full height and proud. Christ forsook worldly glory, we hold it fast. Christ washed

his disciples' feet, we make men kiss ours. Christ came to serve, we seek
to be served. Christ purchased heaven, we give the earth to the rich.

Cardinals dread this pope's goodness because the poor listen to him
instead of them and because he might strip the Church of power.
Fear links man and God, man and man, Gaetani reasons. Celestine
"is good but isn't feared, so he cannot hold and," repeating Clement
VI's phrase in *Red Noses*, "who knows what hellish chain of events
will result from just one act of unconsidered goodness? [. . .] A Pope
is too much in this world, of this world, to risk being good" (1.8).

Some factions try to persuade Celestine to resign from the papacy,
others to be steadfast. Torn by self-doubt, he asks Gaetani for advice.
"Man reduced to his own resources is too wicked to be free," is the
reply. "He must be governed. The indispensable check can only be
found in papal authority. But if that authority doubts its own authority, then respect disappears, Church and worlds slide to ruin." Since
the Church may remain "doomed to falsehood and decay" if Morrone
resigns, Gaetani begs him to remain Pope (1.11). Clarifying the basic
issue, Celestine agrees not to abdicate if only one cardinal "stands
up and shouts, 'I believe in goodness and virtue. I believe in truth,
purity, justice and mercy!'" When the response is silence, he concludes, "Another Pope will do as well." He names Gaetani, whom
he gives the mitre, robes, and ring, and who takes the name Boniface
VIII (1.12). Is the result of giving a good man power simply ineffectu-
ality? If so, the comic drama would end here—a one-act play.

Whereas the first half of *Sunsets and Glories* revolves around a
pope who is a good man, the second half turns on a pope who,
understanding realpolitik, cannot therefore be a good man. To con-
solidate his authority, Boniface VIII nullifies all of Celestine's acts
and appointments. He moves to Rome, which has the "apparatus of
power"—by implication, if one recalls act 1, scene 3, all becomes
"right with the world" once more. Before going there, he orders the
murder of an admirer of Celestine—to the approval of a cardinal and
king, who call the deed "swift and decisive justice" and evidence of
"greatness of soul" (2.2). Unlike Celestine, who renounces earthly
power, Boniface—who, one recollects, follows his whore's advice in
act 1, scene 4—finds, like Marlowe's Tamburlaine, whom Barnes has
him quote, "perfect bliss" in the "sweet fruition of an earthly crown!"
(2.3). Fearing conspiracies behind disobedience, however, he impris-

ons Morrone lest his virtue prove contagious. In his cell, innocently impervious to the intrigues outside, Morrone becomes a magnet for disputes among figures and groups who contend for power.

Boniface worries that "the people will shout 'Celestine! Celestine!'" to fill a vacancy in the college of cardinals. Montefelto, one of his secular allies, urges the pope to send him to kill Morrone, but Boniface warns that he has given no specific command to do so. "There is at most a glance, a half smile, an unfinished gesture. But no orders." Before Montefelto can kill Morrone, an admirer of the former pope, still loyal to him, kills Montefelto instead (2.5).

Former and present popes, exemplars of goodness and of ruthless power, face each other again. In contrast to *The Ruling Class*, wherein Jack succeeds J. C. but does not argue with him, and like *Noonday Demons*, wherein the Tempter and St. Eusebius talk to each other, Boniface and Morrone debate. The true nature of men, who "live in a night without dawn," contends Boniface, is imbecility. "But God looked over the world and found it good," Morrone points out. "He should've been more demanding," says Boniface, who claims he would have done better. "Then start work," Morrone challenges him. Morrone's spiritual presence, Boniface contends, frustrates his efforts. "According to the Gospel of Peter," he asserts, with accuracy, "Jesus didn't say on the cross 'My God, My God, why hast thou forsaken me!' but 'My power, my power, thou hast forsaken me!' He knew power, not love, saturates the earth. And it flows to the strongest."[11] To Morrone, the Christian Church is "the river of life." To Boniface, "it is a centralized, coherent and structured movement with objectives and rules, disciplines and prerogatives. It cannot be governed by saints. Its lower orders may be made up of good men but it can only flourish in the world by installing Judas as chief steward." Protesting that he does not rule, Morrone asks what more he can do. "Die," replies Boniface, who proposes to do the angel of death's job. To make it easier, Morrone obligingly turns his back. Boniface discovers he cannot strangle him. "I'm not fit to be Supreme Pontiff," he concludes. These "mincing niceties of scruple unman me and I cannot play my role. I've failed and plant the seeds of destruction of the one true Church." Since Boniface remains Christ's vicar, says Morrone, if the pope commands him to die he will submit, certain the angel of death will also obey. "The God I serve," says Boniface, "created this whirling world where the strong must slay the weak and enslave the living, where men and women're slaughtered and I am soaked." Morrone's God "is Love and nothing but Love." At Boniface's command, he releases his soul to God, but not before he tells his antagonist:

> You live and win and lose by winning. I die and lose and win by losing. In due time I will come to harvest. What I plant will be grown and the world will change and the day will come when [. . .] the earth [will be] without those dire miseries which destroy its peace and beauty and mankind will be without the briars and thorns of pride, greed and violence. Evil will be blown away [. . .] But others must gather in these fruits, these fruits of love.

Recalling Clement VI's statement about Flote in *Red Noses*, Boniface determines to wrap Morrone "in oblivion" and asks God to "blot out his example and his name, else men and women will know how near they came to Paradise" (2.12).

In an epilogue set in 1303, seven years after Morrone's death and the year of his own death, Boniface reports he had Celestine canonized. To defend the Church's unity, to bring peace to Europe, and to make its people happy, "I used force, Pope Celestine love, Pope Nicholas [IV] force and love. We all failed—but I got the best notices." He quotes and paraphrases laudatory comments from histories and encyclopedias of Catholicism. "Of course, Dante consigned me to Hell," he admits. "But what do you expect? He was a poet."

> In my reign, the Papacy declined and the way prepared for Luther. I made a mess of it but my mess had muscle. So I'm remembered with respect, oh yes. Pope Celestine's deep in oblivion's pit. The Church condemns him for incompetence, as if that had ever been a bar to high office. They're ashamed of him because he shamed them [. . .].

He prays to God to redeem human beings. "Men and women can't go on living and dying like this. "We've reached the end."

As we know, the beginning of the fourteenth century was not the end. Indeed, it preceded the years of the Black Death, the historical period for *Red Noses*. In the introduction to *Red Noses*, Barnes mentions that its first performance took place seven years after he wrote the play and that if it were written in 1985 "it would be much less optimistic" (7). Yet *Sunsets and Glories* is not considerably less optimistic. It dramatizes how goodness can tempt those with power, haunt those who destroy it, pave the way for change, and perhaps win by losing. Pope Boniface VIII may love the good and pursue the worst, yet lose to the good. The good Celestine may renounce power, yet be influential. In *Sunsets and Glories*, in which the problem of goodness is more thematically important than in any other play by Barnes since *The Ruling Class*, goodness and power dispute each other, as the play explores the complex issues between them with perhaps greater clarity than in any of the author's previous plays.

NOTES

1. In early 1978, Albert Wertheim invited me to contribute to a book of original essays on contemporary British dramatists that he and Hedwig Bock had contracted to edit. Because of the vagaries of publishing, my essay, a pilot for a book on Barnes, appeared in *Essays on Contemporary British Drama* (Munich: Max Hueber, 1981) on the eve of my book *The Theatre of Peter Barnes* (London: Heinemann, 1981). Although the present essay borrows some material from the book, its subject and treatment are new.

2. Peter Barnes, introduction to *Collected Plays* (London: Heinemann, 1981), viii. Unless otherwise indicated, quotations from the plays and introductions are from this edition; they will be cited parenthetically in the text. Since all but one of the plays this essay treats are published, I will not summarize their plots. A brief synopsis of *Sunsets and Glories* (London: Methuen, 1990) will be incorporated in its interpretation. *Sunsets and Glories* was produced in the new Leeds Playhouse in summer 1990.

3. Bertolt Brecht, *Selected Poems*, trans. H. R. Hays (New York: Grove, n.d.), 165.

4. Interview, in Yvonne Shafer, "Peter Barnes and the Theatre of Disturbance," *Theatre News* 14 (December 1982), 8.

5. Letter, Fyodor Dostoyevsky to Sofya Aleksandrovna Ivanova, 1 (old style) / 13 (new style) January 1868, in *Selected Letters of Fyodor Dostoyevsky*, ed. Joseph Frank and David I. Goldstein, trans. Andrew R. MacAndrew (New Brunswick, N.J.: Rutgers University Press, 1987), 269–70.

6. Told about a homosexual affair between two actors, Mrs. Patrick Campbell quipped, "I don't care what people do, as long as they don't do it in the street and frighten the horses!" See, e.g., Margot Peters, *Mrs. Pat* (London: Bodley Head, 1984), 211.

7. Introduction to *The Real Long John Silver and Other Plays* (London: Faber and Faber, 1986), ix.

8. Peter Barnes, *Red Noses* (London: Faber and Faber, 1985), 49–50. Quotations from *Red Noses*, from this edition, will be cited parenthetically in the text.

9. Conversation with the author, February 1985. Barnes had completed the play two months earlier. Quotations from *Sunsets and Glories* are from the typescript. Citations, parenthetically in the text, will be to acts and scenes.

10. Milton Rokeach, *The Three Christs of Ypsilanti* (London: Arthur Barker, 1964). See Dukore, *The Theatre of Peter Barnes*, 50–51, 153n.

11. A fragment of a Greek translation of the noncanonical Gospel of Peter, written in the first half of the second century, was discovered in 1886. The extent to which this fragment, which contains Boniface VIII's quotation, is or represents the original is unknown. However, the quotation is accurate, not an invention of Barnes: this gospel was known for a long time by its refutation. As Barnes says in his introduction to *Leonardo's Last Supper* and *Noonday Demons*, "Nothing a writer can imagine is as surrealistic as the reality" (122).

A Trick of the Light: Tom Stoppard's *Hapgood* and Postabsurdist Theater

HERSH ZEIFMAN

In a 1974 interview with the editors of *Theatre Quarterly*, Tom Stoppard was questioned about the genesis of his playwriting career. *A Walk on the Water*, written in 1960 (but not staged in England until 1968, as *Enter a Free Man*), was considered "an unusual kind of first play" by the interviewers, containing little that was "autobiographical or seminal." Stoppard responded:

> I don't think a first play tends to be that—it tends to be the sum of all the plays you have seen of a type you can emulate technically and have admired. So *A Walk on the Water* was in fact *Flowering Death of a Salesman*. . . . *I don't think it's a very true play, in the sense that I feel no intimacy with the people I was writing about. It works pretty well as a play, but it's actually phoney because it's a play written about other people's characters.*[1]

The "other people's characters" Stoppard was referring to were abducted, as he himself pointed out, from Robert Bolt's *Flowering Cherry* and Arthur Miller's *Death of a Salesman*: a strange theatrical amalgam that perhaps explains the play's uncertain tone. For his second play Stoppard turned to an entirely different source: "The next play I wrote, *The Gamblers*, was over-influenced by Beckett, set in a con-

175

demned cell with only two people in it."[2] While this imitation of
Beckett was originally likewise "a kind of feint,"[3] it has proved to be
of more lasting significance: Samuel Beckett has remained an important influence on Stoppard's drama.

Stoppard has expressed his intense admiration of Beckett on numerous occasions. "There's just no telling," he has written, "what
sort of effect *[Waiting for Godot]* had on our society, who wrote because of it, or wrote in a different way because of it. . . . Of course it
would be absurd to deny my enormous debt to it, and love for it."[4]
Precisely what Stoppard loved in Beckett was, first of all, the structure of Beckett's humor: "There's a Beckett joke which is the funniest
joke in the world to me. It appears in various forms but it consists of
confident statement followed by immediate refutation by the same
voice. It's a constant process of elaborate structure and sudden—and
total—dismantlement."[5] Stoppard was also heavily influenced by
the poetic cadences of Beckett's language, especially the stichomythia
characteristic of much of Gogo's and Didi's dialogue. But his greatest
"debt" was to Beckett's absurdist vision (hence his ironic description
of *The Gamblers* as *"Waiting for Godot in the Condemned Cell"*).[6] As he
wrote while still a theater critic in a review of Jack MacGowran's
Beckett compilation *End of Day*: "[Beckett's] characters vacillate in a
wasteland between blind hope and dumb despair. . . . Everything is
canceled out; Beckett (see Martin Esslin's *The Theatre of the Absurd*) is
much impressed by St. Augustine's words, 'Do not despair—one of
the thieves was saved. Do not presume—one of the thieves was
damned.' "[7]

The characters of Stoppard's next stage play similarly "vacillate in
a wasteland between blind hope and dumb despair." *Rosencrantz and
Guildenstern Are Dead*, the work that established Stoppard's fame (and
fortune), is a deeply Beckettian play—as almost every critic who has
analyzed it has acknowledged. (That acknowledgment has not always been a positive one. Robert Brustein, for example, labeled the
play "a theatrical parasite" and dismissed its author as a mere "university wit," offering audiences "a form of Beckett without tears."[8]
But whether positive or negative, Beckett's influence on the play is
clearly evident.) Mirroring "the Beckett joke," the structure of *Rosencrantz and Guildenstern Are Dead* is a series of comic "statements"
constantly refuting themselves, playing in effect "a sort of infinite
leap-frog."[9] ("I write plays," Stoppard has noted, "because dialogue

is the most respectable way of contradicting myself.")[10] Further, the stichomythic exchanges of the title characters eerily echo the language of *Godot*'s tramps; what Stoppard wrote in a 1963 review of James Saunders's *Next Time I'll Sing To You*—"Some of his dialogue is so Beckettian as to be pastiche"[11]—proved to be prophetically applicable to Stoppard's own play, not yet written. And the play's central conceit—two shadowy courtiers on the fringes of *Hamlet*, trapped in the margins of a "text" about which they know nothing, adrift in a world that makes no sense—embodies the heart of a Beckettian endgame, the quintessence of Camus's definition of the absurd:

> A world that can be explained even with bad reasons is a familiar world. But, on the other hand, in a universe suddenly divested of illusions and lights, man feels an alien, a stranger. His exile is without remedy since he is deprived of the memory of a lost home or the hope of a promised land. This divorce between man and his life, the actor and his setting, is properly the feeling of absurdity.[12]

Beckett's absurdist influence is equally strong in *Jumpers*, Stoppard's next full-length work for the theater. The argument of the play has been neatly summarized by the philosopher A. J. Ayer: it is "between those who believe in absolute values, for which they seek a religious sanction, and those, more frequently to be found among contemporary philosophers, who are subjectivists or relativists in morals, utilitarians in politics, and atheists or at least agnostics."[13] (It was mischievous of the *Sunday Times* to commission this review from Ayer, the preeminent logical positivist [i.e., relativist] of his generation, whose first initials just "happen" to be reflected in the name of the play's "arch-villain," Archibald Jumper.) Although many of the play's characters "seek," however, they do not find: nothing in *Jumpers* appears certain, least of all absolute values. As I have argued elsewhere, *Jumpers* is a parodic mystery play, in both senses of the term. There are in fact two linked mysteries at the core of the play: (*a*) Who killed Duncan McFee? and (*b*) Does God exist?[14] The play's central character, a professor of ethics named George Moore, thinks he knows the answers, but in neither instance can he prove his case: the physical mystery and the metaphysical mystery remain equally unsolved (and unsolvable). (As the prisoner wryly informs the jailer in *The Gamblers:* "I think you may have stumbled across the definition of divine will—an obsession with mystery.")[15] The world of *Jumpers* is thus maddeningly, absurdly ambiguous, with both the earth and the heavens refusing to divulge their secrets.

The metaphysical absurdism of *Jumpers* is dramatized not simply in the play's theme but in its structure as well: if the world is "divested of illusions and lights," if it no longer makes sense, why then should plays that attempt to reflect that world? In absurdist theater, as Martin Esslin proclaimed in his seminal study, form mirrors content: "The Theatre of the Absurd has renounced arguing *about* the absurdity of the human condition; it merely *presents* it in being—that is, in terms of concrete stage images."[16] One of the first stage images we encounter in the play's bizarre prologue sets the tone for everything that follows: a (progressively) naked lady is seen swinging from a chandelier. *"Like a pendulum between darkness and darkness, the* Secretary *swings into the spotlight, and out . . . , in sight for a second, out of sight for a second, in sight for a second, out of sight for a second. . . ."*[17] Now you see it, now you don't; the audience is in effect "ambushed" from the play's opening moments. Reflecting the play's theme in a maze of mirrors, the structure of *Jumpers* is rife with ambiguity, a conjuror's trick that has the audience echoing George's baffled "How the hell does one know what to believe?" (62). Just when we think we "know" where we are, just when the picture finally seems to come into focus, the angle suddenly shifts and we are left once more with a blur.

Take, for example, the first postprologue encounter between George and his "dotty" wife Dotty.[18] From the darkened space of her bedroom, Dotty has been uttering piteous, and increasingly urgent, cries for help: "Murder—Rape—Wolves!" (18). George, feverishly attempting to "invent" God in his study, is convinced she is merely "crying wolf" ("Dorothy, I will not have my work interrupted by these gratuitous acts of lupine delinquency!" [18]), but he finally breaks down and decides to look in on her. As he enters the bedroom, the lights come up to display Dotty's nude body *"sprawled face down, and apparently lifeless on the bed."* Dotty *appears* to be dead, and the audience is allowed a brief interval to register the shock of that fact. But even as we are jumping to that conclusion, George's reaction to the scene puzzles us: "George *takes in the room at a glance, ignores* Dotty, *and still calling for* Thumper *goes to look in the bathroom.*" Is this professor so absent-minded that he fails to notice the nude corpse of his wife? Is he so indifferent that he doesn't care? While we are pondering, George returns from the bathroom and suddenly addresses the "corpse":

> *George:*   Are you a proverb?
> *Dotty:*   No, I'm a book.
> *George:*   *The Naked and the Dead.* (21)

An audience invariably laughs at this point, partly in relief that Dotty is alive and partly in embarrassment at having been so easily misled: Dotty was simply "acting out" a charade, as she will continue to do throughout the play.[19] Now you see it, now you don't: the whole play is, structurally, a series of "charades" that constantly challenges our perceptions of "truth."

And yet, though the truth in *Jumpers* proves to be elusive, though the world appears meaningless and absurd, there is a significant counterthread of optimism running defiantly through the fabric of the play. On the surface, the absurdist vision originally "inherited" from Beckett is brilliantly sustained, but *under* the surface that vision is continually being eroded and sabotaged. The source of the play's optimism is George's heartfelt belief that, whether he "knows" it or not, God *does* exist, that moral absolutes are valid. Camus would have argued that George is suffering from what he termed "the fatal evasion" of hope: "Hope of another life one must 'deserve' or trickery of those who live not for life itself but for some great idea that will transcend it, refine it, give it meaning, and betray it."[20] It is an evasion practiced by almost all of Beckett's characters as well, desperately attempting to wrest meaning out of the very heart of meaninglessness. ("How one hoped above, on and off," comments the speaker of one of Beckett's "Texts for Nothing" from beyond the grave. "With what diversity.")[21] The crucial difference is that everything in a Beckett play conspires to invalidate that hope: in a circular text reflecting the unattainability of desire, Godot will never come. Unlike his characters, Beckett has no illusions; the absurdity of his dramatic world continually denies man's "pernicious and incurable optimism."[22] Stoppard, on the other hand, *shares* George's faith: "Our view of good behaviour *must* not be relativist. . . . I wanted to write a theist play, to combat the arrogant view that anyone who believes in God is some kind of cripple, using God as a crutch."[23]

The faith expressed by George (and Stoppard), however, is never allowed to wrench the play completely out of its absurdist framework. Stoppard is careful not to sentimentalize George, to "vindicate" him: despite his faith, George is frequently buffoonish and ineffectual, and his values by no means triumph. George's belief in moral absolutes, for example, cannot save Thumper and Pat from their spectacularly absurd deaths, deaths that George himself, however unwittingly, causes. Thus the play comes full circle, ending as it began with the anguished cries of "Help! Murder!" ringing in our ears (72). Nor—in spite of Stoppard's attempts to "soften" George's inertia in his latest revision of the play's coda—is George's belief translated into the kind of action that might prevent (or, at the very least, *try* to prevent) the murder of Clegthorpe.[24] And finally, although George's closing argument in the coda is emotionally moving, it is Archie who not only scores points (literally) for his intellectual "bounce," but, in the debate between relativism and absolutes, is given the last word:

> Do not despair—many are happy much of the time; more eat than starve, more are healthy than sick, more curable than dying, not so many dying as dead; and one of the thieves was saved. Hell's bells and all's well—half the world is at peace with itself, and so is the other half; vast areas are unpolluted; millions of children grow up without suffering deprivation, and millions, while deprived, grow up without suffering cruelties, and millions, while deprived and cruelly treated, none the less grow up. No laughter is sad and many tears are joyful. At the graveside the undertaker doffs his top hat and impregnates the prettiest mourner. Wham, bam, thank you Sam. (78)

As many critics have noted, there is something deeply cynical and offensive about Archie's Beckettian/Augustinian parody, especially as it immediately follows the shooting of Clegthorpe. Previously Archie employed the phrase "do not despair" as a prelude to bribery (62); now it serves as a cover under which to dismiss murder. If the "Wham, bam, thank you Sam" refers to *Sam* Clegthorpe, the saying is hideously apt, for Clegthorpe has indeed been screwed—royally (note the coda's ironic allusions to the murders commissioned by Richard III and Henry II) and briskly.

But there is also a strange sense in which Archie's closing words are meant to be taken "straight," as a kind of consolation. *Jumpers* clearly dramatizes metaphysical anguish, the anguish underlying Beckett's absurdist view of the world; at the same time, however, it suggests that, despite that absurdity, there are genuine grounds for optimism, for not giving in to despair. If Beckett sums up existence in haunting images of death (Pozzo's mournful "They give birth astride of a grave, the light gleams an instant, then it's night once more," later expanded by Vladimir: "Astride of a grave and a difficult birth. Down in the hole, lingeringly, the grave-digger puts on the forceps"),[25] Stoppard focuses instead on life: "At the graveside the undertaker doffs his top hat and impregnates the prettiest mourner." Archie's "Wham, bam, thank you Sam" is directed, then, more at Sam Beckett than at Sam Clegthorpe, but the acknowledgment is double-edged. While the "thank you" is obviously sincere—Stoppard has much to thank Beckett for—it also denotes a leave-taking: Stoppard's salute to Beckett is both a hail and a farewell. *Jumpers* thus marks a demarcation point in Stoppard's drama, his reluctant parting of the ways from the all-encompassing absurdism of Beckett's vision. The metaphysical optimism felt so insistently as an undercurrent in the play, pulsing faintly but tenaciously beneath its absurdist surface, produces a powerful tension. And it is out of this tension—a manifestly absurd "text" just as manifestly subverted by its own subtext—that Stoppard has created what is in effect a distinctively postabsurdist theater.

Hapgood, Stoppard's most recent play, which opened in London in the spring of 1988, brilliantly exemplifies his unique brand of postabsurdist theater. On the surface, the play is filled with all manner of dazzling absurdist trappings, but the tension produced by the play's subtext continually undermines that surface. Like its radio predecessor *The Dog It Was That Died*, *Hapgood* is, on the most obvious level, a play about espionage. (Stoppard frequently uses short media plays as "trial runs" for his longer and more complex stage plays: thus *Jumpers* derives from the earlier television play *Another Moon Called Earth*, while much of *Travesties* was anticipated in the radio play *Artist Descending a Staircase*.) In *The Dog It Was That Died*, the absurdities of the espionage world are instantly evoked by the play's title, an allusion to Goldsmith's "An Elegy on the Death of a Mad Dog":

The dog, to gain some private ends.
Went mad, and bit the man.
. . . .
The man recovered of the bite—
The dog it was that died.[26]

As the radio play opens, a dog indeed has died—an unfortunate
mutt that just happened to be lying on a barge that just happened to
be passing under Chelsea Bridge at the precise moment Purvis, a
double agent who no longer knew which side he was spying for,
decided to jump off it in a suicide attempt. Purvis recovered; that dog
it was that died. Like the comic reversal of Goldsmith's elegy, there
is thus something immediately topsy-turvy about the play and the
world it is dramatizing, a world so absurd that the whole concept of
espionage ultimately becomes meaningless.

Hapgood opens in a similar absurdist vein: what Stoppard once said
of *Jumpers* and *Travesties*—"You start with a prologue which is slightly
strange"[27]—is true of *all* his full-length stage plays. Set in the men's
changing room of an old-fashioned municipal swimming-bath, the
opening scene of the play resembles a Feydeau farce peopled by the
characters of a John LeCarré novel on speed. In a totally confusing
"ballet" impossible to make sense of (and choreographed, in Peter
Wood's production, to the limpid strains of Bach's *Brandenburg Con-
certo*), spy chases counterspy chases countercounterspy in and out
of slamming cubicle doors and all around the Burberry bush (for the
still center of this storm is the raincoat-clad Elizabeth Hapgood, code-
named "Mother," waiting patiently in the men's shower under a pink
umbrella). Adding to the bewilderment are identical briefcases, identical towels, and—crucial to the plot but impossible to detect at this
point—identical twins. The confusion of this opening scene is deliberate; there is no way an audience can possibly follow all those com-
ings and going, and Stoppard knows that. We are thus immediately
made to experience, structurally, what the play's characters are suffering from thematically: an inability to figure out what's going on,
to determine precisely who is the traitor in their midst.

For it turns out that the mayhem of the opening scene is the result
of a complicated espionage operation designed to trap that traitor, a
"mole" who is passing sensitive scientific data to the Russians. The
"prime" suspect (a word we shall return to later) is the defector

Joseph Kerner, a physicist and double agent: a Soviet "sleeper" apparently spying for the KGB, he is in fact, unbeknownst to the Russians, a British "joe" who has been "turned" by Hapgood and is working for British Intelligence. Or is he? Could he be, unbeknownst to the British, a *triple* agent? Hapgood is convinced he is loyal— "*Kerner is my joe!*"[28]—but Blair, a senior colleague,[29] and the American Wates, representing the CIA, have their doubts. As the action of the play progresses, a second major suspect emerges in the figure of Ridley, another member of the intelligence unit. Ultimately, however, everyone in the unit becomes suspect. "How are you at telling lies?" Wates asks Hapgood at one point; "I make a living," she replies (39). When lying is a part of the job description, how does one know whom to believe? And what if the problem is not about lying per se (which implies that there is a specific truth deliberately being obscured), but rather about the very nature of "truth" itself?

This difficulty in determining the truth is emphasized in the play through an analogy with physics (specifically, quantum mechanics)—an analogy continually pointed out by Kerner, who, as both spy and physicist, is uniquely qualified to make the connection. During an early "interrogation" scene set at the zoo, Blair confronts Kerner directly about his suspect allegiances, expecting the Russian to provide him with an unequivocal answer. Despite his professed ignorance of physics, Blair has, paradoxically, a "scientific" perspective on life: obviously Kerner must be working for one side or the other.

Blair: One likes to know what's what.
Kerner: Oh yes! Objective reality.
Blair: I thought you chaps believed in that.
Kerner: "You chaps?" Oh, *scientists*. *(Laughs)* "You chaps!" Paul, objective reality is for zoologists. "Ah, yes, definitely a giraffe." But a double agent is not like a giraffe. A double agent is more like a trick of the light. (10)

In the London production, Kerner's point was cleverly underlined by Carl Tom's witty set design: this conversation at the zoo occurred directly in front of an enormous giraffe—or, rather, a pair of giraffes, positioned in such a way that we seemed to be seeing a two-headed giraffe emanating from a single body. "Ah, yes, definitely a giraffe"—but *nothing* is definite in this play when even a giraffe appears to be a "double agent."

Kerner then proceeds to clarify what he meant by the phrase "a trick of the light," launching into a minilecture on whether light is wave or particle. Confused by this apparent digression, Blair tries to return to the ostensible subject, "Joseph—I want to know if you're ours or theirs, that's all," only to have Kerner reply, "I'm telling you but you're not listening" (11). Kerner *is* answering Blair's question, but by analogy:

> [We scientists] watch the bullets of light to see which way they go. . . . Every time we don't look we get wave pattern. Every time we look to see how we get wave pattern, we get particle pattern. The act of observing determines the reality. . . . Somehow light is particle and wave. The experimenter makes the choice. You get what you interrogate for. And you want to know if I'm a wave or a particle. (11–12)

There is a conundrum here: light appears to have the mutually exclusive properties of *both* wave *and* particle. As the physicist Richard Feynman has written, in a passage Stoppard selected as the epigraph to the play, "We choose to examine a phenomenon which is impossible, *absolutely* impossible, to explain in any classical way, and which has in it the heart of quantum mechanics. In reality it contains the *only* mystery. . . ."[30] If light is both wave and particle (depending on who's looking, or not looking), then can a double agent be both "sleeper" and "joe"? The "mystery" within the espionage plot is as baffling as the "mystery" in physics: both are explicitly referred to as a "puzzle" (11, 14), and both seem impossible to solve.

The analogy in the play between espionage and physics depends—and becomes even more disturbing—as Kerner goes on to describe the strange behavior of electrons ("Electrons," Feynman notes, "behave just like light"):[31]

> The particle world is the dream world of the intelligence officer. . . . An electron . . . is like a moth, which was there a moment ago, it gains or loses a quantum of energy and it jumps, and at the moment of the quantum jump it is like two moths, one to be here and one to stop being there; an electron is like twins, each one unique, a unique twin. (48–49)

A true double agent, then, like an electron, defeats surveillance because he's a "twin," seemingly in two places at the same time: now
you see it, now you don't. Kerner, for example, appears to be both
"sleeper" and "joe"; but which is the "mask" and which the "face"?
Or, to phrase the question in slightly different terms that are more
familiar to students of Stoppard's drama, which is "the real thing"?
Does "the real thing" even exist? And can we ever hope to plumb the
depths of so complex a mystery?

Although Stoppard has great fun immersing himself (and us) in
the unsettling world of quantum mechanics, the analogy between
particle physics and espionage in *Hapgood* extends far beyond espionage specifically to embrace a much more general concept: the "puzzle" of human identity itself. Confronted once more with Blair's accusations near the end of the play, Kerner responds, "So now I am a
prime suspect":

> A prime is a number which cannot be divided except by itself. . . . But
> really suspects are like squares, the product of twin roots. . . . You . . .
> think everybody has no secret or one big secret, they are what they seem
> or the opposite. You look at me and think: *Which is he?* Plus or minus? If
> only you could figure it out like looking into me to find my root. And
> then you still wouldn't know. We're all doubles. . . . The one who puts
> on the clothes in the morning is the working majority, but at night—
> perhaps in the moment before unconsciousness—we meet our sleeper—
> the priest is visited by the doubter, the marxist sees the civilizing force of
> the bourgeoisie, the captain of industry admits the justice of common
> ownership. (71–72)

Like electrons, like espionage agents, all human beings are "doubles": "squares," not primes; "the product of twin roots," each of us
embodying our own "sleeper." And of no one is this more true than
the enigmatic eponymous heroine of *Hapgood*. Kerner recalls,
significantly, that he never saw Hapgood sleeping: "Interrogation
hours, you know. She said, 'I want to *sleep* with you.' But she never
did. And when I learned to read English books I realized that she
never said it, either" (74). Yet Hapgood, too, is a "sleeper," a "double
agent"—not in terms of the espionage plot but in the ontological
sense for which espionage (and physics) acts as a controlling metaphor in the play.

Who and what is Hapgood (that all our swains commend her)? In the "technical," macho world of espionage, she is Mother: a crack shot with both a gun and a quip, a coolly intelligent and efficient executive who plays chess without a board and is fiercely protective of her "joes." But at the same time she is also a mother with a conflicting set of "Joes": her eleven-year-old son Joe, and *Joseph* Kerner. (Kerner is not only Hapgood's agent, he is also the father of her son; not only, then, one of her "joes" but also, as he explicitly reminds her, "one of your Joes" [46].) Hapgood's "schizophrenic" existence is neatly dramatized structurally in our first glimpses of her. In scene 1 she is Mother anxiously watching her espionage joe (Kerner) deliver a possibly incriminating briefcase to his Russian contact; in scene 3, the next time we see her, she is mother anxiously watching her son Joe play a rugby game at his school. This "personal" Hapgood is both deeply attached to her son ("He's the handsome one with the nicest knees" [15]) and deeply guilty that her demanding work consigns Joe to a boarding school, alienating her from the day-to-day activities of his life.

The two "worlds" of Hapgood—mother and Mother—wage a constant battle throughout the play: in order to accommodate the former, she must repeatedly jeopardize the latter, thereby blurring the boundaries and breaking all the rules. But this collision course between the split sides of her character is only one sense in which Stoppard dramatizes the enigma of her identity. For Hapgood is many different things to many different people, a multiple personality reflected in the various names by which other characters address her; if one's name is the "key" to one's identity, then Elizabeth Hapgood is truly protean. To agents Ridley and Merryweather, she is "Mother"; Blair refers to her as "Elizabeth"; Joe calls her "Mum" or "Mummy"; her secretary Maggs says "Mrs Hapgood"; Wates calls her "ma'am"; her "sister" Celia speaks of "Betty"; and Kerner uses the Russian form of her first name, "Yelizaveta," along with various endearments derived from it: "Lilya," "Lilitchka."

The question of Hapgood's identity becomes even more complex with the appearance of Celia Newton, the "twin sister" she fabricates in order to expose Ridley as the unit's traitor. Hapgood's impersonation of Celia links her with all the other "reflectors" in the play, scientific and human—decoys designed to deceive. Having been informed by Kerner that the only logical solution to the apparent contradictions of the opening scene is to posit twin Ridleys, Hapgood sets out to trap him (them?) with the aid of her own "twin." She thus makes a quantum jump, "impossibly" present in two places at the same time: as Ridley will discover to his peril, "she's here and she's not here" (84). In terms of personality and behavior, Celia and Hapgood are as different as (to allude to yet another Stoppard play title) night and day. To cite just one example: prim and proper Hapgood never swears, as Blair for one points out both directly—"Do you never use bad language, never ever?" (23)—and indirectly, in his constant teasing: "Oh, f-f-fiddle!" (19); pot-smoking, "bohemian" Celia, on the other hand, swears a blue streak (indeed, the first word out of her mouth is scatological).

Faced with a physically identical Hapgood who is nothing like Hapgood, Ridley is dumbfounded. On one level, this non-Hapgood in Hapgood's body excites him. Earlier in the play, having been re-buffed by Hapgood's "You're not my type," he exploded: "You come on like you're running your joes from the senior common room and butter wouldn't melt in your pants but . . . if you could have got your bodice up past your brain you would have screwed me and liked it" (44). Now his fantasy seems to have been made flesh; the battle between bodice and brain is, for Celia, not much of a contest. On another level, however, the transformation terrifies him. "Who the hell are you?" he cries out in anguish. "I'm your dreamgirl, Ernie—," Celia replies, "Hapgood without the brains or the taste" (83). "Who the hell are you?" is, of course, the key question in the play. Celia is not only Ridley's "dreamgirl" but Elizabeth's: her "sleeper," her "dou-ble." The complicated trap Hapgood has sprung for Ridley hinges on his being totally convinced that Celia is not Hapgood, and it works: despite his espionage training, despite his street smarts, de-spite his suspicions, Ridley is taken in. (He calls her "Auntie," Mother's sister.) But in order to "become" Celia so convincingly, there must be something of Celia locked deep within Hapgood. Ironi-cally, Celia is Hapgood's "twin"; Kerner may have never seen her "sleeping," but we have. Who, then, is the "real" Elizabeth Hapgood? Is it possible to answer? Ridley is fooled the way all of us are ulti-mately fooled, expecting people to be "what they seem or . . . the opposite," to be either "particle" or "wave."

As always in Stoppard's plays, the elusiveness of the truth proves to be a matter of form as well as of content: just as the characters are constantly being "ambushed" in *Hapgood*, so too is the audience. Thus, when the lights come up on the second scene of act 2 and "Celia" suddenly comes flying out the kitchen door to answer Ridley's ring, we are in the same shocked position as he is: who *is* this creature who looks exactly like Hapgood but who dresses, speaks, and behaves so differently? When she identifies herself as Hapgood's twin, there is no real reason to doubt her—especially since we have not been told the exact details of Hapgood's plan to trap Ridley. As far as we know, Hapgood's having a twin may be part of the plan. After Celia exits briefly, allowing Ridley to contact Hapgood on his two-way radio and thus enabling us to hear Hapgood's voice, we are even more convinced that Celia is legitimate: can one person, after all, be in two different places at the same time? (There is an obvious answer to this apparent impossibility, but the pace of the theater production is such that we don't have the time to work it out.) Celia seems so different from Hapgood that, despite ourselves, we get taken in.

This adds immeasurably, of course, to the humor of the later scene in which Celia, now dressed like Hapgood and occupying her office, finds herself having to impersonate Hapgood when Maggs unexpectedly enters the office with important classified documents from Australia:

> Maggs: I was in the pub. . . . I got the desk to bleep me if you came in—just the top one, really, it's green-routed and Sydney's been on twice this morning.
>
> Hapgood: Has he? (75)

We laugh because Celia is way out of her depth and trying desperately to disguise that fact. When Ridley attempts to help her out by reaching for one of the documents, Maggs cautions her, "It's yo-yo, Mrs Hapgood." "Is it, is it really?" Celia replies. "Yes, indeed. It's yo-yo, Ridley, you know what yo-yo is" (75). Luckily, Ridley does, since Celia, treading cautiously through the minefield of this foreign language, clearly doesn't have a clue. Nor can she respond when Maggs passes on the cryptic message "Bishop to queen two" (76)—a move in one of Hapgood's ongoing boardless chess games with McPherson in Canada, played via the security link with Ottawa. At the very end of the scene, however, Ridley departs before her, leaving her alone on stage for a moment; as she prepares to follow him, Maggs enters once more wondering if everything is all right:

> *Hapgood:* Yes, Maggs—everything's fine.
> *(She heads through the open door.)*
> Queen to king one. (80)

Like pawns rooked by a grand master, we have suddenly been check-mated: Hapgood's "Celia" turns out to be the queen of disguises.

This structural dislocation of the audience's perspective is by now a Stoppardian signature: an absurdist world, after all, defies compre-hension. The scene transitions in *Hapgood* exemplify this conundrum brilliantly. At the end of scene 1, for example, Blair, in the municipal baths, speaks into his two-way radio: "I want Kerner in Regent's Park, twelve o'clock sharp. *(He puts the radio away and looks at his wrist-watch. The next time he moves, it is twelve o'clock and he is at the zoo)*" (9). Blair has made, in effect, a quantum jump; like an electron or a "twin" moth, he is one moment at the baths and then "instantly" at the zoo. Blair's "elusiveness" sets the pattern for the majority of the play's scene changes, the most stunning of which involves Ridley in act 2. At the end of his first encounter with Celia, "Ridley *stays where he is. The next time he moves, he's somebody else. So we lose the last set without losing* Ridley. *When the set has gone,* Ridley *is in some other place . . . , a man arriving somewhere. He carries a suitcase. He is a different* Ridley. *It's like a quantum jump*" (69).[32] What we are seeing, in effect, is Ridley's literal twin materializing out of "nowhere." But as we have seen, all the play's characters are "twins," literally or metaphori-cally: the audience's difficulty in determining who is who on the physical plane simply mirrors its confusion on the ontological plane. Thus, in the play's climactic scene, set once again full-circle in the municipal baths, we see, "impossibly," two Ridleys at the same time. The illusion is created, significantly, through lighting: the flashlight Ridley is carrying at the beginning of the scene (allowing much of the stage to be in darkness) and the strobe light at the end (distorting our perception). But then, as *Hapgood* has dramatized so convincingly, all human identity is finally "a trick of the light."

The unmasking of the Ridley twins as the play's traitors seems to solve one of the major mysteries posed by *Hapgood*, at least on the surface level of its espionage plot; unlike *Jumpers*, say, this mystery play *does* offer a "dénouement" in which the guilty party is identified. But Stoppard's surfaces are deceptive, and his surprises never stop. For Ridley, as his name suggests, is, like all the play's central characters, a riddle: both "wave" and "particle." On the one hand, he is indeed a traitor who has been spying for the Russians, and he can certainly be extremely ruthless. On the other hand, the motives behind his "selling out" to the Russians are complex: feeling betrayed by the English class system ("We're in a racket which identifies national interest with the interests of the officer class" [82]), he has come to distrust all ideology, viewing espionage as a round dance of futility, a "game" that nobody ever wins. When he falls into Hapgood's trap, then, and agrees to help her hand over secret scientific data to the Russians, he acts not so much for ideological reasons as for "personal" ones: his genuine concern both for Hapgood's son, who he believes has been kidnapped by the KGB, and, more important, for Hapgood herself. In Ridley's view, the information they are meant to be passing on to the Russians is worthless ("It's a joke" [60]), especially when weighed against the safety of Joe. Given the absurdist nature of espionage dramatized in the play, it is hard not to sympathize with Ridley's point of view—especially with his feelings for Joe. Hapgood's son is the latest in a long line of "wise children" in Stoppard's drama; a template of ethical behavior, he serves, like young Alastair in *Night and Day*, "as a catalyst for revealing the moral propensities of others."[33] And Ridley's feelings for Hapgood are likewise a mitigating factor. When he precedes her into the darkened baths with flashlight in hand, thus initiating the events that will expose him as a traitor, the torch he is carrying exists on more than one level: Ridley's "treason" here stems primarily from his love for Hapgood.

This ambiguity surrounding Ridley's identification as the play's traitor is mirrored in Stoppard's treatment of the other "prime" suspects in the unit, Kerner and Blair. Although the exposure of Ridley as a double agent would appear to let them both off the hook, Stoppard's surprises are not yet over. For we ultimately discover that Kerner too has been spying for the Russians. The story he told about being blackmailed into betraying the British (the KGB figured out Joe's paternity and were threatening to harm the boy)—a story we initially viewed as a fabrication, a web in the strand of Hapgood's trap for Ridley—turns out to be genuine; as Hapgood paradoxically observes, "You made up the truth" (88). The ground keeps shifting beneath our feet: Kerner's sardonic comment to Hapgood earlier in the play—"You think you have seen to the bottom of things, but there is no bottom" (55)—is meant equally as a warning to the audience. Kerner is thus as much a riddle as Ridley. "When things get very small," Kerner once noted when discussing the atom, "they get truly crazy" (49); the enigma of Kerner's identity, like Ridley's, is embodied in his very name (German *Kern:* the nucleus of an atom). And yet, can treason resulting from blackmail—motivated, even more than Ridley's, by love for Hapgood and their son—really be considered treason? Technically, perhaps, but then the "technical," as opposed to the "personal," is one of Stoppard's central concerns in the play.

Thus Blair, while "technically" the only one of the three men to emerge "clean" from the espionage betrayal plot, proves to be, in yet another surprise, the most significant "traitor" of all. As an accomplished Intelligence agent, Blair is a master of "Newspeak," the lies that posed as truth in Orwell's *Nineteen Eighty-four*. (Orwell, we recall, was born Eric *Blair*.) Blair's doublespeak, however, extends to friends as well as enemies, to the "personal" as well as the "technical." But then for Blair it's *all* technical, as Kerner had sensed from the beginning. Proclaiming his concern for Hapgood's safety, Blair at one point threatened Kerner: "I've got one of my people working on the inside lane on false papers and if she's been set up I'll feed you to the crocodiles. . . ." But Blair's language gives himself away. "One of your *people?*" Kerner replies. "Oh, Paul. *You* would betray her before I would. My mamushka" (73). Kerner's prediction turns out to be correct: perfectly willing to deceive Hapgood and jeopardize Joe's safety for the "larger," fictive safety of British security, Blair is technically loyal but personally traitorous. Kerner's "mamushka" is, for Blair, only Mother.

As Hapgood (and the audience) discovers, then, the quest to determine the play's "real" traitor is a deeply enigmatic one: everybody is a "double agent" one way or another—even, as we have seen, Hapgood. Especially Hapgood. In the struggle between the "personal" and the "technical," between heart and brains, between mother and Mother, Hapgood has consistently sacrificed the former—has sacrificed, in effect, her Joes for her joes. Joseph Kerner was finally more valuable to her as a spy than as a father for Joe; as Ridley taunts her: "We aren't in the daddy business, we're in the mole business" (81). And while she clearly loves her son, he too gets subsumed in "the mole business": when Hapgood phones Joe to check that he is safe and closes the conversation, ominously, with "Yes, Joe, I'm here to be told" (64)—the precise words she has addressed throughout the play to her operatives—a shudder passes through the audience. Who is speaking here: mother or Mother? And if Hapgood no longer knows the difference, is it any wonder that— even without her direct knowledge—Joe gets sucked in as "bait" in the espionage trap she is setting? What, finally, is Hapgood accomplishing that is so worthwhile that it could justify the sacrifice of Joe? In a quantum world that is random, quixotic and indeterminate, espionage is merely another "trick of the light." As Ridley informs Celia:

> Telling lies is Betty's job, sweetheart—... so Betty can know something which the opposition thinks she doesn't know, most of which doesn't matter a fuck, and that's just the half they didn't *plant* on her—so she's lucky if she comes out better than even, that's the edge she's in it for, and if she's thinking now it wasn't worth one sleepless night for her little prep-school boy, good for her, she had it coming. (81)

"Maybe she did," Celia agrees, and then proceeds to deride the madness of the espionage world: "Everybody's lying to everybody. You're all at it. Liars. Nutters' corner. You deserve each other. . . . You're out on a limb for a boy she put there, while she was making the world safe for him to talk properly in and play the game . . ." (82).

But this is Celia talking, not Hapgood: the "sleeper," not "the working majority." In the play's penultimate scene, Ridley gives Hapgood one last chance to awaken that "sleeper":

> Listen, be yourself. These people are not for you, in the end they get it all wrong, the dustbins are gaping for them. Him [Blair] most. He's had enough out of you and you're getting nothing back, he's dry and you're the juice. We can walk out of here, Auntie. (85)

Ridley persists in addressing her as "Auntie," as Celia, even though at this point he has discovered the ruse. But "Celia" won't, or can't, respond; feeling betrayed, Ridley reaches for his gun and Hapgood shoots him. "Oh, you *mother*" (86), Wates spits at her in a particularly well-chosen epithet; by betraying her Joes, Ridley, and "Celia"—by choosing Mother over mother—Hapgood has become an obscenity. The sight of Ridley's dead body, coupled with her anger at Blair for placing Joe at risk, finally shocks Hapgood to her senses. Responding to Blair's attempt to justify his actions—"It's them or it's us, isn't it?"—Hapgood's scorn is withering, an acknowledgment of her "personal" treason: "Who? Us and the KGB? The opposition! We're just keeping each other in business, we should send each other Christmas cards—oh, f-f-fuck it, Paul!" (87).[34] That final phrase is, of course, Celia's, not Hapgood's; the "sleeper" has at last awakened, with an outraged howl of despair.

What Hapgood awakens to is, paradoxically, an absurdist nightmare, a world "suddenly divested of illusions and lights." The play's analogy between espionage and quantum mechanics, then, seen on one level as a metaphor for the elusiveness of human identity, is, on the deepest level, a metaphor for the structure of the universe itself, for the elusiveness of cosmic identity: the mystery of physics mirrors the mystery of metaphysics. As Kerner explains to Hapgood:

> It upset Einstein very much, you know, all that damned quantum jumping, it spoiled his idea of God. . . . He believed in the same God as Newton, causality, nothing without a reason, but now one thing led to another until causality was dead. Quantum mechanics made everything finally random, things can go this way or that way, the mathematics deny certainty, they reveal only probability and chance, and Einstein couldn't believe in a God who threw dice. . . . There is a straight ladder from the atom to the grain of sand, and the only real mystery in physics is the missing rung. Below it, particle physics; above it, classical physics; but in between, metaphysics. All the mystery in life turns out to be the same mystery. . . . (49–50)

"If it's all random, then what's the point?" cried Bone, the forerunner of George in Stoppard's television play *Another Moon Called Earth* (the "original" of *Jumpers*).[35] And George later echoes his lament: "Coper-

nicus cracked our confidence, and Einstein smashed it: for it one can
no longer believe that a twelve-inch ruler is always a foot long, how
can one be sure of relatively less certain propositions, such as that
God made the Heaven and the Earth . . ." (65).

In the quantum world of *Hapgood*, a world where light is both
wave and particle, a twelve-inch ruler may not always be a foot long.
This is indeed a terrifying concept, for the pragmatist Blair, such
conclusions are not acceptable. When Kerner mocks his belief in objective reality, Blair replies: "What other kind is there? You're this or
you're that, and you know which. Physics is a detail I can't afford . . ." (73). Orwell's Winston Smith sought psychic security in
certain immutable scientific laws: "The solid world exists, its laws
do not change. . . . *Freedom is the freedom to say that two plus two make
four*,"[36] a claim reiterated (though "halved") by Alexander, the hero
of Stoppard's *Every Good Boy Deserves Favour:* "One and one is always
two."[37] But Winston and Alexander were struggling against repressive totalitarian regimes that cynically distort truths for their own
power-driven ends; the characters in *Hapgood*, on the other hand, are
struggling against an absurdist universe in which the very essence
of such "truths" has been exploded. Despite George's impassioned
belief in the original coda of *Jumpers* that "it remains an independent
metaphysical truth that two and two make four,"[38] the most one
seems able to say in a post-Newtonian world is Dotty's "two and two
make *roughly* four" (77; my emphasis).

The sweet security of Newtonian physics has thus been forever
shattered, destroying in its wake such complementary consolations
as "*God's in his heaven—/ All's right with the world!*"[39]—in an absurdist
universe, Pippa has passed on. The resulting randomness is ironically acknowledged in Hapgood's choice of an alias when imperson-
ating her "twin sister": portraying a "decoy," a "trick of the light,"
she slyly names herself *Celia* [Latin *caelum:* heaven] *Newton*. The joke,
however, is ultimately on Hapgood, for "Celia Newton" turns out to
be an illusion in more ways than one: the certainties that name once
embodied no longer apply, replaced by a God rolling dice. "What's
the game?" queried a bewildered Rosencrantz, a "*voice in the wilder-
ness*"; "What are the rules?" added Guildenstern.[40] The characters
of *Hapgood* appear equally forlorn. Invited by Celia to play a deckless
game of cards while waiting for Joe's "ransom" call, Ridley responds,
"Well, what are we playing?" (78). Celia's silence forces Ridley to

guess, to plunge blindly into the void. Unfortunately, Ridley guesses wrong: "*Snap!!* Bad luck . . ." (79). When the "game" of life proves to be so inscrutable, so arbitrary, what are the chances of winning? Certainly the dice never roll in Ridley's favor; in the program of the London production of *Hapgood,* Stoppard casually informs us that the fateful day on which Ridley plays and loses the game of "Snap"— and, later, his life—is a Friday the thirteenth: "bad luck" indeed. The question twice posed in *Hapgood* about a particular espionage scheme, "Who's in charge and is he sane?" (17, 46), might thus well be asked of the universe; the mocking laughter that serves as an answer—the sound of rolling dice—echoes repeatedly through the play.

And yet, for all its absurdist trappings, Stoppard's drama refuses to succumb to despair. In Beckett's ironically titled *Happy Days,* Winnie's desperate mask of cheerfulness keeps slipping, exposing the face of pain underneath; as Winnie notes, "sorrow keeps breaking in."[41] In *Hapgood,* by contrast, it is happiness that keeps breaking in: the optimistic note sounded continually as the play's counterthread beats a muted but persistent refrain. Kerner, for example, while acknowledging his "estrangement" (72) in a seemingly absurd and pointless universe, nevertheless continues to make value judgments, continues to believe in *something.* Against the theorems of quantum mechanics suggesting randomness, Kerner places an opposed set of "theorems":

> The West is morally superior, in my opinion. It is in different degrees unjust and corrupt like the East. Its moral superiority lies in the fact that the system contains the possibility of its own reversal—I am enthralled by the voting,[42] to me it has power of an equation in nature, the masses converted to energy. Highly theoretical, of course. . . . (73)

"The masses converted to energy" implicitly evokes Einstein's celebrated equation $e = mc^2$; Kerner's equation transposes it into the social and political sphere and discovers consolation. Similarly consoling is Kerner's transformation of Einstein's metaphysical angst, his shattered faith in God. Einstein's inability to believe in a God who threw dice is, for Kerner, "the only idea of Einstein's I never understood. . . . He should have come to me, I would have told him, 'Listen, Albert, He threw *you*—look around, He never stops' " (49). The world may be random, uncertain, but hopelessness and despair are certainly not the inevitable response.

The subtext of optimism running through *Hapgood* is at its clearest—and, because of the structural position, its strongest—in the play's brief final scene. On the surface, we seem to have reached the nadir of despair. All of Hapgood's illusions have been totally shattered: her espionage work has been exposed as a farce; Ridley is dead, killed by her own hand; Blair has "betrayed" her; Kerner is about to return to Russia ("[Blair] thinks I was a triple, but I was definitely not, I was past that, quadruple at least, maybe quintuple" [88]). Having repudiated espionage and resigned her job, Hapgood is now simply a mother: the final scene is set once more at Joe's school as Hapgood watches her son play rugby. When Kerner, who has come to say farewell before departing for Russia—to Hapgood and, not so incidentally, to his son, whom he is seeing for the first time—turns to leave, Hapgood cries out: "How can you go? *How can you?*"

> (*She turns away. The game starts. Referee's whistle, the kick. After a few moments* Hapgood *collects herself and takes notice of the rugby.*
> *When the game starts* Kerner's *interest is snagged. He stops and looks at the game.*)
> Hapgood: Come on St Christopher's!—We can win this one! Get those
>   tackles in!
> *She turns round and finds that* Kerner *is still there. She turns back to the game and comes alive.*)
> Hapgood: Shove!—heel!—well heeled!—well out—move it!—*move it,*
>   Hapgood—that's good—that's *better!* (89)

Like everything else in the play, the ending is enigmatic but charged with hope: Kerner does *not* leave; Hapgood, registering his hesitation, "*comes alive.*" Kerner's interest has been snagged specifically by the "game." The "game" of espionage may be elusive and futile, but *this* game—Joe's "game"—is worth playing. As Hapgood herself has discovered in her "liberating" impersonation of Celia, there *are* values worth believing in, the values noted by Michael Billington in his astute review of the play: "that democracy is better than dictatorship, that love is a possibility and that—a persistent Stoppard theme—children anchor one in the real world."[43] The universe may be random and subject to chance; the metaphysical "game" may be purely arbitrary, played by a God capricious as a child ("Snap") or made giddy by the sound of rolling dice; but not every Friday, luckily, is the thirteenth. Chance may be positive as well as negative, a belief embodied in the very name of Stoppard's title character: Hap (defined by the OED as "Chance or fortune . . . ; luck, lot") is specifically linked to *good*. The clouds of absurdism are dispersed in the play by Stoppard's postabsurdist search for silver linings; "the need to make things better," Stoppard noted in a 1981 interview, "is constant and important. Otherwise you're into a sort of nihilism."[44] Temperamentally opposed to nihilism, Stoppard has chosen to write plays in which a "crazy" world is, crazily but persistently, imbued with hope. And so *Hapgood* closes with both Elizabeth and Kerner facing front, facing the audience, as they recommence their journey of faith, rooting for St. Christopher's (the patron saint of travelers, the bearer of divinity) and cheering on *Hap-good*. The last word we hear when all is said and done, echoing in our ears as the curtain falls, is, significantly in this postabsurdist play, *"better!"*

In the addendum to Beckett's early novel *Watt*, we find the following little poem:

who may tell the tale
of the old man?
weigh absence in a scale?
mete want with a span?
the sum assess
of the world's woes?
nothingness
in words enclose?[45]

This is the daunting task absurdist writers like Beckett have set for themselves: the dramatization of "negatives" (age, absence, want, woes, nothingness). Beckett's plays—frequently, like the *Watt* poem, couched in the interrogative—are thus a series of paradoxes; it is enormously difficult to make absence present on stage, to concretize a void, to create something out of nothing, to "eff" the "ineffable."[46] In doing so they explore, in Esslin's words, "the ultimate realities of the human condition. . . . Like ancient Greek tragedy and the medieval mystery plays and baroque allegories, the Theatre of the Absurd is intent on making its audience aware of man's precarious and mysterious position in the universe."⁴⁷

Tom Stoppard is similarly concerned in his drama with the metaphysically "precarious" and "mysterious"—thus his attraction to the Theater of the Absurd. But while frequently exhibiting an absurdist outer shell, Stoppard's plays contain at their core a subversive "sweetness" that ultimately bursts forth and cracks that shell; this unique blend of shell and core produces the distinctive postabsurdist tone of much of Stoppard's theater. The measure of Stoppard's departure from true absurdism can be gauged partly by comparing the humor of his plays with that of Beckett. Beckett's is almost literally graveyard humor, the rueful laughter of skeletons littering the road to Calvary (as Nell observes in a quintessentially Beckettian line in *Endgame:* "Nothing is funnier than unhappiness, I grant you that").⁴⁸ At the close of Shakespeare's *Love's Labour's Lost*, a sudden shadow blots the merriment of that last act in the figure of Marcade, an emissary of death. Infected by the darkness of his presence, Rosaline delays for a year the expected comic resolution by imposing a "service" on her lover Berowne:

> *Rosaline:* You shall this twelve month term from day to day,
> Visit the speechless sick, and still converse
> With groaning wretches; and your task shall be,
> With all the fierce endeavour of your wit
> To enforce the pained impotent to smile.
> *Berowne:*   To move wild laughter in the throat of death?
> It cannot be; it is impossible:
> Mirth cannot move a soul in agony.⁴⁹

"Wild laughter in the throat of death" precisely sums up the humor of Beckett's plays. Stoppard's humor, by contrast, is "tomfoolery," marked by its buoyancy, its exultation in life—a torrent of unstoppable puns and hilarious jokes, full-throated and irrepressible.

This disparity in the tone of their humor leads us to the heart of Stoppard's divergence from Beckett and genuine absurdism. Although I disagree with much of Brustein's criticism of *Rosencrantz and Guildenstern Are Dead*, his assessment of the "derivative" nature of Stoppard's despair in that play strikes me as accurate: "[Stoppard's insights] all seem to come to him, prefabricated, from other plays—

with the result that his air of pessimism seems affected, and his philosophical meditations, while witty and urbane, never obtain the thickness of *felt* knowledge."[50] As admiring as Stoppard is of the art of Beckett's absurdism, that art is, finally, not Stoppard's. In the "arguments with himself" that constitute his drama, part of him clearly acknowledges the absurdism of man's existence in a world "divested of illusions and lights," but another part of him—a major part—consistently subverts that acknowledgment. In the last analysis, Stoppard's eschatology is ameliorist; the rich vein of optimism running through the subtext of his plays thus converts what could easily be a threnody into an aubade. There is light at the end of the tunnel of Stoppard's drama—elusive, inscrutable, perhaps even deceptive, but still light. Whereas Beckett's absurdist theater fearlessly explores the darkness, the "black hole" of nothingness ("The fable of one with you in the dark. The fable of one fabling of one with you in the dark. And how better in the end labour lost and silence"),[51] the postabsurdist plays of Tom Stoppard hopefully explore this "trick of the light."

NOTES

1. Stoppard, "Ambushes for the Audience: Towards a High Comedy of Ideas," *Theatre Quarterly* 14 (May-July 1974): 4–5.

2. Charles Marowitz, "Tom Stoppard—The Theater's Intellectual P. T. Barnum," *New York Times*, 19 October 1975, sec. 2.

3. Ibid.

4. Stoppard, "Something to Declare," *Sunday Times* (London), 25 February 1968.

5. Quoted in Ronald Hayman, *Tom Stoppard* (London: Heinemann, 1977), 7.

6. Stoppard, "Ambushes for the Audience," 4.

7. Stoppard, "Crying Till You Laugh," *Scene* 7 (25 October 1962): 19. Stoppard was similarly impressed by Augustine's words; in one of his early short stories, the narrator wryly comments, "Do not despair: one of the thieves was saved. Do not presume: one of the thieves was damned. Very nice, that. St Augustine, I believe" (Stoppard, "Life, Times: Fragments," in *Introduction 2: Stories by New Writers* [London: Faber and Faber, 1964], 128).

8. Robert Brustein, "Waiting for Hamlet: *Rosencrantz and Guildenstern Are Dead*," *New Republic*, 4 November 1967, 25, 26.

9. Stoppard, "Ambushes for the Audience," 7.

10. Quoted in Jon Bradshaw, "Tom Stoppard, Nonstop Word Games with a Hit Playwright," *New York*, 10 January 1977, 51.

11. *Scene* 18 (9 February 1963): 46.

12. Camus, *The Myth of Sisyphus*, trans. Justin O'Brien (New York: Vintage, 1955), 5.

13. Ayer, "Love Among the Logical Positivists," *Sunday Times* (London), 9 April 1972.

14. Zeifman, "Tomfoolery: Stoppard's Theatrical Puns," *Yearbook of English Studies* 9 (1979): 204–20.

15. Stoppard, *The Gamblers* (unpublished typescript), 29.

16. Martin Esslin, *The Theatre of the Absurd*, 3d ed. (Harmondsworth, Eng.: Penguin, 1980), 25.

17. Stoppard, *Jumpers*, rev. ed. (London: Faber and Faber, 1986), 9. All further page references to *Jumpers* will be cited in the text.

18. Like all the play's characters, Dotty suffers from what Archie terms the Cognomen Syndrome.

19. The charade, however, is not merely "whimsical," for it encapsulates Dotty's dilemma: the naked (Dotty's vulnerability) and the dead (the corpse of the murdered jumper) are precisely what Dotty is worried about.

20. Camus, *Myth of Sisyphus*, 7.

21. Beckett, "Texts for Nothing Two," in *Stories and Texts for Nothing* (New York: Grove, 1967), 84.

22. Beckett, *Proust* (London: John Calder, 1965), 15.

23. Quoted in Oleg Kerensky, *The New British Drama: Fourteen Playwrights since Osborne and Pinter* (London: Hamish Hamilton, 1977), 170.

24. In both the first and second editions of *Jumpers* (London: Faber and Faber, 1972; 1973), George explicitly fails to respond to Clegthorpe's direct plea for help ("Professor—it's not right. George—help"), rationalizing his inertia until the gunshot renders the whole question "academic" (86–87 [1972]; 85–86 [1973]). In the most recent edition (1986), Stoppard cuts both Clegthorpe's appeal and George's rationalizations; George now speaks for the first time only *after* the murder (76).

25. Beckett, *Waiting for Godot* (London: Faber and Faber, 1965), 89, 90–91.

26. Oliver Goldsmith, "An Elegy on the Death of a Mad Dog," in *The Vicar of Wakefield* (London: Dent, 1979), chap. 17, pp. 93–94.

27. Quoted in Hayman, *Tom Stoppard*, 12.

28. Stoppard, *Hapgood* (London: Faber and Faber, 1988), 43. All further page references to *Hapgood* will be cited in the text.

29. Blair is likewise the name of a senior spymaster in the British intelligence—Purvis's immediate boss—in *The Dog It Was That Died*.

30. Feynman, *The Feynman Lectures on Physics: Quantum Mechanics* (Reading, Mass.: Addison-Wesley, 1966), chap. 1, p. 1.

31. Ibid., p. 1. Most of Kerner's "lecture" is derived directly from Feynman. See especially Feynman, "Probability and Uncertainty—the Quantum Mechanical View of Nature," in *The Character of Physical Law* (Cambridge: MIT Press, 1967), 127–48.

32. In production, this "inter-scene," as Stoppard terms it, was shifted from act 2 to act 1, immediately following scene 3 (the scene in which suspicion first centers on Ridley). Stoppard presumably wanted to "visualize" the concept of Ridley's being a twin much sooner in the text (though an audience, at this early stage, may not quite

get the point). Still, wherever it is placed, we sense from the "inter-scene" that Ridley is something other than he claims to be.

33. Richard Corballis, "Tom Stoppard's Children," in *Tom Stoppard: A Casebook*, ed. John Harty (New York: Garland, 1988), 266.

34. The same conclusion is reached by the chief in *The Dog It Was That Died*. As he attempts to clarify the value of Purvis's espionage activities as a double agent, his "explanation" becomes more and more tortuous and impossible to decipher. ("These double and triple bluffs can get to be a bit of a headache"), resulting in the following summation: "In other words, if Purvis's mother had got kicked by a horse things would be more or less exactly as they are now." Stoppard, *The Dog It Was That Died and Other Plays* (London: Faber and Faber, 1983), 43, 45.

35. Stoppard, *Another Moon Called Earth*, in *The Dog It Was That Died and Other Plays*, 101.

36. Orwell, *Nineteen Eighty-four* (Harmondsworth: Penguin, 1954), 67.

37. Stoppard, *Every Good Boy Deserves Favour and Professional Foul* (London: Faber and Faber, 1978), 36.

38. George's line appears in the (unpublished) rehearsal typescript of *Jumpers* (79) but was omitted in performance and in all published editions of the play.

39. Browning, "Pippa Passes," part 1, "Morning," ll.227–28, in *Selected Poetry of Robert Browning*, ed. Kenneth L. Knickerbocker (New York: Random House, 1951), 15.

40. Stoppard, *Rosencrantz and Guildenstern Are Dead* (London: Faber and Faber, 1968), 32.

41. Beckett, *Happy Days* (New York: Grove, 1961), 34.

42. Dotty, in *Jumpers*, is far more cynical on this point: "It's not the voting that's democracy, it's the counting" (26).

43. Billington, *The Guardian*, 9 March 1988, quoted in *London Theatre Record* 8, no. 5 (1988): 288.

44. David Gollob and David Roper, "Trad Tom Pops In," *Gambit* 10, no. 37 (1981): 14.

45. Beckett, *Watt* (New York: Grove, 1959), 247.

46. Ibid., 62.

47. Esslin, *Theatre of the Absurd*, 402.

48. Beckett, *Endgame* (New York: Grove, 1958), 18.

49. Shakespeare, *Love's Labour's Lost*, ed. Richard David (London: Methuen, The Arden Shakespeare, 1963), 5.2.840–47.

50. Brustein, "Waiting for Hamlet," 25.

51. Beckett, *Company* (New York: Grove, 1980), 63.

Hen in a Foxhouse: The Absurdist Plays of Maria Irene Fornes

TOBY SILVERMAN ZINMAN

"Where do female playwrights stand in relation to the tradition of the theater of the absurd?" This question was posed to me by the editors of this volume. Never mind its invitation to tokenism. Never mind its invitation to specious, gender-based generalizations. Better to say something than nothing.

I went back to Martin Esslin's *The Theatre of the Absurd* to find some clues; scanning the index yielded only one female playwright's name: Gertrude Stein, and she is described as a precursor, linked to dadaism and surrealism rather than absurdism, and Esslin points out that the works she describes as "plays" are really "short abstract prose poems in which single sentences or short paragraphs are labelled act I, Act II, and so on. . . . When, towards the end of her life, Gertrude Stein wrote a play with plot and dialogue, *Yes Is for a Very Young Man*, it turned out to be a fascinating but essentially traditional piece of work. . . ."[1] So the question remained.

reductio ab Absurdo:

The theater of the absurd revolutionized the modern stage in both form and content; that is, absurdist drama is distinguished by its "metaphysical anguish"[2] stemming from our culture's loss of meaning, value, and certitude, as well as by the way such drama communicates this vision through its concrete images, its abandonment of rational discourse, and its insistence on showing rather than saying that life is senseless, thereby revealing a profound mistrust of verbal language. Using these basic ideas, which Esslin provided us all with nearly thirty years ago, it was easy to eliminate many of the most visible women playwrights—Marsha Norman, Beth Henley, Pam Gems, Tina Howe, Wendy Wasserstein, and Nell Dunn, for example—because they are obviously writing varieties of realistic drama. Even when they violate those conventions (as Wasserstein does in *Heidi's* interior monologues) it is within a realistic framework. Even when they exaggerate the conventions of realism, as Emily Mann does in *Still Life*, it is to press theater more toward the journalistic (this happened; they live in Minnesota; they said these words to me) and further from the imagistic. Even when they depart from realism through song and dance, as Ntozake Shange does in *Colored Girls*, it is discursively. When Shange and Mann recently collaborated on a musical play, *Betsey Brown*, which tries to raise both racial and feminist issues, the results were so blatantly discursive as to seem sophomoric.

It is necessary to acknowledge at this juncture that Americans have never gravitated toward absurdist drama—perhaps because, as Esslin argues,

> the convention of the absurd springs from a feeling of deep disillusionment . . . which has been characteristic in countries like France and Britain in the years after the Second World War. . . . [but] The American dream of the good life is still very strong. In the United States the belief in progress that characterized Europe in the nineteenth century has been maintained into the middle of the twentieth. It is only since the events of the 1970's—Watergate and defeat in Vietnam—that this optimism has received some sharp shocks. (311)

The logic of this reasoning would lead us to believe that women *would* have embraced the theater of the absurd, since they have experienced "deep disillusionment," but this is not the case. Thus, it becomes even more interesting to see that although many women writing for the stage use many of the methods of the theater of the absurd, testifying to the power of the inheritance, they do not share its vision.

Many of the overtly political women dramatists, of whom Caryl Churchill and Joan Holden are brilliant examples, could be eliminated from my "answer" to the editors' question by virtue of their commitment to radical social change. This is necessarily an optimistic position, while theater of the absurd assumes the Beckettian premise "Nothing to be done," the line with which *Waiting for Godot* begins. The new feminist theater, too, obviously believes that there is much to be done. The very enunciating of the polemic—despite an absurdist framework or technique—has, surely, at its base, a belief that remediation of societal as well as individual attitudes is feasible.

On the other hand, Adrienne Kennedy, who in some way shares the absurdists' metaphysic of despair, uses methods far closer to expressionism. To see life as symbolic nightmare, heavily invested in and with Christianity as Kennedy does, is, almost certainly, to miss out on the humor. And a strong sense of the ludicrous is essential in—and to—the absurdist playwright.

So it was with a sense of relief that I answered the editors' question with the works of Maria Irene Fornes. To consider Fornes within the absurdist tradition becomes even more interesting when one considers that she is usually regarded as a feminist playwright, despite her rejection of the label. While it is certainly plausible to read her plays as feminist documents, recognizing them as absurdist theater shifts their meanings and effects considerably. Fornes is, to my mind, committed to the theater, not to politics, and she has said, "When we start respecting imagery and sensibility, the gender of the writer will be the last thing we think of."[3]

In *Feminist Theatre*, Helene Keyssar mentions Fornes's administrative work in founding the Women's Theatre Council, which collapsed in 1973 and gave rise to a new group called Theatre Strategy, of which Fornes was president. It is important to note that this group's commitment was not to feminism but "to sending experimental plays across the country."[4] But Keyssar insists that it is in "Fornes's fifteen or more plays that we see the best evidence of the theatrical weapons she deploys in the service of feminism" (122). Gayle Austin comes to a similar conclusion; choosing three of Fornes's plays, *Fefu and Her Friends*, *Sarita*, and *The Conduct of Life*, she declares: "Examining these plays through a feminist lens focused on the madwoman figure shows Fornes to be a playwriting exemplar in both form and content."[5] W. B. Worthen, who discusses Fornes's ongoing theatrical experiment, her "eclectic, reflexive theatricality,"[6] centers his discussion on the sexual politics of the stage-spectator relationship. Although he acknowledges that "Fornes refuses to be identified solely as a 'feminist' playwright" and that her work "resists formal or thematic categorization,"[7] he nevertheless reads *Fefu and Her Friends* in a strong feminist light. The way Fornes's drama changes if one changes the lens or the light is most clearly revealed by reexamining *Fefu*, her best known play.

The action of this play takes place in Fefu's New England house where eight women, many of whom are old friends, have met to plan and rehearse a fundraising program for an educational project. It is a spring day in 1935. This location in time and space creates an immediate disjunction, in that these women seem contemporary—in their verbal as well as their body language—and, given that this is 1935, in that there are no signs of financial hard times in these women's circumstances (cars, jobs, travel, clothes, sense of leisure). It is, nevertheless, croquet, not frisbee, that they go out to the lawn to play, but they may be using flamingos for mallets.

Fornes's characteristic emphasis on the visual rather than the verbal, a crucial absurdist preference, may well stem from the fact that she spoke Spanish before she spoke English (she emigrated from Cuba when she was fifteen) and that she saw the original Roger Blin production of *Waiting for Godot* in Paris when she did not understand any French.

> I felt that my life had been turned around. . . . I felt I saw clarity. Maybe that night something in me understood that I was to dedicate my life to the theatre. . . . If you'd asked me then what it was I'd understood, I couldn't have told you. If I had understood the text it still wouldn't have been clear.[8]

And, too, Fornes was a painter (she studied with Hans Hoffman)[9] before she was a playwright. Fornes, who teaches playwriting at INTAR, the Hispanic American Arts Center in New York, uses visualization exercises as her primary pedagogic technique, designed to "get past thinking of writing as 'how to phrase something,' "[10] since her own creative process hinges on the visual:

> But then there is the point when the characters become crystallized. When that happens, I have an image in full color, technicolor. And that *happens!* I do not remember it happening, but I get it like *click!* At some point I see a picture of the set with the characters in it—let us say a picture *related* to the set, not necessarily the exact set.[11]

The most startling "picture of the set with the characters in it" we are given in *Fefu* is an image early in act 1: Fefu picks up a double-barrelled shotgun and shoots her husband, who is offstage, outside on the lawn; he then, we are told, gets up and brushes himself off.

Fornes tells us that the idea for *Fefu* began with the image of a woman shooting her husband, and it took her years to get from that scene to the whole play. She writes:

> Most of my plays start with a kind of a fantasy game—just to see what happens. *Fefu and Her Friends* started that way. There was this woman I fantasized who was talking to some friends. She took her rifle and shot her husband. Also there is a Mexican joke where there are two Mexicans speaking at a bullfight. One says to the other, "She is pretty, that one over there." The other one says, "Which one?" So the first one takes his rifle and shoots her. He says, "That one, the one that falls."
> So in the first draft of the play, Fefu does just that. She takes her rifle and she shoots her husband. He falls. Then she explains that they heard the Mexican joke and she and her husband play that game. That was just my fantasy: thinking of the joke, how absurd it was.[12]

Although the joke was eliminated from the finished play, the absurdity was not. The game Fefu and Phillip play, which so scandalizes Christina and Cindy, is an absurdist image of their marriage—of, perhaps, marriage itself, of the universal, permanent warfare of male/female relationships. Consider the opening dialogue of the play:

> *Fefu:* My husband married me to have a constant reminder of how loathsome women are.
> *Cindy:* What?

Fefu: Yup.
Cindy: That's just awful.
Fefu: No it isn't.
Cindy: It isn't awful?
Fefu: No.
Cindy: I don't think anyone would marry for that reason.
Fefu: He did.
Cindy: Did he say so?
Fefu: He tells me constantly.
Cindy: Oh, dear.
Fefu: I don't mind. I laugh when he tells me.
Cindy: You laugh?
Fefu: I do.
Cindy: How can you?
Fefu: It's funny.—And it's true. That's why I laugh.
Cindy: What is true?
Fefu: That women are loathsome.
Cindy: . . . Fefu!
Fefu: That shocks you.
Cindy: It does. I don't feel loathsome.
Fefu: I don't mean that you are loathsome.
Cindy: You don't mean that I'm loathsome.
Fefu: No . . . It's something to think about. It's a thought.
Cindy: It's a hideous thought. . . .
Fefu: Cindy, I'm not talking about anyone in particular. I'm talking about . . .
Cindy: No one in particular, just women.
Fefu: Yes.
Cindy: In that case I am relieved. I thought you were referring to us.
        (They are amused. Fefu speaks affectionately.)
Fefu: You are being stupid.
Cindy: Stupid and loathsome. *(To* Christina.) Have you ever heard anything more . . . [13]

One might write a play about how "loathsome" men find women and about the self-loathing that is both cause and effect of this, and about how women deeply resent loving men, about the terrible interplay of dependence and self-assertion, about the terrible interplay of sexual passion and contempt, but then, one might be Strindberg. To contain all that in one image of Fefu's shooting Phillip with a rifle, into which *he* may have placed real bullets instead of blanks, is to make the stage speak in the powerful shorthand of concrete images. Further, to read the play as a feminist call to arms is to respond as Cindy does—it is to take the cosmic joke personally. Fornes theatrically demonstrates that it is naive and profitless to assume that the complex enmity inherent in such relations is remediable. The Mexican joke is funny and grotesque and horrible all at once, because it is about brutality and self-defeating stupidity, about simultaneous wish fulfillment and wish denial, about the random victim and the victimizer, about the privileging of action over speech and how powerful and dangerous that can be; it is about the Absurd.

All of this is contained in the stage image of Fefu with her shotgun, an image repeated at the close of the play, in the controversial concluding scene wherein Julia, in a wheelchair since her "hunting accident," begins to bleed from the forehead, as though the bullet with which Fefu kills a rabbit has struck her. This scene undoes the tacit realistic explanations of the earlier mysterious story of the deer hunter. Julia, we have been told, fell to the ground in the woods when the hunter shot a deer. There is no medical evidence of harm, yet she can no longer walk. The audience's easy, reassuring diagnosis of psychosomatic paralysis is reinforced, especially since we and Fefu see Julia walking in one scene. Look, the spectator can say, see how the male establishment has victimized her and how she has internalized that victimization. This is to assume realism; that is, such a peculiar event must be accounted for, and psychological exegesis is the one most comfortable to our culture. It is, further, to assume that Julia is a symbolic character whose meaning can be expressed. This is fundamental to the feminist readings of the play; for example, Keyssar sees Julia as the symbol of feminine yielding in the face of the "enormity of the struggle women must undertake," and that "woman-as-victim must be killed . . . in order to ignite the explosion of a community of women."[14]

But the bleeding wound on Julia's forehead after Fefu shoots the rabbit has also been viewed as "miracle" by Susan Sontag,[15] which also suggests the play is realistic and that the only way of explaining such a "violation of the quotidian" is mystically. This, too, I think, mistakes the vision and therefore mistakes the genre. But, if we see the play as absurdist, then the images do not have to be explained;

they are theater, not life, and speak with the language of the contemporary stage. Consider, for example, a startlingly similar image: the bleeding forehead at the conclusion of Sam Shepard's *Red Cross*.

It may be useful to note here that the only play Fornes had read before she started to write plays was *Hedda Gabler*,[16] and one might see Fefu's shotgun as an absurdist transmutation of Hedda's pistol; Fefu is not about to shoot herself to escape male dominance, but she may, in the shooting of the rabbit/Julia at the end, have shot the Hedda principle. This is to suggest not only the feminist act of destroying that female character who symbolizes a yielding to male dominance (or the equally self-destructive suicidal refusal to yield to male dominance), but also the destruction of the Hedda principle in theatrical terms: the rejection of the well-made, realistic play replete with explanations and meaningful actions; the well-furnished house party revisited and revised.

Perhaps the play's most subtle yet radical assault on the realistic is that its characters spring from different modes of theatrical creation: the naturalistic, the symbolic, the histrionic, and the absurdist. This is not merely to say that they exist on different levels of fictive reality—the difference, say, between the actors and the characters in Pirandello's *Six Characters in Search of an Author*. It is also that they belong to different kinds of playwriting, and the play is, formally, built on the collision of these modes.

Julia's long speeches explaining her torment at the hands of her male oppressors—

I told them the stinking parts of the body are the important ones. . . . (24)

and

The human being is of the masculine gender. . . . (25)

and

I feel we are constantly threatened by death. . . . (35)

—are discursive lumps in the texture of the play. It might be useful to note here that in explaining why she dislikes Arthur Miller's and

Tennessee William's plays, Fornes said, "I don't romanticize pain. In my work people are always trying to find a way out, rather than feeling a romantic attachment to their prison."[17] They do not, of course, find it; this quest for escape and the defeat of the quest is fundamental to the absurdist vision. By extension of these remarks, one might assume that Julia is a character out of a Miller or a Williams play. Julia defines herself as neurotic, suffering heroine, while Julia as character is defined by Fornes as a manifestation of symbolic realism. Fefu, on the other hand—by far the least verbal character in the play—is an absurdist character; she speaks as well as acts in presentational images.

Thus, it is through an image rather than an argument that Fefu shows Christina that she, too, is "fascinated with revulsion," the image of the smooth, dry stone whose underside is "slimy and filled with fungus and crawling with worms. It is another life that is parallel to the one we manifest" (9). This is more than an appeal to Christina to open her mind to the excitement of grappling with uncomfortable ideas; it is a testimony to theatrical possibilities, an assertion that the stage can show us the life beneath the realistic surface. Fefu's account of the monstrous, mangled cat whom she feeds and fears and who fouls her kitchen is really an image, not a story; like Albee's dog in *Zoo Story*, Fornes's cat is full of unarticulable meaning; it speaks Fefu's "constant pain," which is far less explicable than Julia's.

Like an audience that has come for realism and found absurdity, the guests in Fefu's house find her shocking and puzzling. The refined Christina, who is new to the group, expresses much of the honest, dismayed reaction of audiences to theater of the absurd and to Fefu who is the incarnation of it:

> She confuses me a little. . . . I don't know if she's careful with life. . . . I suppose I don't mean with life but more with convention. I think she is an adventurer in a way. . . . Her mind is adventurous. I don't know if there is dishonesty in that. But in adventure there is taking chances and risks, and then one has to, somehow, have less regard or respect for things as they are. That is, regard for a kind of convention, I suppose. I am probably ultimately a conformist, I think. And I suppose I do hold back for fear of being disrespectful or destroying something—and I admire those who are not. But I also feel they are dangerous to me. I don't think they are dangerous to the world, they are more useful than I am, more

important, but I feel some of my life is endangered by their way of thinking. (22)

This defines the play's mode—or collision of modes, as they are embodied not just in the minds of the characters themselves but in the very way the characters have been conceived.

That the play is about theater rather than politics is most straightforwardly suggested by the plot—the planning of the fundraiser, which is far more a rehearsal than a meeting. The star of the show the next day will be Emma, the most flamboyant character of the group, whose clothing is costume and whose speech, the centerpiece of their meeting, is performed for us rather than just assigned to a position in the program as the others are. Her speech uses a long passage from "The Science of Educational Dramatics," by Emma Sheridan Fry, an early twentieth-century teacher, full of inspirational phrases and the passionate belief that theater can teach—not as a pulpit for a particular ideology, but as a liberating catalyst of the human spirit. The rousing image that concludes Emma's speech enjoins her audience—and, by extension, us—to intrepid action: "Let us, boldly, seizing the star of our intent, lift it as the lantern of our necessity, and let it shine over the darkness of our compliance. Come!" (32). And the image of the "constant stars" of Shakespeare's sonnet 14, which Emma recites in the second act, suggests the same human capacity to convert "truth and beauty" to the storehouse of art, thus forestalling doomsday. The star image is linked to Fefu, for it is she who asks, "Have you been out? The sky is full of stars" (39).

If we read this in pursuit of a feminist interpretation, we see that Fefu sends them all out of doors, into that realm designated by the play as the male domain. Only Julia cannot or will not go, and remains confined indoors, in her wheelchair, in her timidity and terror. Fefu tries to rescue Julia ("Fight, Julia!" [40]) but when Julia retreats into weakness and fear, Fefu must reject her: "You're contagious. . . . I'm going mad too" (40). Politically, Fefu rejects Julia's paralyzing deference, although the concluding scene, Julia wounded or dead and the women gathered around her, remains ambiguous. Are they lending their support to the murder? Are they appalled? Mystified? Sorry? Glad? The text does not tell us, although there is nothing to suggest that this is a triumphant moment. If anything, there is clearly madness on both "sides." There is no escape in this play; both Julia and Fefu are victims and victimizers; in Fornes's version of the Mexican joke, it does not matter which end of the rifle you are on.

The image functions as a metadramatic analogy as well. Aesthetically, Fefu's shooting of the rabbit/Julia is Fornes's rejection of the confining conventions of symbolic realism. She sends her friends out into the brilliant night, rejecting "the darkness of our compliance" and accepting the theatrical adventure of the theater of the absurd.

Perhaps even more bizarre than the collision among kinds of characters is that between "educational dramatics" and the theater of the absurd, since many of Fornes's plays are about teaching and learning, and since theater of the absurd is distinguished by its nondidacticism. Like the joyful, histrionic Emma and her namesake, Emma Sheridan Fry, Fornes believes in theater as a liberating force. In an interview she said that

> the play is there as a lesson, because I feel that art ultimately is a teacher. You go to a museum to look at a painting and that painting teaches you something. You may not look at a Cezanne and say, "I know what I have to do." But it gives you something, a charge of some understanding, some knowledge that you have in your heart."[18]

And, although the plays are various in size, shape, and style, one of the patterns that can be traced from the early (*Tango Palace*, 1960) to the recent (*Mud*, 1983) is the repeated use of the teaching/learning pattern; as Susan Sontag points out,

> People requiring or giving instruction is a standard situation in Fornes's plays. . . . (Fornes's elaborate sympathy for the labor of thought is the endearing observation of someone who is almost entirely self-taught.) And there are many dispensers of wisdom in Fornes's plays, apart from those—*Tango Palace, Doctor Kheal*—specifically devoted to the comedy and the pathos of instruction.[19]

Dr. Kheal (1968) is her most obviously absurdist play. Flagrantly indebted to Ionesco's *The Lesson*, it lacks both the intellectuality and the sexual menace of its precursor. But *The Lesson* is an absurdist play about power and language, while *Dr. Kheal* is an absurdist play about absurd theatre itself, a totally self-reflexive piece. In it, the professor, dwarfed by the set composed of blackboard, water glasses, and demonstration charts—Fornes specifies that "he is small, or else the furniture is large"—plays both questioner and respondent, actor and audience, as he attempts to instruct on a range of subjects from poetry to brussels sprouts. The conclusion of Dr. Kheal's lesson is "Man is a rational animal,"[20] while the conclusion of *Dr. Kheal's* lesson is to have demonstrated how foolish and pedantic the rational can be. This entire short play becomes a concrete stage image indicting rationality, and thereby also indicting the sort of drama that assumes the viability of the conventional elements of drama—dialogue, action, conflict—all of which are parodied here.

A far more subtle and disturbing treatment of teaching and learning happens in Fornes's first play, *Tango Palace* (1960), a two-hander about Isidore, "an androgynous clown," and Leopold, "an earnest youth." It, too, indicts rationality, although it is harder to tell how. One would do well to be guided by Fornes's preface:

> To say that a work of art is meaningful is to imply that the work is endowed with intelligence. That it is illuminating. But if we must inquire what the meaning of a work of art is, it becomes evident that the work has failed us. . . .
> To approach a work of art with the wish to decipher its symbolism, and to extract the author's intentions from it, is to imply that the work can be something other than what it demonstrates, that the work can be treated as a code system which, when deciphered, reveals the true content of the work. A work of art should not be other than what it demonstrates. It should not be an intellectual puzzle. . . . If there is wisdom in the work it will come to us. But if we go after it, we become wary, watchful. We lose our ability to taste.[21]

This is a critical caveat indeed. It also sounds like a substantial manifesto of the theater of the absurd. If we apply it to *Tango Palace*, it provides a gloss on the play. Both Isidore and Leopold are interested in wisdom: Isidore mockingly asserts his possession of it; Leopold urgently wishes to acquire it. Isidore's gaudy appearance (he is stout, with long hair, men's clothes, high heels, lots of makeup, and a corsage) announces, among other things, the refusal to let us know who we are looking at (surely the most basic, instantaneous perception of another person is to identify gender), but lack of clarity is

Isidore's stock in trade. In contrast, Leopold, who is born into the play by crawling out of a canvas sack ("Look what the stork has brought me" [13]), is young, handsome, and wearing a business suit; we know exactly who he is. Once again, Fornes builds a play on jarring incongruities rather than old-fashioned conflict.

The vehicle of instruction in *Tango Palace* is a limitless pack of cards, each inscribed with a cliché ("All is fair in love and war") or with a piece of the play's dialogue. The cards seem to be cue cards after the fact, or perhaps they suggest that there is nothing new under the sun, that all dialogue is a rerun, thereby discrediting both written and spoken language. Isidore offers them, pompously, to Leopold: "These cards contain wisdom. File them away. *(card)* [is flipped.] Know where they are *(card)* Have them at hand. *(card)* Be' one upon whom nothing is lost. *(card)*" (16). When Leopold mishears or missays a cliché—"All's fair . . ." in the vulgar, common fashion ("Not love *in* war. Love *and* war!"), Isidore smacks him. Once the communication battle becomes physical, it escalates quickly, and soon both characters have been stabbed, although nothing is permanent here, not even death. Nothing is sacred either, since the religious images and allusions are bandied about lavishly, as Isidore opens his arms wide and is killed with a sword, but it is Leopold who says, solemnly and incorrectly, "It is done." If "cleanliness is close to godliness *(card)*," both "stink." The contest continues in a preposterously clichéd heaven, complete with harps and clouds and angels; Fornes's first play is its own theatricalized manifesto.

The no-exit set, complete with giant padlock on the door, is made far more interesting by Isidore's collection of eighteenth-century furniture (suggesting the museum room in Stanley Kubrick's film *2001*), and forms a visual contrast to Isidore's outlandish shrine filled with bullfighting equipment and the beetle masks (debt to Kafka's "Metamorphosis"?). The image of the two men (?) playing (?) at bulls and matadors suggests the grotesque cruelty of the "astounding elegance" of blood sport, which is supposed to yield wisdom and truth. "As I stick each banderilla on your back I'll reveal the answer to a mystery. And then. . . . *(taking the sword)* the moment of truth. . . . As eternal verity is revealed to you, darkness will come upon your eyes . . ." (28). (Debt to Kafka's "The Penal Colony"?[22]

The nature of this strange play is finally emblematized in itself; Isidore gives Leopold a drawing lesson on the blackboard, teaching him how to draw a "portrait of a mediocre person" by connecting three dots and adding an eye dot and a mouth line to the resulting triangle. But this easy system will not yield a portrait of Leopold, since

> all we can establish is that I am at the top. And way down at the bottom is you. There is no other point. We therefore can't have an angle. We only have a vertical line. The space around us is infinite, enclosed as it may be, because there is not a third person. And if the space around us is infinite, so is, necessarily, the space between us. (20)

This oxymoronic image of the infinity of enclosed space is, to my mind, the image of the absurdist stage. The lack of a third character, one that might resolve the tension of two points symmetrically suspended, is the hallmark of absurdist drama as it theatricalizes absence and redefines linearity and chronology. That it takes two to tango is precisely the point here.

In another early play, *The Successful Life of Three* (1966), easily recognized as absurdist, the teaching/learning motif reappears to show us that stupidity and ignorance allow for a "successful life"— whereby rivalry, greed, criminality, incompetence, and ineducability allow these two men and one woman to tolerate their existence. Fornes requires in her headnote to the play that each character has one characteristic facial expression—She has a "stupid expression," He "looks disdainful," and Three looks "with intense curiosity"; the note further specifies that these are to be played "very deadpan."[23] The required lack of emotional range clearly rejects the traditional theatrical aesthetic, and creates an absurdist version of Greek masks (absurdist partly because they miss the importance and clarity of comedy and tragedy, and partly because live human faces are being used as masks).

The Successful Life of Three begins with the literalizing of a cliché:

> *Three takes a shoe off and drops it. At the sound of the shoe, He becomes motionless, his arms suspended in the air. Three looks at He, and freezes for a moment.*
> Three: What are you doing?
> He: Waiting.
> Three: What for?
> He: For the other shoe to drop.

Three: Ah, and I was wondering what you were doing. If I hadn't asked, we would have stayed like that forever. You waiting and me wondering. . . That's the kind of person I am. I ask . . . That's good, you know.

He: Why?

Three: *** [Asterisks signify their characteristic expression.]

He: Why?

Three: It starts the action.

He: What action did you start?

Three: We're talking. (43–44)

After this metadramatic opening, each of the play's conventional dramatic situations—middle-aged man and young man as rivals for "a sexy young lady," a thief getting caught by the police, the achievement of financial success with an invention—is meaningless, devoid of the emotional component convention demands. The other shoe never drops, as it never does in absurdist drama.

Sontag asks us to "consider the twenty-year trajectory that goes from *The Successful Life of 3* to *Mud*, about the unsuccessful life of three."[24] Although this play, typical of Fornes's recent work, seems far more naturalistic than the earlier plays, both Sontag and Bonnie Marranca[25] have been at pains to define the redefinition of realism these later plays, *Mud* and *The Conduct of Life* (1985), imply. Just as these two plays continue Fornes's career-long discussion—and celebration—of learning and teaching (and, thus, of the viability of received wisdom), so they also continue her interest in the stage as visual field.

Mud pulls against its apparent realism by creating a series of seventeen scenes, each of which ends with a *tableau vivant*, an eight-second freeze "which will create the effect of a still photograph."[26] Thus the play becomes a photograph album, ironically using the art form most easily associated with realism to break the stage realism.

Like *The Successful Life of 3*, this is a play about a love triangle of two men—one older, one younger—and one woman, but here the play ends in the woman's death, as Lloyd, who refuses to let her leave, shoots her with a rifle. This play, like most of Fornes's others (*Tango Palace, Fefu, Conduct of Life, The Danube, Sarita*), ends with a murder. Fornes has said, "I don't know how to end a play unless . . . who's going to kill whom?"[27] This seems to me more a function of an ontology than of politics; the violence is emblematic of a catastrophic vision of human life rather than of tyranny and oppression. The catastrophe at the end of *Mud* is still another reworking of the appalling Mexican joke discussed earlier—the literalizing of the metaphor to create a new image, far more powerful than the easily laughed-off metaphor of the joke.

Mud's capacity to move us deeply lies in Mae's human longings to learn, the value of different kinds of knowledge, and the eloquence of the poetic language that speaks that knowledge. Mae reads from a textbook about starfish—"The starfish is an animal, not a fish. He is called a fish because he lives in the water. The starfish cannot live out of the water..." (27)—and this information is transformed into the beauty of her final speech as she lies dying on the kitchen table: "Like the starfish, I live in the dark and my eyes see only a faint light. It is faint and yet it consumes me. I long for it. I thirst for it. I would die for it. Lloyd, I am dying" (40).

It would be easy to read this as a feminist play, but Fornes has specifically rejected her idea of the feminist interpretation:

> I think usually the people who have expressed to me their dismay at Mae's being killed are feminist women who are having a hard time in their life. They hang onto feminism because they feel oppressed and believe it will save them. They see me as a feminist and when they see Mae die, they feel betrayed."[28]

Mud is not immediately recognizable as an absurdist play; nevertheless, it participates in the most basic premises of the theater of the absurd: structurally, it builds on inaction at the conclusion of each scene; theatrically, it conveys, through images rather than explanations, the terrible conflicting human needs inherent in human relationships; linguistically, it demonstrates simultaneously both the inadequacy and the dazzling beauty of words.

Just as *Mud* can be mistaken for a conventionally realistic play or a conventionally feminist play, *The Danube* (1982) is often mistaken for a conventionally absurdist play, along the lines of Ionesco's *The Bald Soprano*, since it depends on foreign language tapes and seems to depict people as puppets. It would be equally easy to read *The Danube* as a feminist work as well, but in fact, although both elements are present, such exclusionary interpretations diminish the play's range and power. Rather than a reductive post-Edenic diatribe, Fornes gives us glimpses into the male-female relation in all its dangerous symbiosis. Similarly, she avoids a prefabricated indictment of the failure of devalued language.

In a statement that seems worthy of an absurdist in the widest and deepest meaning of the term, Fornes has said:

> A way of expressing your awe is to say, "Words fail me." That's language.[29]

NOTES

1. Martin Esslin, *The Theatre of the Absurd*, 3d ed. (New York: Doubleday, Pelican, 1983), 397.

2. Ibid., 23.

3. *Performing Arts Journal*, "Women Playwrights Issue," 7, no. 3 (1983): 91.

4. Helene Keyssar, *Feminist Theatre* (New York: Grove, 1985), 121.

5. Gayle Austin, "The Madwoman in the Spotlight: Plays of Maria Irene Fornes," in *Making a Spectacle*, ed. Lynda Hart (Ann Arbor: University of Michigan Press, 1989), 76.

6. W. B. Worthen, "*Still Playing Games:* Ideology and Performance in the Theater of Maria Irene Fornes," in *Feminine Focus: The New Women Playwrights*, ed. Enoch Brater (New York: Oxford University Press, 1989), 167.

7. Ibid., 180.

8. Quoted in David Savran, *In Their Own Words: Contemporary American Playwrights* (New York: Theatre Communications Group, 1988), 54.

9. Ibid., 51.

10. Quoted in Neena Beber, "Dramatis Instructus," *American Theatre*, January 1990, 24.

11. Maria Irene Fornes, "I Write These Messages That Come," *Drama Review* 21, no. 4 (December 1977): 27.

12. Ibid., 30.

13. Maria Irene Fornes, *Fefu and Her Friends* (1978), in *Word Plays* (New York: PAJ Publications, 1980), 7–8. All further page references will appear in parentheses in the text.

14. Keyssar, *Feminist Theatre*, 125.

15. Susan Sontag, preface to *Maria Irene Fornes Plays* (New York: PAJ Publications, 1986), 8.

16. Savran, *In Their Own Words*, 51.

17. Ibid., 55.

18. Ibid., 56.

19. Sontag, *Fornes Plays*, 8.

20. Maria Irene Fornes, *Dr. Kheal*, in *A Century of Plays by American Women*, ed. Rachel France (New York: Richards Rosen Press, 1979), 184. The play's title, although often written *Doctor Kheal*, appears with the abbreviation *Dr.* in this edition, as it does in its more recent publication in the collection titled *Promenade and Other Plays* (New York: PAJ Publications, 1987).

21. Maria Irene Fornes, *Tango Palace*, in *Playwrights for Tomorrow*, vol. 2, ed. Arthur H. Ballet (Minneapolis: University of Minnesota Press, 1966), 9. All further page references appear in parentheses in the text.

22. Fornes has said that *The Trial*, like *Godot*, gave her "an experience of incredible energy inside me" (Savran, *In Their Own Words*, 56).

23. Maria Irene Fornes, *The Successful Life of Three: A Skit for Vaudeville*, in *Playwrights for Tomorrow*, vol. 2, ed. Arthur H. Ballet (Minneapolis: University of Minnesota Press, 1966), 42. All further page references appear in parentheses in the text.

24. Sontag, *Fornes Plays*, 9. Writing the title as Sontag does, with the figure 3 rather than the word *Three*, eliminates the ambiguity that it may be the character, Three, whose success the play is about. It is worth noting, too, that this play is dedicated to Susan Sontag. The word *Three* is used in the play's first publication in *Playwrights for Tomorrow*.

25. Bonnie Marranca, "Maria Irene Fornes and the New Realism," *Performing Arts Journal*, no. 22 (1984): 29–33.

26. Maria Irene Fornes, *Mud*, in *Maria Irene Fornes Plays*, 16. Further page references appear in parentheses in the text.

27. Savran, *In Their Own Words*, 56–57.

28. Ibid., 57.

29. Ibid., 65.

The Internationalization of the Paris Stage

Rosette C. Lamont

Paris is talking about the year 1992, when the United States of Europe (the "Europe of the Twelve") will become a political and economic reality. President Mitterand's dream of melding small, militarily weak countries together with former imperial powers into what he calls "the Great Market" is at hand. On the cultural level, national borders have already been erased.

In this formerly ethnocentric country, chauvinism, no longer considered chic, is the province of Le Pen's National Front, of French rednecks, and of some retrograde blue-collar workers. The intelligentsia is proud of its spirit of open-mindedness and American-style empiricism. The internationalization of French cultural institutions, a result of entrusting the highest jobs in the country to foreigners, could not have taken place before the Socialists came to power in the 1980s. Mitterand and his minister of culture, Jack Lang (with his own international-looking name), must be given credit for this phenomenon. Their plan means making use of the best talents available, enriching the cultural life of their country by opening it up to the rest of the world.

In all fairness, even before Mitterand's success in the 1981 elections there were signs of a new national policy regarding the use of foreign artists. President Giscard d'Estaing, for example, appointed a German, Rol Liebermann, to head the Opéra. But a more recent controversy, what some call "L'affaire Barenboim," involved two foreign artists vying for the post of director for the new opera house, L'Opéra de la Bastille. This was one of Mitterand's "Grands Projets"; even the entries for the building's design competition were to be anonymous. Mitterand favored the American architect Richard Meier, but the jury picked a design by the obscure Uruguayan-born Canadian architect, Carlos Ott. Rumor has it that the jury thought the design looked like Meier's work—and that then it was too late to back down.

But the real cause célèbre was not the design of the house but its artistic directorship. During that curious political period known as "La Cohabitation" (June 1986 through March 1988), when Mitterand had to appoint someone from the Right to be his prime minister (he named the mayor of Paris, Jacques Chirac, who hoped to become the next president), the minister of culture, Léotard, approached the Jewish-Argentinian pianist Daniel Barenboim about taking charge of the "modern and popular" opera house. Unlike the elitist Palais Garnier, the Bastille was supposed to appeal to a mass audience, and to provide inexpensive tickets. When the Socialists won a landslide election in 1988, Léotard was at once replaced by his predecessor, Jack Lang, who then named Pierre Bergé chairman of the Opéra. Bergé fired Barenboim, who had been promised seven million francs for his position. After a world-wide search, the position of music director (but not artistic director) was offered to a young Korean artist, Myung Whun Chung, born in Seoul in 1953 and educated at the Mannes School of Music in New York. Myung, a former assistant to Carlo Maria Giulini at the Los Angeles Philharmonic, had never spent any time in France before assuming his new duties. Another development at the Paris Opéra concerned the artistic directorship of the ballet corps: from 1983 to 1989 it was in the hands of Rudolf Nureyev, the Soviet-born dancer with Austrian citizenship who has based his international career mostly in Manhattan. Nureyev was succeeded by Patrick Dupond, the internationally known French ballet star.

In other open, international competitions, especially in architecture, France's greatest commissions have also gone to foreigners. An Italian, Gae Aulenti, was entrusted with the 1986 interior renovation of the Gare d'Orsay, which now houses a museum for nineteenth-century art. And what has been called "the most gratuitous abstract state monument of the late twentieth century," the big arch of La Défense, was designed by the Danish architect Johan Otto von Spreckelsen (after his death, however, the work was completed by the Frenchman Paul Andreu). The "big arch" is a cube measuring 360 feet on each side, sheeted in Carrara white marble. It can be seen from the heart of Paris, in line with the Arc de Triomphe.

The most controversial of the "Grands Projets" has been the glass pyramid designed by the Chinese-American I. M. Pei and erected in the central courtyard of the Louvre to serve as an entrance to the remodeled, enlarged museum. Paul Goldberger of the *New York Times* calls it "the virtual symbol of the remaking of Paris." The Parisians hated it (just as they had hated the Eiffel Tower one hundred years before), even when Pei's work was shown as an elegant maquette in the Orangerie museum. Pei described himself as a "garden architect" when he spoke of this project at the New York Metropolitan Museum. "The splendid glass and metal-cable structure," according to Goldberger, "demonstrates that I. M. Pei is a master at producing large-scale work with refinement and excellence of detail." The new landmark, which looks less like a building than a crystallized fountain, has also been hailed as "a triumph of urbanism." Its archetypal form is both older and newer than the Louvre. Its transparency allows one to see the blond stone enclosing it, but its placement defines the southeastern end of the axis running up the Champs-Elysées through the Arc de Triomphe. Thus, from the pyramid of the big arch at La Défense we follow a trail built by two foreign architects: one born in China, the other from Denmark.

The same international perspective has also been operating in the theater. In the late 1980s, Jack Lang invited Giorgio Strehler to bring his Théâtre de l'Europe to the building that served as the second house of the Comédie Française, the Odéon. Strehler shared the space with Jean le Poulin until the latter's death in March 1988, but since March 1990 has been the sole master, assisted by Luis Pasqual, former director of the national theater of Spain. A fascinating development along the same lines is the creation of a new national theater in Paris, Le Théâtre National de la Colline, in the twentieth arrondissement, which at the time of this writing is in its third season. The director, Jorge Lavelli from Argentina, specializes in presenting modern and experimental works. A fellow Argentinian, Alfredo Arias, runs Le Théâtre de la Commune D'Aubervillers, one of the best "théâtres périphériques" surrounding Paris. Recently he has staged his own "Famille d'Artistes" with the music of Astor Piazzola.

The result of such integration within the European community can be that even when the director is French, the accent is often foreign. The late Antoine Vitez, who left the directorship of Chaillot to head the Comédie Française, set a repertory for the company's final season at the Odéon that included *La Celestina*, Goethe's *Torquato Tasso*, *As You Like It*, directed by Pasqual, and Molière's *Le médecin malgré lui*, staged by Dario Fo. And Jérôme Savary, the new director of the TNP, recently invited the Germans Matthias Langhoff and Hans Peter Closs to stage *Macbeth* and *Le Malade Imaginaire*.

Traditionally, France has always welcomed foreign artists and granted refuge to political exiles. People endlessly debate whether Picasso ought to be considered French or Spanish. What about Picabia, Juan Gris, Modigliani, Giacometti, Man Ray, Chagall? In literature there is a plethora of nation-straddling names: Julien Green, Witold Gombrowicz, Arthur Adamov, Samuel Beckett, Eugene Ionesco, Fernando Arrabal. However, when it came to words spoken or sung from the stage, the French insisted on clear diction and the elimination of foreign intonations; the beauty of their language was sacrosanct. Yet the most striking phenomenon of today's French stage is its verbal tapestry of accents, visual metaphors, and exotic musical instrumentation.

The director who initiated this movement in Paris, carrying it throughout the world by means of his fluid, adaptable, peripatetic company, the Centre International de Recherches Théâtrales (CIRT), is a Russian-Jewish Englishman, Peter Brook. His Théâtre des Bouffes du Nord in Paris is the nest whence issued the multiracial, multicultural cast of the *Mahabharata*.

When I interviewed Brook in Paris (1 May 1986) about the way in which he had formed a company whose members speak only a rudimentary French, often bordering on the incomprehensible, he explained:

Think of a forest: it is composed of different species of trees and inhabited by all kinds of animals and birds. Some are gentle, others fierce, but all of them exist together, if not always peaceably. This is essential for ecological balance. I seek to establish this kind of natural balance on the stage.

It is fundamentally natural for an Indian, an African and a European to share the same space, our planet. Why not bring them closer together, upon the same stage, or in the same performance space? Despite their differences, actors blend with one another as they reach the core of their roles. Collectively and individually they then achieve the right rhythm.

Peter Brook's revolutionary aesthetics are rooted in the vision of the French surrealist of Greek ancestry, Antonin Artaud. When Artaud began his essays and manifestoes (1931–35; published in 1938 under the title *Le Théâtre et son Double*), his pronouncements about the superiority of Oriental culture and theater were taken as acts of provocation. Artaud's crisis of conscience occurred in 1931, when he saw the Balinese dancers perform at the Paris Coloniale Exposition. It seemed to him that this theater, with its amalgam of dance, song, and pantomime, was not cut off from its sacred roots, that it was in fact closer to ancient Greek theater than classical French drama. Profoundly repelled by bourgeois boulevard theater, Artaud embraced this total, metaphysical spectacle in which each participant becomes "an animated hieroglyph."

In the theater world of "l'entre-deux-guerres," Artaud was not the only artist to wish to explore the possibilities of creating a poetic stage vocabulary. In the early 1920s he had been trained in rhythmic gymnastics, diction, and improvisation at Charles Dullin's "research laboratory." In his Ecole Nouvelle du Comédien, Dullin explored bringing together ancient Japanese theater with the plasticity of commedia dell'arte techniques. At approximately the same time, Louis Jouvet wrote that the actor is "double," since he or she must live "between being and appearance." Another member of the Cartel des Quatre, Gaston Baty, also advocated the metaphysics of the theater by means of physical expressiveness, the use of marionettes, and the development of a larger-than-life language, one that transcended text. The fourth member of "les Quatre," Georges Pitoëff, did not feel that his Russian accent stood in the way of bringing to France the works of Chekhov and Pirandello.

There was, however, a fundamental difference between these masters and Artaud. The latter was, as Jean-Louis Barrault stated, "un homme théâtre." Roger Shattuck, in the November 11, 1976, *New York Review of Books*, called him "the whirling dervish of literature and self-performance." Artaud advocated dramatic expression as a form

of collective shock treatment. In January 1947, fourteen months before his death, he appeared on the stage of the Vieux Colombier
shuffling a pile of papers. This was reading in the form of a happening. He declaimed, whispered, roared; denounced language, sex,
and himself. He hurled neologisms as javelins: "Klaver striva / Ca-
vour Tavina / Scaver Kavina / Oskar Triva." As Jacques Derrida explained in a series of lectures delivered at the graduate school of City
University of New York in September 1986, Artaud felt that French
was a moribund language laboring under the illusion that it had
reached some peak of perfection. It was up to him to repossess it, to
turn words into things, his own things, objects of his making.

Those were the years when a revolution in artistic sensibility was
wreaked by the surrealists (André Breton, Picasso, Artaud). They
brought to the intelligentsia's attention the powerful impact of "l'art
nègre" and of Polynesian masks. (Most of them traveled only as far
as the Musée de l'Homme, where the artifacts of "primitive art" could
be viewed.) At approximately the same time, Claude Lévi-Strauss
began to formulate his structuralist thesis in *Tristes Tropiques*. Together, artists and ethnologists were discovering the relativity of the
concept of culture.

Our contemporary artists and theoreticians have embarked on a
new adventure, that of exploring what Richard Schechner calls
"points of contact between anthropological and theatrical thought."[1]
A link is established between "two realms of experience" (6), but
there is no attempt made to see "with native eyes," or feel with "a
native heart" (13). Although such critics as Gautam Dasgupta have
posed the problem of "Orientalism,"[2] it would be a mistake to see in
these endeavors a sign of an imperialist appropriation of a Third
World culture. As Schechner states: "I prefer to let the 'natives' speak
for themselves. For my part I acknowledge that I am seeing with my
own eyes. I also invite others to see me and my culture with their
eyes. We are then in a position to exchange our views" (13). The
second of these possibilities has found an eloquent exponent in the
Japanese director Tadashi Suzuki, whose postmodern *Tale of Lear* was
presented at the Berkeley Repertory Theatre and at the Arena Stage
in Washington, D.C. In America these "exchanges" are shaping the
aesthetics of experimental theater, as in Mabou Mines's use of Bun-
raku and Noh, Julie Taymor's Javanese masks, and the influence of
Balinese dance theater on Islene Pindar's *Night Shadows* and Ron

Jenkins's *One Horse Show*. All of these testify to a learning process, one that Schechner diagnoses as "metabolism" (24).

As the founder in 1964 of the London Theatre of Cruelty, Peter Brook raised the Artaudian banner. This took him on the path of "theatre anthropology."[3] For Brook, the stage is the realm of the "between" where various cultures clash, but also mesh. However, he does not intend to achieve a bland international style, the concretization of "a belief in a syncretic cultural universe."[4] On the contrary, his wish is to create a vast collage of cultures in which each one would still retain its particular traits. Thus, he puts the actors of his intercultural company through a rigorous training not unlike that of ethnographers or archaeologists. They participate in the paces of t'ai chi and the exercises of martial arts. They are also taught to deal with passages from the ancient Greek dramatists, learning them phonetically. Thus, the practice of reciting a speech from Aeschylus led to the invention of *Orghast*. To speak a language one does not know, or an invented tongue, forces the actor to communicate more forcefully what lies in his subconscious and to listen with his inner ear to the subtext. It may be unfair to accuse Brook of remaining outside "the theological value system"[5] of a work such as the *Mahabharata*. He cannot—nor does he wish to—become an Indian artist, be assimilated by his material. As a director, he would say that he is simply a reader; as a teacher, he is an interpreter and a guide. As to his production of the great Sanskrit epic, it must be viewed as a gesture of friendship, the outsider's willingness to reach out and touch the unknown, perhaps the unknowable.

The same international spirit is present in Hélène Cixous's recent historical epics written for Ariane Mnouchkine's Théâtre du Soleil: *The Unfinished Story of Norodom Sihanouk, King of Cambodia*, and the *Indiade*. The latter's title echoes the greatest of all Western epics, the *Iliad*.

Like Peter Brook, who likes to joke, "I'm not a director who travels, but a traveler who directs plays," Mnouchkine and Cixous are inveterate explorers. Like Brook they embark on these study voyages with members of their acting and technical staff. For *Sihanouk* they chose Cambodia as the locus of their collaborative effort for two reasons: their desire to present a noble, gentle people (the Khmer), and their equally strong wish to show the genocidal destruction of a people by power-mad ideologues. For Cixous, a Jewish woman from

North Africa, the insane project of the Khmer Rouge echoes the mass murders characteristic of our century.

No longer centered on a single figure such as the beguilingly crafty Sihanouk, the *Indiade* is still concerned with the whirlpool of political intrigue. It explores the struggle for independence by diverse religious and ethnic Indian groups. In the process, unity is compromised by partition. Carved from India's body, the state of Pakistan severed western Punjab from eastern Bengal. As Cixous states in her preface to the published script: "August 1947 marked an implacable surgical operation." Two polar figures represent the struggle between purity and political expediency: the saintly Mahatma Gandhi, played as a clever holy fool by Andres Perez Araya, and Nehru, given great dignity by Georges Bicot, who had played Sihanouk. In his Western white suit, Nehru cuts a different figure from the half-naked, hairless, toothless Gandhi.

The *Indiade* begins before the audience settles down on the tiered, upholstered benches facing the vast, low platform of the Cartoucherie. As the people climb up to their seats, actors, dressed as Indian villagers, trickle onto the village square, sweeping away the morning dust and sprinkling it with fresh water. Filtered through an airy canopy, the morning light suggests the start of an ordinary day in the Far East.

While this is going on, a Bengali itinerant female beggar, Haridasi, played by Baya Belal, runs up and down the aisles, asking members of the audience to identify themselves by name and nationality so that she may introduce them to her friends, the villagers. Since the Cartoucherie's audiences are unfailingly international, or at least European, the breakdown of national barriers is established at once. To be addressed by Haridasi in highly accented Indian English contributes to the sense of estrangement people experienced at the moment they stepped into the huge foyer, with its back wall covered by a map of India. A saffron curry, cooked by members of the company, was served by costumed, made-up actors who would later be seen on the stage. Past the huge, bright-red doors of the Cartoucherie, the audience becomes a group of travelers who have left Paris behind.

Ariane Mnouchkine practices a special "politique d'accueil" in her theater. She is present at every performance, greeting every member of the audience at the door, often by name. The actors are not "des

monstres sacrés" in the tradition of nineteenth-century French theater. In fact, the audience is invited to watch them dress and apply
makeup in a communal room clearly visible through a curtain made
up of split, floating panels. Mnouchkine's community of actors, musicians, and technicians aims at creating a bond of complicity and
friendship with the audience, a relationship full of respect, but
stripped of awe.

Beginning with her Kathakali/Noh Shakespeare performances,
Mnouchkine has developed a broad, almost caricatural acting style
for her international cast of actors. Artaud, Brecht, and Peter Brook
are her artistic ancestors in her work for the Théâtre du Soleil. What
is astonishing is the ensemble work of the company: the actors enter
and exit on the run, as though carried by the tidal wave of historical
events. There is a fluidity throughout the spectacles as flowing
garments are unfurled, sparkling bed linen is spread upon the
ground, and carpets are rolled out to define a sacred spot or a place
for diplomatic encounters.

The Brook/Mnouchkine phenomenon testifies to a creative breakdown of cultural boundaries, to the public's acceptance of an international stage language. Although the plays are performed in French,
it is the kind of French under which one hears a medley of other
tongues. It comes close to the glossolalia Artaud envisioned as the
perfect poetic language, a tongue free of rational Occidental forms.
The voices are only one element. Both Brook and Mnouchkine use
complex music that involves instruments from every part of the
world. In the *Mahabharata* we hear a *ney* (Turkish flute), a *cmanche*
(Iranian violin), a *nagaswaram* (South Indian oboe), and numerous
percussion instruments. Specifically Indian instruments, such as the
sitar, have been avoided, in order for the music to have only a
vaguely Indian coloring. The music is an aural metaphor that parallels the images created on the stage.

Peter Brook's and Ariane Mnouchkine's colossal undertakings are
not the only form of internationalization in Paris, known for its an-
nual Festival d'Automne, which attracts foreign companies and
dance groups. There is, however, a theater that has become a permanent international festival: Giorgio Strehler's Théâtre de l'Europe at
the venerable Odéon, a branch of the Comédie Française. Strehler
has done bold things for France and Europe. The Théâtre de
l'Europe, as its name indicates, plays host to foreign companies. To

attract to the Odéon a public willing to listen to a play in English or Italian is one thing, but Strehler has brought over plays in German, Swedish, and Russian. Moreover, the character of the productions themselves is highly international. To give one example, two years ago Strehler presented a magnificent production, *John Gabriel Bork-man*. It was performed in German translation and directed by Ingmar Bergman for the Munich Bayrisches Staatschauspiel-Residenz Thea-ter with Hans Michael Rehberg in the title role. Rehberg imparted a tragic grandeur to the role, playing it as though the dishonored em-bezzler were a kind of King Lear. Bergman's production was beauti-fully stark, concentrating on the conflict between the twin sisters who vie for possession of Borkman's only son. Paris flocked to this production of a Norwegian play in German translation, directed by a Swede. The Ibsen-Bergman-Rehberg combination was an artistic triumph and a social event.

In the same spirit, Strehler directed an Italian translation of Strind-berg's *Storm (Temporale)* with his Piccolo Teatro actors. Created in Milan, the production was brought over to the Odéon. Strehler im-parted an Italian verve to the production, creating an atmosphere that was not in the least northern. The stormy clash between the estranged spouses evoked Pirandello's *Six Characters in Search of an Author*. At a climactic point in the play, the protagonist, losing all self-control, leapt upon a chess table as if he were going to strangle the woman on the other side of it. Strehler took this late Strindberg play (1907) in the direction of symbolic action. In Ezio Frigerio's ele-gant, shimmering set, players in white frocks and summer suits were pitted against those wearing black; they became life-size pieces on the chess board. Lines were delivered deliberately and slowly. Styl-ized speech and movement lent a hieratic quality to the proceedings.

In the spring of 1986, Strehler invited his colleague Jean-Pierre Vincent, the director at that time of the Comédie Française, to stage Pirandello's *Six Characters* in French. Despite the translation, a for-eign coloring was imparted by the presence of the Italian actor Ugo Tognazzi in the role of the Father. Tognazzi managed to convey the feeling that the play, or at least his part of it, was being acted in Italian. He made us hear the original text behind the translation. Vincent emphasized what the critic Jean-Pierre Léonardi called "une latinité assumée et datée." Tognazzi's Franco-Italian vocal apparatus and his robust build lent the role of the Father Personaggio an unusual "thickness." Vincent also conveyed the disquieting aspect of the Characters by having them emerge slowly out of a black void at the back of the stage and walk up an invisible slope as though rising out of some unseen inferno. This image altered the one in the memory of those who saw the famous Pitoëff production of 1923, when the stage elevator of the Comédie des Champs-Elysées brought the Characters to the stage during "rehearsal." Pitoëff's elevator "made enigma palpable," wrote the *Nouvel Observateur* drama critic Guy Dumur. In Vincent's staging, the Characters remained enigmatic, haunting, yet they were—as they ought to be—more compelling than the so-called real actors in the process of rehearsing. The Father's gravelly voice suggested the horror of a human conscience caught in a past moment. Fifty years after Pirandello's death, the playwright's avant-garde drama proved to be ageless.

Still in the spirit of remembering this anniversary, Strehler invited the Teatro Stabile di Cantania to present its production of an early Pirandello, *Ciampa, Il Berretto a Sonagli (Cap and Bells)*. This splendid production of the rarely seen 1917 drama attracted the attention of the Parisian audience to a powerful, aging Sicilian actor, Turi Ferro, in the role of Ciampa, who vividly crystallizes the moral and artistic values of Pirandello's dramaturgy. The play posits the question, What is conscience?

Il Berretto a Sonagli is the story of a cuckolded husband, aware of his wife's betrayal, yet willing to endure the situation out of love for her. For a Sicilian male this is an astonishing compromise. Nor is there anything comical about Ciampa. He is in no way the figure of fun "wearing horns" that appears in French and Italian farces. One senses in this man a great inner strength coupled with bitter realism and metaphysical despair. On the other hand, the self-righteous spouse of the injuring party, Beatrice Fiorica, has no intention of practicing patience and abnegation. She lays a trap for her adulterous husband and Nina Ciampa and has them arrested. Ciampa, who wishes to avoid the outbreak of a public scandal that would force him to assert his rights, suggests to Beatrice's family that if they wish to avoid a major tragedy, the truth-clamoring woman must be declared mad and put away in an asylum.

Who is this Ciampa? No longer young, he has never made a success of his life. He is known as a public scribe, a kind of writer. Pirandello has imbued this character with mystery and ambiguity.

Ciampa knows that what is important is not the spoken word, but the realm of the unstated, the subtext. Certainly Beatrice has the facts on her side. The lovers (or are they?) have been caught in a room and arrested by Spano, the comical police officer. What will happen now? Ciampa explains calmly that a scandal will leave him with no recourse but to avenge his honor—he will be forced to kill his own wife and Beatrice's husband. In Sicily, he would undoubtedly go free after this crime of passion. There is, however, an alternative to this "solution": to have Beatrice declared mad, since only a crazy woman would entrap her own husband. If she is put away, the adulterous couple will be freed. Once declared officially insane, Beatrice could be allowed the pleasure of proclaiming the truth, of shouting it from the rooftop of her asylum, but nobody would lend an ear or give a second thought to what she says.

Thus, it is the cuckolded husband, who may at first have seemed foolish, who emerges as the powerful character. He imposes his will on a whole family, and this is made easy for him because he has nothing more to lose, having already lost the only thing he treasured. It is Pirandello's philosophy that we hear from Ciampa's lips: Society can work only by making use of hypocrisy.

Strehler's love for Pirandello informs many of his choices, particularly what he calls his "tetralogy" on the subject of illusion: Shakespeare's *Tempest*, Corneille's *L'Illusion Comique*, Eduardo de Filippo's *La Grande Magia*, and, most recently, Pirandello's rarely performed *Come tu mi vuoi (As You Desire Me)*. When Strehler was named director of Le Théâtre de l'Europe at the Odéon, he embarked on the French play in the tetralogy.[6] The work was postponed a year because of a mysterious virus that almost caused his death. After he recovered, he presented *L'Illusion*, one of Corneille's few comedies, as the opening program of his directorship. Then he moved his French production to the large Lyric Theatre in Milan. The play enjoyed an immense success. Thus, Strehler proved that a director's empire can spread freely, ignoring national boundaries and the limitations of linguistic barriers.

It is the fourth panel of the tetralogy, however, that expresses fully Strehler's program in founding Le Théâtre de l'Europe. Written in 1930 for the great actress Marta Abba, *Come tu mi vuoi* was presented a year later in the United States. It was made into a film in 1933, with Greta Garbo in the role of the Unknown Woman and Eric von Stroheim in that of her lover, the writer Carl Salter.

In January 1987, exactly one year before Strehler staged *Come tu mi vuoi* at the Piccolo Teatro, he delivered a lecture at the Paris Instituto Italiano on Eduardo de Filippo as writer and actor. He said: "Pirandello, and later Brecht, are the two dramatists who broke the mold, set the theatre free. We are all deeply in their debt." After his talk, Strehler revealed that he was at work on a rarely performed Pirandello play. He mentioned the Hollywood film *As You Desire Me*, judging it harshly, but he called Garbo "another Duse."

As he concluded the question period, he greeted a few acquaintances. We walked out together, and Strehler continued to talk about the work in progress. He explained that he found the play intriguing because it was not, as he saw it, only about illusion, but about mystery and self-knowledge, about the structuring and destructuring of the human personality. Set in Berlin a decade after World War I, the play presents a lost generation. It was inspired by an actual case of amnesia (the Bruneri-Canella affair) in which two families identified the same man as their relative; Pirandello based his Unknown Woman on this man. Strehler said that the "Garbo character" might be an Italian from the region of Venice who speaks perfect German and has somehow been carried to Berlin by the tides of war, or she might be a German woman who speaks perfect Italian. "The point is," he added,

> that we will never find out the truth about her origins. . . . I will have some of the characters speak German, particularly in Act I, in Berlin. I plan to invite some German actors to join the Piccolo company for this production. There will be constant shifts from German to Italian, Italian to German. This is essential for the preservation of the ambiguity surrounding the main character's origins. If I fail to identify a suitable translation, we will do it ourselves. The play has never been staged in this way before, but the situation is very familiar to me; it was in fact that of my Triestine family.

I recalled that when I interviewed Strehler for the *New York Times* in connection with his production of Shakespeare's *The Tempest*, he told me that there was always a process of translation going on at the family table. An uncle had to translate for his Austrian wife what was being said in Italian, or the German comments of some member of the family had to be repeated in Italian. "We had epic fights in two languages," he said, "and even some dialects were thrown in. I grew up completely bilingual, as most descendants of the Austro-Hungarian empire. Later I added French and English." Strehler's wife, the actress Andrea Jonasson, is German. She is a member of the Vienna Burg Teater, but she also appears with the Piccolo, as she did in the role of the Unknown Woman. "We go back and forth between Milan, Paris, Vienna," the director sighed, adding, "I suppose this is what it means to be a European."

A European man who is now in his early sixties, Strehler spent his formative years caught in the tidal wave of fascism. As an adolescent he joined the Italian resistance movement and went into hiding. While in the underground he could not study. "There's a kind of void, a black hole in my youth," he says. Hard as they were, those years shaped his character and determined his leftist political commitment. Thus, Strehler brings a special understanding of Pirandello's Unknown Woman to his production. "She's a creature destroyed by the war," he explains. The play does not reveal what had actually happened to her, although she hints at all kinds of indignities and violence. Between the lines we decipher mass rape, followed by years of wandering and uprootedness. The Unknown Woman is the perfect symbol of twentieth-century Europe. Because she seems to have no knowledge of who she was and is, and has in fact become a nonperson, she is able to step into any role waiting for her. Mentally and culturally, she stands at the crossroads, the eternal stranger and wanderer, the actor par excellence. For the length of Pirandello's drama, playing many roles will be her only self-definition.

When we meet the Unknown Woman a few minutes into Act 1, she is a night-club entertainer, one of the many "dancers and vice-ridden young girls" Pirandello himself encountered during his stay in Berlin (1929–30). She is living with the writer Carl Salter, who has left his wife for this seductress. Dispatched by her mother to get Salter out of the clutches of this femme fatale, Mop, Salter's daughter, has fallen in love with her father's mistress. Life between these rivals— the failed, sterile writer and the masochistic lesbian—has become unbearable for the Unknown Woman, whose German name is Elma. The name means "water" in Arabic, and indeed the Unknown Woman is as fluid, as elusive, as this element. Water, however, is not what the lady drinks; day after day she is high on champagne. She drinks to forget some terrible past, to escape from a tormenting present.

When she bursts into Salter's apartment, dressed in a shimmering gold lamé gown and a sumptuous fur coat, she is followed by four reeling young suitors, each one speaking a different language (English, French, Spanish, German). A strange Italian man slips in with them, observing the woman. He is a famous photographer, the inventor of the "stereoscopic portrait." Physical likeness, the reproduction of reality, is this man's métier and passion. When he calls Elma by another name, Madame Lucia (this name means "light"), and assures her that he has known her from the time she was a child, everyone, including the object of his attention, is taken aback. Boffi, the photographer, states that Madame Lucia's loving husband, Bruno Pieri, has been called by him to Berlin and now awaits his wife's telephone call. Elma could become Bruno's "little Cia," the bride who was raped by German officers in her home near Venice, and who disappeared for years somewhere in Germany. The Unknown Woman embraces these memories, which may or may not be hers. A new path appears under her wandering feet: a new life opens.

Pirandello explores in depth the theme of the double in this play. Elma/Lucia leaves with Bruno, abandoning Salter, who melodramatically tries to shoot himself. In Strehler's production, she turns and turns, whirling at the center of the stage, unable at first to make up her mind whether to follow Boffi or to stay at the side of her wounded lover. Then she walks down into the audience; and from the center aisle whispers: "I'm nothing but a body, a nameless body, waiting for someone to take hold of it. Let him create me anew, give to this flesh the soul of his little Cia . . . let him pour new life into me, since I am nothing but despair."

In Italy, Lucia's closest relatives recognize her in the Unknown Woman, as did Bruno the moment he saw the beautiful stranger. No one seems to realize that after ten years of unbearable physical and emotional pain, Bruno's bride would not be likely to look like the radiant creature in the formal portrait whose hairstyle and old-fashioned lace dress the Unknown Woman copies after her arrival. Their peaceful family life is shattered, however, by the news that Salter, who has recovered from his failed suicide attempt, is arriving with a madwoman he has found in a Vienna hospital—the "real" Lucia.

When the latter appears in act 3, no one believes she is Lucia, even though she calls to Lena, the kind aunt who brought her up. Lena herself, though deeply shaken, turns away from her. At this point, the Unknown Woman, now dressed in simple black like the madwoman, walks up to her, saying, "I am the first to say that Cia might also be this woman. No certainty can exist the moment it is sapped by doubt." Having restructured her personality through the supreme art of acting out a role, Elma/Lucia, the bilingual double who symbolizes a torn, war-ravaged Europe, is ready to walk out again, to return to Berlin with Salter, whose dogged persistence and readiness to give up his life have won, if not her affection, at least a kind of respect.

Elma/Lucia is also Giorgio Strehler, the European artist, divided in so many ways and yet all the stronger for it. Like Pirandello, whom he admires and has often staged, the director of Le Théâtre de l'Europe is keenly aware that there is no single reality, that one must be able to maintain at least two distinct, often opposite truths at the same time.

World War II and the Holocaust have taught European artists that they cannot settle for simple answers, or even for simple questions. The internationalized stage of today is much more than the McLuhan "global village." Modern thinkers are wary of utopian visions glimpsed through the haze of hallucinatory mushrooms or so-called mind-expanding drugs. More than ever before in the short history of man on this planet, one is aware of the absurd, tragic dimensions of life. In an address at the conference of Nobel Prize winners held at the Elysée Palace in Paris (January 1988), Elie Wiesel made the following statement: "We are assembled here because we know that what happens in one place on our planet affects every other place." He concluded by quoting from one of the Hassidic masters: "If you wish to find a spark, look for it in the ashes." In Europe, the ashes—the memories—are never buried, but hope, phoenixlike, has started to rise again. The internationalization of the stage testifies to the healthy spirit of openness, to the break with narrow nationalisms and rigid traditions. By studying, by traveling, and by inviting to their stage the languages and cultures of many lands, directors are shaping the not-so-absurd dream of reconciliation and peace.

NOTES

Editors' Note: The subject of this essay was first explored by the author in a talk presented at the Guggenheim Museum in New York on October 9, 1986. In March 1988 Lamont further developed these ideas at the Mid-America Theatre Conference.

1. This is the title of chapter 1 of Richard Schechner's *Between Theater and Anthropology* (Philadelphia: University of Pennsylvania Press, 1985). Page references for quotations from Schechner's book will be given in parentheses in my text.

2. Gautam Dasgupta, "The *Mahabharata:* Peter Brook's 'Orientalism,'" *Performing Arts Journal* 30 10, no. 3 (1987): 9–16. See also Patrice Pavis, "Interculturalism in Contemporary Mise-en-Scène: The Image of India in 'The Mahabharata' and 'The Indiade'" in *The Dramatic Touch of Difference,* ed. Erika Fischer-Lichte, Josephine Riley and Michael Gissenwehrer (Tübingen: Gunter Narr Verlag, 1990).

3. The term was first used by Eugenio Barba, founder of the Odin Theater in Denmark and of the International School of Theater Anthropology (ISTA). He spoke of "theater anthropology" in a lecture delivered in Warsaw in 1980. See also Anne-Marie Picard, "*L'Indiade:* Ariane's and Hélène's Conjugate Dreams," *Modern Drama* 32, no. 1 (March 1989): 24–38.

4. Dasgupta, "*Mahabharata,*" 10.

5. Ibid., 13.

6. Giorgio Strehler has staged few French plays at the Odéon other than this initial production of Corneille's *L'Illusion Comique.* Many of the plays at the Odéon are performed in such languages as Hungarian and Russian, which are highly unfamiliar even to very cultured French theatergoers. No overtitles are used, and most of the time there is no recorded simultaneous translation. Occasionally, a foreign director will be invited to offer a French translation of a play written in his or her native language, but this is the exception rather than the rule.

Framing Actuality: Thirty Years of Experimental Theater, 1959–89

Theodore Shank

One of the most striking artistic developments since the publication of Martin Esslin's definitive book on the theater of the absurd has been an energetic and inventive experimental theater that is not predominantly text-based, that tends to blur the line between the arts, and that often keeps the spectators conscious of some aspects of their actual physical and/or social environment. Playwrights have put actuality into their work in a variety of ways: (1) by focusing on events in the real world in works advocating social change; (2) by using themselves—their actual mental processes, their reactions, or events from their lives—as the content of their work; (3) by using task acting as the performance mode and having performers present themselves rather than fictional characters; (4) by framing actual events and locales as art; (5) by aiming, even when actors create fictional characters, not to hide the performer but to present both performer and character so that the spectator sometimes relates to both the fictional and the actual person.

There were two other important characteristics of experimental theater work during these thirty years. First, the typical method of making new plays was autonomous creation. Instead of the conventional two-process method—a playwright writing a play and other artists staging it—in the experimental theater of this period the same artists developed the work from initial conception to finished performance. Second, there was a shift from reliance on language as a means of artistic communication; visual means became predominant. In the sixties and early seventies many of the new theaters were part of an alternative culture that not only recognized the shortcomings of language in expressing experiential concepts, but distrusted it as a means of communicating truth.

Despite some similarities, the experimental theater in the United States and in Eastern and Western Europe during the last thirty years has taken a variety of forms as artists have invented and adapted techniques to express artistic concepts reflecting the changing culture. The absurdists themselves had been experimental artists who had rejected old forms for new, and as a consequence the experimental artists of the sixties, seventies, and eighties were relieved of the burden of realism. The conventions of realism, which imply faith in the scientific method, and which were most expressive of how it felt to live in a former time, could not serve the needs of the absurdists, so the absurdists invented nonrealistic, expressionistic forms that embodied their concepts of how it felt to be alive in a world without purpose—a world that, having already lost God as a unifying principle explaining existence, was now losing science. Esslin has discussed with insightful detail the techniques and conventions eschewed by the absurdists and the new techniques they invented to express their conceptions of the world.

At the same time artists working in other media were also rejecting the ways of traditional art. The abstract expressionist painters had given up representational iconography. Their paintings attempted to express more directly the feeling of being alive in absurd times by rejecting conventional technique, composition, and pictorial ideas. Some, going even further, rejected the static nature of conventional painting and sculpture and created works with moving parts sometimes driven by motors. However, the innovation in the visual arts of this period that had the most important impact on the experimental theater was the concept of the "Happening" in which live human beings became part of the work of art.

In 1959, two years before Martin Esslin's *Theatre of the Absurd* was published, the painter Allan Kaprow presented his first Happening. In his book *Assemblage, Environments, and Happenings*, published several years later, he traced the break with convention back to the making of collages and assemblages earlier in the century. The principal innovation in these forms was the introduction of materials and objects that, unlike the neutral medium of paint, had a meaning in the real world. An example is a famous 1913 "ready-made" of Marcel Duchamp, consisting of a bicycle wheel mounted on top of a kitchen stool. In his Happenings Kaprow went beyond assemblage, however, extending his real-world materials to include human activities.

Kaprow set down seven "rules of thumb" for Happenings, guidelines that parallel some of the practices of experimental theater from the sixties to the present (Kaprow, 188–207). The most fundamental of these was that the "line between art and life should be kept as fluid, and perhaps indistinct, as possible." The mode of performance inspired by this objective was "task acting," which became the typical mode in the experimental theater of the late seventies and the eighties. It is noteworthy that formalists such as Robert Wilson and Alan Finneran were visual artists before beginning to work in the theater.

As early as 1964 the Living Theatre used task acting in *Mysteries and Other Pieces*. This work was first presented in Paris, where the directors of the company, Judith Malina and Julian Beck, were voluntary fugitives from the U.S. Internal Revenue Service. The production consisted primarily of theater games and exercises that did not create a fictional illusion. Performers wore their own clothes and did not play characters. The piece was perceived as existing in actual time and place, like other events such as parades, circuses, football games, or weddings. There was no set and no attempt to create an illusion of a place other than the theater or a time other than the actual time of the performance. For example, the performance began with a man standing at attention, unmoving, facing the audience for about six minutes. Other performers walked through the aisles chanting the words inscribed on a U.S. dollar bill. A woman on stage improvised a Hindu raga in Sanskrit. These and other events of the performance were simply tasks that created no fictional illusion of character, place, or time. The only hint of an illusion occurred in the final segment, which was inspired by Artaud. The performers, in the aisles, enacted the physical symptoms of the plague as they crawled, writhed, died, and were arranged in a pile by other performers.

Task acting became more important a decade later; in the sixties another mode of performance was explored by Jerzy Grotowski of the

Polish Laboratory Theatre (formed in 1959) and Joseph Chaikin of the Open Theatre in New York (1963). While these directors did not avoid illusion, their primary focus was elsewhere. They were reacting against the superficiality and pretense of realistic acting; they trained their performers in an expressionistic kind of acting that revealed the genuine subjective responses of the performer. Grotowski put into focus the actual responses of the body and voice by attempting to eliminate the social mask and all other impediments between impulse and reaction. He developed psychophysical exercises to eliminate the disparity between the actor's physical and psychic functions. Chaikin borrowed and invented similar exercises to get beyond realistic, exterior, socialized behavior. He wanted performers to play the "inside" of a situation or character rather than the realistic "outside." Psychophysical exercises and abstract nonverbal improvisation became the principal means of discovering "the inside" and creating material for a production. Thus it was the performance—consisting of the performer's inner, genuine responses—that led to Chaikin's concept of "presence." In the work of the Open Theatre and the Polish Laboratory Theatre it was not the fictional character who was put into focus; it was the actor, stripped of habitual social behavior.

Task acting and the new expressionistic acting developed by Grotowski and Chaikin have some similarities. Both put into focus the performer rather than an illusion of character. Task acting, however, even when physically arduous, made no demands on the psyches of the performers—they simply went through the required motions; the expressionistic actors, on the other hand, were expected to go beneath the socialized surface of their behavior and present their deepest inner responses. Both of these modes of performance have continued to influence experimental theater productions.

The fifties and early sixties were a period of reaction against artistic conventions, whether the restrictions were those of traditional iconography and the confining frame of the visual arts or the realism of the theater. However, by the mid-sixties a more positive focus had come about in some segments of the Western world, and especially in the United States. The main focus was no longer the rejection of conventions or the alienation of the individual in an absurd world. The principle of social justice for all became a rallying cry at the center of an alternative culture. The energy of believers in this culture became concentrated in the civil rights movement, which attempted to bring equal opportunity, justice, and political enfranchisement to all; and, not unrelated, many of the same people were attempting to bring an end to U.S. involvement in the Vietnam War—a war that seemed to be attempting to deprive people in a Third World country of self-determination.

Many of the alternative theaters of the time reflected the attitudes of the alternative culture and created performances they hoped would help bring about the desired change in society. Instead of concentrating on the alienation of the individual in an absurd world, they expressed the solidarity of the community in their social aims. People were fundamentally good; the government was the problem because it failed to reflect the needs of the disenfranchised. Those who were part of the alternative culture tended to focus on the human spirit rather than on appearances or materiality. The artifices of makeup, hairdos, and fine clothes were eschewed. Personal material gain was not important; the group, not the individual, was the important entity. Together, as a community, the people could develop enough political power to bring about the needed changes. It was a period of idealism.

The Activist Years

In the late sixties and most of the seventies many of the experimental theaters reflected the alternative culture. Instead of the individual playwright expressing personal concerns, performances were created by a group working collectively expressing community concerns. Sometimes this community was an ethnic minority. The Free Southern Theatre, formed in Mississippi in 1963, aimed to reflect the cultural and historical experience of blacks. Under the leadership of Gilbert Moses and John O'Neal, the company hoped to develop self-esteem among its black audiences; further, it set out to educate them about the causes of their oppression and to indicate the means for alleviating it. Other black companies with similar intentions were soon formed in other major U.S. cities and in London. El Teatro Campesino was founded in California in 1965 by Luis Valdez to support the Mexican-American agricultural workers who were attempting to form a union; within a few years it expanded its constituency to include urban Hispanic-Americans as well. Other companies were formed in the late sixties and early seventies to present the perspective of a variety of disadvantaged groups—women, gays, and lesbi-ans, to mention the most active. Examples of feminist companies were the It's Alright to Be Woman Theatre in New York, the Women's Theatre Group and Monstrous Regiment in London, and Lilith in San Francisco. Gay companies include the Play-House of the Ridiculous and the Ridiculous Theatrical Company in New York, the Cockettes and the Angels of Light in San Francisco, and the Gay Sweatshop in London, which also supported a lesbian company of the same name. Some of the companies dedicated to social change had a broader political perspective and concerned themselves with a variety of government ills in their own countries—the San Francisco Mime Troupe in the United States, Red Ladder (originally AgitProp Theatre) in England, Théâtre du Soleil in France, Die Grips in Ger-many. The structures of all these theater groups reflected their politi-cal objectives. They were formed as collectives rather than along the lines of a traditional artistic hierarchy, and their creative process was democratic and collaborative rather than authoritarian. These compa-nies shared the conviction of Ariane Mnouchkine of Théâtre du Soleil that the political development of a group cannot be ahead of how the group lives and works. A group advocating the socialist ideal natu-rally considered it important to reflect that ideal in its company structure. This also served as one way to present a model of the better life that could be achieved through political action.

Another way of demonstrating the better life was through the spirit and circumstances of the performance and its relationship to the audience. Joan Holden of the San Francisco Mime Troupe has mentioned the astonished delight of people in a city park who hap-pen upon an energetic group of actors and musicians. The people say, "This is the way it ought to be!" The brightly painted circus caravans that were the homes of the Welfare State Group contrasted sharply with the drab English industrial town in which they were parked and provided a model of a better world, which attracted citi-zens to participate in the preparation of performances. The circus atmosphere of performances by the French group le Grand Magic Circus presented a model of freedom and friendly interaction that contrasted with the isolation and repressive atmosphere of the spec-tators' lives. Such positive models were especially important because the performances were often concerned with the negative aspects of the existing order.

Some theaters for social change were formed to serve specific purposes. The socialist company AgitProp Theatre initially set out in 1968 to organize government housing tenants in London against rent increases. Subsequently they established a relationship with the labor movement in England and presented many of their short plays for trade union organizations at meetings, demonstrations, and strikes; longer plays were developed for a full evening's entertainment at labor clubs. Whenever possible, performances were followed by discussions of the issues raised. Both the short and longer plays presented visual images of the issues at hand in a style similar to that of a political cartoon. One of AgitProp's fifteen-minute collectively developed plays, *The Industrial Relations Act* (1971), responded to specific legislation of the Conservative government headed by Prime Minister Edward Heath. A boss wearing a large top hat decorated with a union jack sits at the top of a tall red stepladder. Three bakery workers wearing white smocks and caps present the boss with a giant cake. He gives them their wages, which they return for a piece of cake. The boss wants productivity increased, so the workers provide additional tiers of cake for which they receive more money, which they pay back to the boss in exchange for a slice of cake. The slice, though costing more, is no larger than before because of rising costs and inflation. The workers take a knife labeled "strike," with which they poke their reluctant union leadership into action. The boss feels faint and requires the assistance of Dr. Heath, who offers to prop up the boss with the Industrial Relations Act, which provides for a cooling-off period, a binding agreement, and a threatened fine. The bakers realize that worker control is the only solution. "We don't just want more cake," they shout, "we want the bloody bakery."

A socialist group in Portugal had more compelling reasons for creating its plays largely from visual images. Communa Teatro de Pesquisa was formed before the revolution at a time when governmental censorship of texts was thorough. To avoid difficulties, the text for *La Cene* (*Supper*, 1972) was taken from such sources as the Bible, the Koran, and traditional Portuguese poets. However, the central visual image consisted of a giant dining table where figures representing the government and the clergy sit down to dine on peasants, workers, and soldiers. In Venezuela the Rajatabla Taller de Teatro, formed in 1971, presented the story of the legendary simple man, Juan Bimba, in the production *La Juanbimbada* (1975). Juan is exploited, tortured, and humiliated, but he never gives up trying to improve his circumstances.

Several companies have involved members of specific social groups in developing plays about the circumstances of those groups. The first performances by Teatro Campesino were actually developed from improvisations by field workers. The production of *It Makes You Sick* (1975) by Red Ladder Theatre was made with the suggestions, criticism, and participation of workers in the National Health Service. *The Lump* (1975), concerning nonunion workers in the construction trade, was developed over a period of three months by the London company Broadside Mobile Workers Theatre, which met frequently with a group of construction workers who supplied many of the ideas. Teatro de la Candelaria in Columbia did its research for *La Ciudad Dorada* (1974) among workers and peasants. This provided the basis for improvisations from which the play was extracted; workers and peasant leaders were then invited to critique the rehearsals and suggest improvements. The play presents the problems of a peasant family that, having lost its tiny farm, moves to "the golden city" where the family is destroyed by the credit system and the tensions and diversions of city life. In Paris, Théâtre du Soleil developed *L'Age d'Or* (1975) from discussions with workers in factories, mines, hospitals, and schools. The National Theatre in Iceland was formed in 1972 to make a play about the culture of the Greenland Eskimos, which was vanishing with the influx of European commercial interests. The group lived among the Eskimos, researching their culture and learning dances and songs from the old people who still remembered them. This research culminated in a collectively developed documentary contrasting the time before the Europeans, when life was integrated with nature, with the disintegration of the culture after the introduction of European products. Mascarones in Mexico lived for more than a year among peasant peanut farmers, studying their indigenous language and culture, before making *Don Cacamafer* (1974), which concerned the way these peasants were being cheated by corporate buyers. Théâtre Quotidien in France developed *Dorénavant (Henceforth,* 1977) after extensive research into the lives of workers living in Bobigny. The performance depicts archaeologists of the future unearthing relics of what might have been Bobigny in the 1970s. The recorded language accompanying the performance is that of the people of Bobigny telling of their daily lives.

The Ambulantes de Puebla (Street Vendors of Puebla) took all of the events for their plays from their own actual experience. These outcast descendants of the indigenous Mexican people, like other street vendors in the city, supported themselves by selling their meager merchandise. However, in 1974 they spent two days each week performing for other street sellers a literal enactment of the harassments they suffered in their daily lives from police and shopkeepers. These performances were presented on the street in a style resembling a naive version of the Keystone Cops, with police helmets made of discarded soccer balls cut in half. The performances served as a means of communicating with other street vendors and organizing them into a united force to improve their impoverished lives.

The style of acting developed for these productions dealing with political issues is quite different from the task acting of the Happenings and the expressionistic acting of Grotowski's company and the Open Theatre. In the case of the Ambulantes, the style was apparently instinctive, in the spirit of play; the more sophisticated companies, however, developed a specific style to serve a particular purpose in addition to the fundamental need to entertain. Unlike the conventional realistic play, which is intended to absorb the audience into the illusion of a fictional world, theater companies advocating social change direct the focus of their spectators to the actual world where the change is to take place. The spectators are intended to relate the events depicted to what they know of the existing world. This requires a style of performance in which the viewers can be conscious simultaneously (or nearly so) of the images of the play, the real-world situation to which the play refers, and the ideological analysis being presented. Nearly always the political theater companies have hit upon a style that in theory is similar to Brecht and in practice suggests a combination of the mime of Chaplin and the style of a modern commedia dell'arte troupe. The performer *demonstrates* the character rather than *becoming* the character and interacts with the audience in such a way that the audience is always aware not only of the fictional character but of the performer creating it. It is as if the performers were saying to the spectators, "We're in the same world and must deal with the same problems. Here is one of the problems; we'll act it out for you." The performance becomes a demonstration, a visualization, of a political issue. The performers try to create a community of themselves and the audience who, it is hoped, having become united by the performance and having acquired an understanding of the issue presented, will be moved to action. The interaction between performers and audience can happen only if the performers are present (not merely the characters) and the spectators are also present (not wholly absorbed in a fictional illusion). Some companies have followed their performances with discussions that help the audience determine a course of action, such as joining a tenants' association, forming a union, or going on strike.

A performance style that allows the spectators to be conscious of themselves and each other makes possible the formation of a community that has the ability to act together as a group. So, as with task acting, the spectators are not absorbed into the illusion; but unlike Happenings, there is a fictional illusion and a clear narrative, even if the characters are no more complex than a boss sitting at the top of a ladder while he is served by workers.

Collective creation was the typical method of the alternative theater companies in the sixties and early seventies. For those socialist groups advocating social change, this democratic process resulted from an insistence that the structure of a company and the working relationships within it be a model of the new society being proposed. Such idealism was not without its problems. For example, at the outset Red Ladder made all decisions by unanimous agreement, which resulted in vast amounts of time being spent in making trivial decisions. In Red Ladder and some other groups, everyone did everything—regardless of training, skill, or interest. A more practical structure was that of the San Francisco Mime Troupe after 1970 when its director, R. G. Davis, was replaced by a collective. While directors and playwrights were not usually identified publicly, internally one or more members were chosen to fulfill these functions and were responsible to the group as a whole. The group, through discussions and research, determined the subject for a play, discussed the scenario as it developed, criticized the script as it was written, and made directorial comments during rehearsal.

Even for groups whose work did not advocate social change, the process by which works were created was as important as the product that resulted. There was no hierarchy. The plays were developed through discussion, improvisation, and rehearsal involving the entire group. This method contrasted strongly with that of the established theater, which had developed a method based on individual specialties, with a hierarchy that aimed at creating a commercial product. The alternative theater companies, while intending to entertain, were not much concerned with the commercial aspects of their work. They were, however, interested in a working process that would improve the quality of their lives and perhaps serve as a model for others.

The Reflexive Years

In the United States, groups of political activists working together as a communal force through the sixties and early seventies exerted sufficient pressure on the government to bring about changes. Civil rights activists achieved legal parity for their constituents, though actual parity is still only a hope. Antiwar activists brought an end to the war in Vietnam. The alternative culture believed in community action; the pronoun of the time was "we." But as time passed through the late seventies and into the eighties, "I" again became the dominant pronoun.

As in the fifties, the artists of the eighties no longer felt themselves to be a part of the dominant culture, but the alternative community of the sixties and early seventies had largely disbanded. As always, the experimental art of the time reflected the experience of the artists. Although the artists of the eighties were self-focused, unlike the absurdists they did not suffer from an existential angst leading to alienation; like others in the eighties, they were disengaged. And, instead of their focus being directed outward toward society, as in the sixties and early seventies, they were more inclined to face inward. They created concepts that were self-focused and reflexive, expressing their individual feelings about themselves and their art. They devised a great variety of individualistic, nonrealistic forms to express their emotive concepts.

A different experimental theater structure began to emerge in the seventies and became dominant in the eighties—a structure reflecting a revived focus on the individual artist instead of the group. The new companies, often formed around a single dominant artist who combined the traditional functions of playwright, director, and designer, were structured as an artistic hierarchy rather than as a democratic group. The result was increased subjectivity and a renewed focus on the expression of individual artists—their attitudes, emotions, and mental processes—rather than collective expression.

Several directors rose to prominence who, even in productions that were strongly text-based, where predominantly concerned with individual artistic expression—André Serban, Peter Sellars, Des McAnuff, Robert Woodruff, Lucian Pintilie, Liviu Ciulei, Luca Ronconi, Yuri Lyubimov, and Anatoli Vasiliev. Sometimes the texts were deconstructed so as to avoid the original concept of the playwright altogether. In some ways the practice was similar to that of Shakespeare and Brecht, who had used earlier material for their own ends. A difference was that these more recent artists were directors rather than playwrights.

Whether the primary artist worked with existing texts or developed new material, the experimental theater of the eighties expressed in nonrealistic form the subjective emotive experience of the artist. In part the shift of artistic responsibility from the theater group to the individual artist was reinforced by the emergence of directors who previously had worked as visual artists, choreographers, or composers. Painters and sculptors such as Robert Wilson, Tadeusz Kantor, Laura Farabough, Chris Hardman, and Alan Finneran were accustomed to having total artistic responsibility and not to working collaboratively. Choreographers such as Pina Bausch, Martha Clarke, Meredith Monk, Anna Teresa de Keersmaeker, Sarah Shelton Mann, and Joe Goode typically created their private artistic visions even though they collaborated with others in making them concrete. Composers such as Philip Glass, Paul Dresher, and Georges Aperghis, because of the nature of musical scores, were accustomed to controlling their works to a much greater extent than was usual in the theater.

Task Acting and Formalism

Improvisation had been one of the principal techniques used by alternative theaters of the sixties and early seventies. It was a chief means of collective creation because everyone could contribute to the work from the earliest formative stage. It also served to train members of the group to work creatively and collectively and to suggest initial concepts for new pieces. It was often the means by which embryonic ideas were developed into finished productions. This was the practice of the Open Theatre and the Performance Group. There are also instances in which improvisation has been used by companies that were not collectives at all but that have had, in fact, rather strict hierarchies. In San Francisco, George Coates chooses for each production performers with particular skills—opera singing, wrestling, mime, etc. In rehearsal improvisations he pushes the performers beyond the rational and scores selected images, activities, and sounds into a production that presents the performers' skills in an unconventional way. Some companies, such as the People Show in London, improvise their performance in front of the audience, following a rough scenario. This practice emphasizes performer presence by putting focus on the task of performing. We become aware of the performer dealing with the concrete, immediate creation of the performance. It involves risk, it gives the work an edge, and it is exhilarating for the performers and spectators, who can interact because the performance is loose enough to accommodate the unforeseen.

In the late seventies and the eighties another mode of performance became prominent—one that gave the director much more control than was possible with improvisation. Improvisation requires a creatively active mind to deal with each moment, while task acting is often relatively perfunctory. The performances of the Living Theatre, beginning with *Mysteries and Other Pieces*, had used task acting in that the performers did not play characters; but insofar as the performers made their own choices in performance, there was an improvisational element. In task acting the performers do not play characters other than themselves, nor do they enact emotions as in conventional realistic acting. Rarely are they required to go beneath the social mask to their own actual responses, as was required by the expressionistic acting of the Open Theatre and Grotowski's company. At its most minimal, task acting simply requires the performers to follow the detailed instructions of the director-playwright as they engage in the manipulation of objects. However, in some instances the tasks may be physically arduous or demand extraordinary concentration.

In its simplest form, task acting is like the mode of performance used in Happenings, where the untrained participants simply followed instructions as they performed unrehearsed activities. In one of the first events of the People Show, formed in London in 1966, each of eighteen spectator-participants received at home a yellow suitcase, two bolts, and a set of instructions. Each was instructed to carry the suitcase around in a certain section of Soho at a particular time until he or she met someone else carrying a yellow suitcase. The

two introduced themselves, bolted their suitcases together end to
end, and continued walking. This process was repeated until all eighteen suitcases were bolted together. Then all eighteen people, carrying their joined suitcases, marched to Trafalgar Square, where they
separated. Each person then intentionally lost his or her suitcase on
some form of public transportation. Such an event created no illusion, and, except for the participant-spectators, the audience happened upon the performance by chance.

The theatrical formalists of the late seventies took over the task
acting of the Happening and such events as the People Show's *Yellow
Suitcases*. It was quite natural to do so, as many of the theatrical
formalists began as painters or sculptors and the Happening had
been invented by visual artists. These visual artists, in rejecting the
conventional limitations of their media, began to incorporate real-
world objects in their collages and then proceeded to incorporate
real-world tasks as well. The formalist directors considered these
tasks to be no more important than other elements of the production,
such as objects, environment, or sound. All elements were strictly
organized into a structure that became the most important content
of the work, regardless of the material used. Allan Kaprow, the theo-
rist and maker of Happenings, wrote that in formal art, "as in a chess
game, the manipulation is intellectual . . . elements of the work are
moved according to strict, sometimes self-imposed regulations. The
weaving of these elements . . . is the fascination of such an art." Kaprow adds that care must be taken not to choose elements with such
powerful overtones that they take the focus from the form and its
manipulation. The impact of the imagery must not be as important
as the moves the imagery is put through (Kaprow, 201).

Robert Wilson's five-hour opera *Einstein on the Beach* (1976) is an
example of a formalist work with a mathematical structure. The opera
has nine scenes, and there are three dominant visual images: (1) a
train and a building, (2) a courtroom and a bed, and (3) a field with
a spaceship. Each of the images appears in every third scene so that
each is used three times. Not only do images recur on a mathematical
schedule, but the postmodern choreography of Andrew de Groat and
Lucinda Childs and the music of minimalist composer Philip Glass
were also precisely constructed on numerical systems. The only
words sung are the numbers one through eight and the *sol* and *fa*
syllables. Glass says that the singers were required to do everything

by numbers, sometimes counting two or three things at once—the numbers they were singing, the measures, and the speed of a movement such as bringing a finger to the upper lip on a count of thirty-two.

The "task-activated landscapes" of Alan Finneran, the playwright-director-designer of SOON 3 in San Francisco, are other examples of formalist structures. The landscape of *Black Water Echo* (1977) was defined by a square of black plastic. At the sides of the square were neatly arranged all of the objects to be used in the performance—doughnut-shaped fluorescent lights, small plexiglass houses, plastic tubes. These were moved around in the space according to a precisely devised scheme. In later work, such as *A Wall in Venice / 3 Women / Wet Shadows* (1978), Finneran might name a place and introduce a fragmented narrative, but these elements were used merely to color the way the other elements were perceived and stimulate the audience's projection onto them. The spectator was led to focus on the actual objects and tasks in the concrete present, not seduced into a psychic involvement with fictional time, place, and characters.

In the case of the French company Atelier Théâtre et Musique (ATEM), the tasks are actual gestures and sounds observed by the artists in a particular environment; these are then precisely scored by composer George Aperghis, the director of the company. Work on *Sans Paroles (Without Words*, 1978) began with acute observation of Bagnolet residents at a café—their gestures, facial expressions, nonverbal sounds, and frequently spoken words. Certain of these gestures, sounds, and words were chosen and structured according to one of the "systems" that are part of the "grammar" developed by Aperghis and his group. The first performance of this piece was presented at a café where the performers were surrounded by unsuspecting customers; subsequently it was performed in other spaces arranged with café tables. Each element in the *Sans Paroles* score below is precisely determined in advance except the "free gestures," which are left entirely to the improvisation of the actors. "Gesture 1," for example, is exactly the same gesture each time it appears in the score. The score for *Sans Paroles*, like those for other works, is performed as a round *(en canon)*. Actor 1 performs the first line alone; when actor 1 begins the second line, actor 2 begins the first line; when actor 1 begins the third line, actor 2 begins the second line and actor 3 begins the first line, etc.

1. Gesture 1
2. Gesture 1 / Sound 1
3. Gesture 1 / Sound 1 / Phrase 1
4. Gesture 1 / Sound 1 / Free Gesture / Gesture 2
5. Gesture 1 / Sound 1 / Phrase 1 / Gesture 2 / Sound 2
6. Gesture 1 / Sound 1 / Free Gesture / Gesture 2 / Sound 2 / Phrase 2
7. Gesture 1 / Sound 1 / Free Gesture / Gesture 2 / Sound 2 / Phrase 2 /Gesture 3

The sounds for this performance included eating potato chips, scraping feet in gravel, belching, gurgling, and whistling for the waiter. Gestures included pouring fruit juice, serving food, offering food to a companion, snapping fingers for the waiter, and standing and dropping coins on the table.

The repetitive tasks in the work of ATEM require great concentration, but they are not physically arduous and do not reveal the performer under stress, as do the tasks in the work of some other companies that use repetition even when the work is not strictly formalist. In *Café Müller*, by Pina Bausch's Tanztheater Wuppertal, a woman is hugged by a man; when he releases his grasp, she slips to the floor. She picks herself up to be hugged again, and again slips to the floor, over and over again. Kate Manheim, the principal performer in many of the productions of Richard Foreman in New York, consciously devises difficult movements that require her to struggle. She is thereby revealed without her social mask, in somewhat the same way as are the performers working in the expressionistic acting style of Jerzy Grotowski or Joe Chaikin.

The Self as Art Object

In the work of Chaikin and Grotowski self-revelation was not the principal objective, though it was an element. However, there were a number of artists who made themselves the primary focus of their work, and task acting was the performance mode they used. For these artists some aspect of self became the principal content of their productions and sometimes the chief material from which the productions were made. In some of the works the content was the artist's own cognitive and perceptual processes, in others it was autobiographical incidents, and in still other the artists presented themselves on stage as themselves, but in such a way that it was not clear what was actual and what was illusion.

Some of those artists who entered theater from the visual arts seemed to pick up where Happenings left off. They created events in which they literally became the art objects and erased the line between performance and life. In some instances the events became works of art only because they were "framed" as art. In 1971 the California artist Chris Burden had himself imprisoned in a locker for five days. In *Shoot* (1971) he arranged for a friend to shoot him in the arm. *Deadman* (1972) consisted of Burden lying under a tarpaulin on a Los Angeles street. These events became performance in the same way that found art becomes art. By placing the object in an art context, for example, putting it on a pedestal in a gallery, it is transformed into an object for perception and loses its concrete efficacy. Similarly, by presenting an event in a performance context, it is viewed as a performance. However, because spectators are aware that Burden's pieces involve genuine risk and pain for the performer and that no fiction or illusion is involved, a tension exists between knowledge of this efficacy and the performance context. Unlike a conventional play in which one relates only to the illusion being created, in these events by Chris Burden one is confronted with an actual event. Because the event is in the context of performance, spectators are given permission to become unblinking voyeurs.

Linda Montano, another California artist, has used her own life as material for her performances since 1973. At the San Francisco Museum of Modern Art she walked a treadmill for three hours while telling the story of her life. Her interest in exploring her responses to various situations led to a number of performances in which these responses were put into focus. In *Mitchell's Death* (1978) she showed a videotape of herself inserting acupuncture needles into her face as she performed live, with the needles in her face. The live performance consisted of reading from an account she had written of her emotional reactions to the death of her estranged husband by a self-inflicted gunshot wound. Beginning in July 1983 Montano and Tehching Hsieh created a yearlong performance in which they were tied together by an eight-foot rope as they went about their lives. For the entire year they never touched, although when they were indoors they were always together in the same room.

The New York director-playwright-designer Richard Foreman has

created productions that reflect his concern with his own consciousness and the structure of his thought. For him writing is a continuous
process reflecting his consciousness. Whenever possible he spends
his days reading and looking at pictures and making notes and diagrams in a notebook. His practice in the late seventies was to use
these notes and diagrams, without alteration or rearrangement, as
texts for his plays. A play text (that is, the notes and diagrams) might
include observations on why he had had a certain thought, warnings
to himself, frequent changes of subject, interruptions, and rebegin-
nings, which Foreman believes reflect the true shape and texture of
his conscious experience. The words from the text would then be
distributed among several characters and he would make a tape recording of the performers reading the lines without coloration. This
tape became the score to which he would "choreograph" the performers, scenery, objects, sounds, and music. When the production
was nearly ready for performance, he sometimes added a tape recording of himself expressing his thoughts in reaction to the work.
His performances consisted of shifting images and associations punc-
tuated by a buzzer, telephone bell, pings, and other disruptive
sounds. The rapid series of displacements and interruptions would
heighten the spectator's awareness; one had to focus acutely so as
not to miss any of the evocative and sensuous images. Performers
would often stare out of the proscenium frame at specific spectators,
making them conscious of their voyeuristic relationship to the performance.

Foreman's productions of the late seventies embodied other ten-
dencies in theatrical experimentation of the time. Some of his theoretical ideas suggest the deconstructionists. He pointed out that we
have a natural inclination to make things cohere, to find connections, to make order out of chaos. He thinks it is important to poke
holes in this order, to disrupt, to avoid going with an emotional flow
or providing a single meaning. His productions are evocative, but
their meanings are open; yet there is a vague situation in each play
that tends to provide a unifying element. In *Pandering to the Masses:
A Misrepresentation* (1975), the central character, Rhoda, receives a
letter with a red seal. It is an invitation to join a secret society that
imparts a very special kind of knowledge. It is never clear what kind
of knowledge is offered, but she is apparently initiated into the society. The fragments can be put together in a variety of ways for differ-

ent meanings. Another evocative aspect of the play is its autobiographical element. As in many of Foreman's productions of the seventies, two of the characters are Max and Rhoda, who are surrogates for Foreman and Kate Manheim, the woman with whom he lived and who played Rhoda in the productions. Foreman's work also has something in common with that of the formalists. In *Pandering to the Masses*, for example, a compositional motif is the images (both visual and verbal) of letters, messages, and envelopes that appear in a variety of forms and seem to refer to the invitation received by Rhoda.

Director-playwright Lee Breuer of the Mabou Mines group in New York has produced a great variety of work, some of which has been self-referential. In the earliest, *The Red Horse Animation* (1970), the performers' bodies create an abstract image of a horse. While speaking as a chorus they join their bodies in various ways until the horse takes shape, gallops, and then disintegrates. The performance is an objectification of Breuer's mental process as he tries to create—his insecurities, his attempts to discover his relationship to objects and events in the world and to the work he is creating. A later work presents the fragmented persona of Breuer. *A Prelude to Death in Venice*, first presented as part of a larger work in 1978, has as its central character John Greed, a puppet three-fifths human size, who is a surrogate for Breuer and is dressed as Breuer has dressed from the age of 16—leather jacket and blue hat. John talks on the telephone to his girl friend, mother, and agent; for each he projects a different persona, and the schizophrenia becomes progressively overt. Breuer valorizes none of these personae; the play was a way of purging himself of them.

The Wooster Group, re-formed from the disbanded Performance Group, began work in 1970 under the direction of Elizabeth LeCompte. Its first three productions comprised the trilogy "Three Places in Rhode Island," which was made in response to remembered events in the life of a fellow company member, Spalding Gray. The events were deconstructed and presented largely as a series of images and verbal material, some of which was taken from actual conversations. For example, in *Rumstick Road* (1977), which focused on the suicide of Gray's mother, a recorded telephone conversation with the mother's psychiatrist was included. The last of the three works of the trilogy, *Nyatt School* (1978), began a practice of deconstructing well-known plays as a beginning point. In this instance T. S. Eliot's

Cocktail Party served as the point of departure. However, the use of such plays by the Wooster Group serves only as a point of focus for presenting the group's own very personal work. *LSD (. . . Just the High Points)* (1983) was partially in response to Arthur Miller's *The Crucible* and used portions of Miller's text, read at a speed that made the words incomprehensible. Later, under threat of a lawsuit, the company dropped Miller's words altogether without really affecting the concept of *LSD*.

The Wooster Group uses several kinds of tasks as means of presenting the actual experience of the performers. In act 1 of *LSD* the performers sit at a long table facing the audience reading short passages from popular counterculture books of the sixties. One of the performers listens on headphones to a taped interview with the babysitter employed by Timothy Leary and reproduces as precisely as possible the voice and phrasing of the original. In act 3 the performers reproduce, second by second, a videotape made of a rehearsal during which they took LSD. At one point in this section the performer Kate Valk holds her nose and spins, imitating her childhood memory of trying to get high. Her increasing unsteadiness as she spins is not an illusion of dizziness; she actually becomes dizzy. The events that make up the production result from tasks that have their expected real-world efficacy. These tasks are framed as performance, yet they project as actual events rather than fictional illusions, in the same way that Duchamp's kitchen stool and bicycle wheel are not illusions of these objects.

The works of Tadeusz Kantor's Cricot 2 Theatre use autobiographical material from the director's life in quite a different way. While Kantor's expressionistic productions are no more realistic than the task-oriented performances of the Wooster Group, there is a fundamental difference. All of his productions, he says, "are personal confessions," and the subjective material drawn directly from his personal experience is used to create a theatrical fiction. Surrogate figures for Kantor are part of the illusion—detailed lifelike puppets of school children carried around by the actors in *The Dead Class* (1975) and a manikin in *I Shall Never Return* (1987). However, lest we become so absorbed in the images that we lose the connection to the actual person, Kantor himself is continually present on stage as a reminder that we are experiencing his subjective world. Sometimes, as in *The Dead Class* (1975), he is visible just outside the acting area conducting the performance; and sometimes, as in *I Shall Never Return* (1988), he is within the action but still outside the aesthetic frame and therefore not absorbed into the illusion.

The members of Squat Theatre in New York explored other ways of using their lives as performance material and reducing the separation between life and illusion. For several years, beginning in 1977, this expatriate Hungarian company lived and performed in the same space—a building with a storefront window looking onto West Twenty-third Street. Those who passed outside became part of the performance for the audience inside, and vice versa. Although the group's work has evolved somewhat, in the late seventies its performances consisted of tasks set in a fictional frame so that illusion and actuality were often confused by the audience. While at times members of the company wore special costumes and performed unusual tasks, they performed as themselves and took risks that had potential consequences for their lives. For the first section of *Andy Warhol's Last Love* (1978), the audience was taken to an upstairs room where group members Eva Buchmüller and Istvan Balint actually lived at the time. The couple was engaged in everyday activities; he was lying on the bed reading, and she was listening to a radio and twisting her hair as she did both on and off stage. Soon, a voice claiming to belong to Ulrike Meinhof came through the static on the radio. Meinhof advised listeners to make their deaths public so that they could be provided with new bodies and taken off to the planet where she now lives. Other bizarre events followed. Buchmüller's dressing gown was nailed to the floor and she was shot, a tablecloth caught on fire, and a man rolled out from under the table in flames. A woman entered from the fire escape wearing a silver cloak, with an erect penis protruding from under her actually pregnant belly. The rest of the performance took place downstairs, where the spectators sat facing the storefront window. Looking in from the sidewalk was a second audience of passersby and a few company members who were taken to be passersby. As these two audiences watched, a man who appeared to be Andy Warhol (he wore a lifelike mask) interviewed (by means of a taped voice) a naked woman who insisted that she was a genuine witch. Apparently she was.

Squat Theatre does not simply replace one level of illusion with another, as in the plays of Pirandello, nor does it simply engage in tasks without a fictional matrix, as in the Living Theatre's *Mysteries and Other Pieces.* Instead, the company intermingles actuality and illusion in such a way that actual persons and events become more mysterious and fictional ones may seem more concrete. This confusion of art and life is risky. Performers have been threatened by both spectators and police who have mistaken illusion for actuality. And they risk arrest for a variety of violations, from breaking fire regulations or obstructing the sidewalk to indecent exposure and the corruption of minors.

In the mixing of actual and fictional elements, theater artists have sometimes employed the technique of putting into focus both the performers and the fictional characters they play. The Performance Group, under the direction of Richard Schechner, explored this concept in its first production in 1968. *Dionysus in 69* was developed by the company using *The Bacchae* of Euripides as a beginning point, but with group members inventing much of the language and action themselves. In performance the actors played characters *and* themselves. Actors were referred to by both their actual names and their character names, and they used a translation of Euripides as well as language they had written or improvised in performance. Thus some parts of the performance were different each night. For example, at one point in the performance William Shepard, who played Pentheus, would go among the spectators to prove to Dionysus that he can seduce a woman without the god's help. The segment that followed was an actual event. Shepard would choose a spectator and attempt to make love to her; usually he was rejected. In one performance Shepard persuaded a woman to leave with him, and they did not return. On the evenings when Shepard failed, he was taken into a pit by Dionysus, where, out of the audience's view, he was forced to make love to Dionysus. The humiliation was not only of the character Pentheus but of the actor Shepard. While the two were away, the other performers would go among the spectators and select individuals to caress. These individuals and the performers would lie intertwined on the floor in the main acting area where they would stroke, hug, and kiss one another. This group caress, which detractors came to call the "group grope," was nearly identical to that of "The Rite of Universal Intercourse" in the Living Theatre's *Paradise Now*, which coincidentally opened in France a month later.

Such physical contact between performers and spectators is a means of making the performance an actual rather than only a fictional event. This technique, which forces the spectators to relate to the performers instead of to fictional characters, was used by several groups, including the Open Theatre (New York), Company Theatre (Los Angeles), and Tréteaux Libres (France). However, there were instances in some productions when a performer made physical contact while in character. In *Zartan, the Unloved Brother of Tarzan* (1971), produced by the French company le Grand Magic Circus under the direction of Jérôme Savary, there is a moment when Zartan rejects a beautiful chanteuse and tells her that he prefers his ape girlfriend. The chanteuse is so distraught that she runs into the audience and looks for comfort on the lap of a male spectator. Soviet director Anatoli Vasiliev used a similar device in his production of *Six Characters in Search of an Author*, presented in 1989 as part of the London International Festival of Theatre. Act 2, set in a brothel, was staged like some of Jerzy Grotowski's productions, with the spectators scattered within the acting area. The stepdaughter, giggling coquettishly, sat on the laps of male spectators, caressing them and declaring her love. Moments such as these tend to break out of the fictional frame even though the performers are presenting fictional characters.

Environmental and Promenade Performances

Another technique that presents both fiction and actuality is environmental staging. This functions somewhat differently depending on whether the environment is constructed specifically for the performance or is a found environment and on whether the audience is stationary or moves from place to place during the performance. Richard Schechner, while directing the Performance Group in the development of *Dionysus in 69*, formulated "6 axioms for environmental theatre" that had grown out of his explorations. The first is similar to the first of Kaprow's rules for Happenings—a rejection of the traditional distinctions between art and life. A second fundamental principle puts the spectator and the performer in the same space, instead of the performance existing in a fictional environment and the audience in a space outside it.

The spectators attending *Dionysus in 69* were stationary for the most part; however, the performers moved among the audience, and there was no attempt to make a distinction between fictional and nonfictional space. Jerzy Grotowski had used similar arrangements for several of his productions. For example, the entire space for *Kordian* (1962) suggested a mental institution. The spectators were scattered throughout the space, some seated in chairs, others on beds. The performance took place among the spectators and used the beds as well. Some of the performances of the Bread and Puppet Theater, founded by Peter Schumann in 1961, take place in a meadow on his farm in Vermont. Here puppets, some as tall as fifteen feet, share the space with masked performers and spectators. Even when performances take place indoors, Schumann's practice of serving bread to the audience involves the interaction of performers and spectators and emphasizes the fact that they are sharing the same space. The standing spectators at Théâtre du Soleil's *1789* (1970) were surrounded by several platform stages, like side shows at a fair or medieval mansion stages. The actors performed on these stages and among the spectators. For their production of *L'Age d'Or* the audience was seated on the floor with some performers sitting among them. After each scene performers guided the spectators to another part of the building where the next scene took place.

In England, under the direction of John Fox, Welfare State International created a production in 1972 around its legendary hermaphrodite hero Lancelot Quail. The performance took place in various found spaces—highways, town squares, pubs, and hillsides—along the 150-mile route to the sea. Finally, having reached the sea, Quail and his friends, including a mermaid, were taken by boat to a submarine awaiting them a mile off the coast. They boarded the submarine and disappeared. *Beauty and the Beast* (1973) was created on the site of a former municipal rubbish dump where the company lived in caravans. The environment for the production consisted of a village constructed from discarded junk found there. The audience was conducted through the village by Lancelot Quail, who told the story of his capture by those living in the village and of his escape in a flying machine. He pointed out in the distance other actual villages that seemed no more real than the fictional one the spectators had just explored.

Snake Theater in California, in its site-specific productions, made similar use of actual environments as settings for fictional events. Initially this company's productions were influenced by Peter Schumann's Bread and Puppet Theater, with whom Chris Hardman, one of the directors, had worked; but soon the company developed its own unique style of performance, using commonplace characters rather than mythological ones. The site for *Somewhere in the Pacific* (1977) was a beach near San Francisco. The audience, seated on the sandy beach, saw a giant puppet, Carol, standing above them on a cliff, looking out to sea awaiting the return of her dead sailor boyfriend. The sailor, wearing the grey makeup of death, sat at the water's edge writing a letter to Carol, and the words appeared on placards that attendants placed in the sand. Snake Theater's production of *Auto* (1979) was presented in an abandoned service station. In 1980 Snake Theater disbanded, and its directors, Laura Farabough and Chris Hardman, formed two new theaters.

Laura Farabough has continued to create environmental productions for her Nightfire Theater. Unlike the site-specific work of Snake Theater, however, Farabough's productions have been created for generic nontheatrical settings and have toured to the same kinds of settings in other locales. Such works have been created for a beauty salon, a high-school girls' locker room, a cocktail lounge, an army barracks latrine, a warehouse, and a swimming pool.

Chris Hardman, in forming Antenna Theater, aimed to put the audience in the action of his productions, which use both site-specific and constructed environments. While all environmental pro lductions put the audience in the same perceptual space as the performance, Hardman developed a technology intended to make each spectator a participant in the action; he calls it Walkmanology, after the small tape players manufactured by Sony. Individual tape players and headsets are attached to each spectator, who is individually guided through the environment by the tape. The spectators are given instructions over the headsets telling them to perform certain tasks, and consequently they participate like characters in the play. In *High School* (1981) each spectator is guided through a high school campus at night, and finally, with band playing (through the headset), marches down the aisle of the campus amphitheatre and receives a diploma. Other site-specific Walkman productions have been created for a World War II liberty ship anchored in San Francisco Bay and for Alcatraz Prison.

Antenna Theater's productions for constructed environments have taken two forms. The first of these derives from what Hardman refers to as the maze concept. In *Amnesia* (1984), a "Walkman walk-through play with masked actors," each spectator/participant, wearing a tape player and headset, spends an hour as a patient being treated for amnesia. The therapy involves sorting out memories from the character's past as the participant is guided through a specially designed environment and directed to engage in a series of tasks, sometimes involving interaction with masked actors or sculpted figures. These tasks include breaking up a dogfight, posing for a photograph, assisting at a childbirth, and being sedated by a nurse with a large hypodermic needle. The second of the forms using constructed environments is what Hardman calls café theater because food and drink are available and the environment is arranged like side shows at an amusement park. The spectators can stroll on the midway, stop to buy refreshments, and participate in the side shows in whatever order they choose. *Adjusting the Idle* (1984) has seventeen of these sideshows. In each the participant puts on a headset and for five to ten minutes interacts as instructed. The tape, as in other Walkman shows, combines music and sound effects with excerpts from interviews. In this instance the interviews are with people whose professions involve them with automobiles—mechanics, pedestrians, hitchhikers, police, streetwalkers, and others. In the various interactive installations a participant can design the car of the future, pay homage to the car idol, make a used-car commercial, service a car on the grease rack, and sit in the back seat of a car to watch a drive-in movie and listen (over the headset) to a young woman describe her sexual experiences at drive-in movies. With the café theater model Hardman found a form that stimulated spectator interaction and a sense of community. In the maze form each participant experiences the entire work alone. While there may be interaction with masked actors, the actors are perceived as nonrealistic characters, not as actual persons. In the cafe theater productions, on the other hand, some of the short events are experienced by five or more participants at once, and there is opportunity for participants to interact as they stroll among the side shows watching others experience the events. Thus, somewhat as in Squat Theatre's storefront-window performances, the spectators become part of the performance for other spectators.

In recent years a few of the established theaters in England have used environmental theater techniques for what they call promenade performances. *The Mystery Plays* (1977), derived in three parts from the York and Wakefield medieval cycles, was presented in the Cottesloe Theatre by the National Theatre Company in London. The audience stood and the performance took place in the midst of it, with the spectators being directed to make room for the performers. A similar arrangement was used for the National's production of *Lark Rise* (1978) and *Candleford* (1979), which were adapted by Keith Dewhurst from the work of Flora Thompson. In 1983 the Royal Shakespeare Company at Stratford presented *The Dillen*, based on the true story of a working man in Victorian Stratford. The performances were presented outdoors in the fields of Stratford and on the banks of the Avon. Spectators were led from place to place to view scenes from the life of George Hewins, enacted in some of the settings where the actual events may have taken place. The Royal Court Theatre in London staged Jim Cartwright's *Road* (1986) as a promenade performance—initially in its small Theatre Upstairs and then in the larger main auditorium where a flat floor was installed. A difference between these productions by established theaters and those by the more experimental companies is that none of the latter used a realistic style of performance while all of the former did. The realism of these productions suggests that those who created them were intent on seducing the spectators into the fictional worlds of the plays, where they would relate empathetically with the characters rather than communally with the performers. Aside from the novelty of environmental staging, use of the technique by the established theaters was apparently aimed at decreasing the physical distance between spectator and character, in the hope that such intimacy would decrease the psychic distance and thereby involve the audience more deeply in the illusion. These objectives seemed to obtain even in *The Mystery Plays*, where actors made a point of speaking to audience members before performance began. The contact between spectator and performer ended when the performance started; the only relationship then was between character and spectator.

Performance and Danger

Other promenade performances have been less friendly in that they have created circumstances that give the audience a sense of physical danger. This is another technique that causes the spectators to focus on the concrete here and now and colors their experience of the total performance. In part that was the case in Luca Ronconi's *Orlando Furioso* (1969), when rolling platforms carrying actors were pushed at top speed through a dense standing audience. The technique has been used more recently by La Fura dels Baus (The Vermin of the Sewers), a Catalan group from Barcelona. Imbued with the violent expressionistic spirit of punk rock music, this company's *Suz O Suz* (1986) was presented in a warehouse in London's docklands as part of the London International Festival of Theatre. With a live rock band playing throughout and the audience standing and milling about, the atmosphere was something like a rock concert. The performers wore only jock straps and their heads were shaved in the manner of skinheads. For this reason and because they threw blood (red paint) at each other and at the audience, they were reminiscent of the Kipper Kids in the United States, who engaged in such antics in a spirit of fun. But the actions of La Fura were violent and potentially dangerous to company members and to unwary spectators. Performers ran through the crowd, sometimes pushing or pulling metal barrels and other heavy metal objects. One performer would swing a metal object around his head and let it go (hitting a spectator in the knee at a performance I attended). As in Ronconi's *Orlando Furioso*, carts five feet high were pushed through the crowd, and the performers standing on them attacked each other with buckets of "blood" and balls of ashes in expressionistic war. On each of two towers was a large plexiglass container of water, inside of which was a naked man breathing through a tube like a fetus in his amniotic fluid attached to an umbilical lifeline. Another man on each tower would poke the man in the tank with a stick; after a time the water would become bloody and the body would float to the surface. The image was undeniably violent, but while it may have suggested both torture and the killing of a fetus, it was intended to be abstract enough so as not to have a single interpretation. In the final action of the performance two men were suspended upside down from a scaffold and swung, like pendulums, through fire. Again, the image suggested torture, such as went on in Spain under Franco, but it also suggested medieval images of hell. Several times the violence was accompanied by frenzied eating of raw animal viscera. Throughout the performance the spectators were highly energized as they attempted to avoid buckets of "blood," metal objects, running performers, animal guts, carts, and water. By the end of the eighty-minute performance the concrete floor was afloat with water, blood, and pieces of animal innards. It looked and smelled like a slaughterhouse.

Survival Research Laboratories (SRL), a group formed in 1979 in San Francisco, creates works with some of the same qualities as La Fura dels Baus, but without human performers. Under the direction of Mark Pauline, SRL rebuilds obsolete industrial equipment into self-propelled, radio-controlled, animalistic machines that perpetrate acts of violence on each other and, in a few instances, inadvertently, on spectators and the human members of the company (the director lost the fingers of his right hand in an explosion). The performances are presented outdoors in parking lots or other unobstructed areas. Following a scenario, six or eight machines, some weighing more than a ton, destroy one another. The atmosphere is something like that of a traffic accident in process. Each of the machines has its own engine, so it can crawl or jump or walk, and together they create general mayhem as they attempt to crush each other, fire bowling-ball cannons and flame throwers, and even blow themselves up, taking their foes with them. Mark Pauline is a selective anarchist of the punk generation who is opposed to structures that tend to limit creativity and promote hypocrisy. Among these he includes art galleries, the government, and universities. He thinks established artists fall into this category because they are in complicity with these organizations. He considers the performances of SRL to be metaphors for our destructive and decaying industrial culture. This view is reflected in ironic titles such as *SRL Views with Regret: The Unrestrained Use of Excessive Force.*

A performance by La Fura dels Baus or Survival Research Laboratories consists of a series of tasks enacted by human or machine performers who do not play characters. The environmental arrangement, the risk to spectators and performers, and the bizarre images create a world that is evocative, even metaphorical, but *not* fictional. Because of the environmental arrangement we are in this world, and we experience it directly rather than vicariously experiencing a fictional world that can have no risk for us.

Breaking Through the Fictional Frame

Other companies present a fictional frame and then break through the illusion to achieve a confrontation. Two companies in London have employed this technique; they create fictional worlds and then introduce elements that are so shocking or repulsive to audience sensibilities that the spectators are put into direct relationship with these elements.

Lumiere and Son was formed in 1973 by playwright-performer David Gale and director Hilary Westlake to "explore the extremes of human appetite that are evident in secret desires, anarchic impulses, messianic fervours and destructive lusts." The productions project the personal obsessions of company members—especially of David Gale—and sometimes refer to individual performers by accentuating their mannerisms. In *Passionate Positions* (1977) there is an ironic level because the playwright performs the role of a narrator who controls the actions of the other characters. Gale wrote the part for himself, he says, because he likes to play sadistic roles, and he was interested in the ambiguity it presents to the spectators, who find it difficult to distinguish between the fictional and the actual. Gale also wanted to goad the audience with an uncomfortable dilemma. Spectators, when presented with material they find repulsive, have to choose either to ignore theatrical manners and walk out or to stay and be offended. The play is structured as a series of entertainments by four inept entertainers. One female entertainer, for example, does impersonations, including one of a person with a "rat up his asshole"; she also demonstrates the difference between a dunce and a child with brain damage. Another woman tries to make the audience tense by smashing plates together at unexpected moments. The narrator mesmerizes the entertainers and mimes cutting their hearts out. The hearts—genuine raw lamb hearts—are put on sticks like lollipops and offered to the audience. The entertainers have become zombies, and the narrator offers to have them do anything the audience requests; but there are no requests. The zombies are told that their hearts have been eaten by the audience. In an attempt to get their hearts back, each of the zombies goes into the audience and attempts seductively to make friends with a spectator. Eventually, back on stage, the narrator orders the zombies to masturbate each other using a gloved hand on a pole. When two of the women are caught trying to complete the job themselves, the narrator makes them stick the offending fingers down their throats, and they retch repeatedly. In the end the narrator presents each of the zombies with a raw lamb heart, which they begin to eat as blood runs down their arms. The chief interest for the audience probably derives from uncertainty concerning what is theatrical illusion and what is actual. The audience does not know the performers are following a script, so some probably believe David Gale as the narrator is satisfying his own manipulative interests in giving orders to the entertainers and punishing them. And, of course, the audience is partly right, because Gale made these decisions when writing the script. However, if some spectators find Gale's behavior unethical, what about the behavior of those who stay and watch it? At times the performance breaks through the fictional illusion, making the spectators believe they are watching actual efficacious events. Everyone realizes that the performers are actually retching involuntarily when they stick their fingers down their throats; are they also actually stimulated sexually by the gloved hand? The performers actually eat raw lamb hearts; are they really willing to do anything that a spectator might request? These ambiguities result, says Gale, from presenting "real material mixed up with imagined material." In all of the company's plays, he says, there is "a leak from the capsule of the illusion."

The Pip Simmons Theatre Group, also in London, has used similar techniques toward a different end. The objective of director-playwright Pip Simmons in *An die Musik* (1975) was neither the fulfillment of sadistic fantasies nor an attempt to present the audience with a dilemma. He wanted to find a way for the audience to experience the cruelty of the Nazi concentration camps more directly than would be possible in a dramatic fiction that would end with the performance. His solution was to present actual performer responses to physical abuse as a metaphor for the Nazi concentration camp experience. The punishments were actual, just as they were in the Living Theatre production of Kenneth Brown's *The Brig* (1963), set in a Marine Corps prison. The idea for *An die Musik* came from the fact that Jewish orchestras were formed in the camps to play traditional German music such as Schubert's musical setting for Goethe's "An die Musik." The hourlong performance is divided into two segments and consists entirely of a concert performed by such an orchestra under the supervision of an SS guard. The first part, an "operetta" entitled "The Dream of Anne Frank," burlesques in grotesque fashion a Jewish family at a seder table. The second part consists of orchestral pieces by Schubert, Liszt, and Beethoven performed by an orchestra of eight Jewish prisoners. The guard announces each piece, and the performers play and sing the music as best they can. The guard amuses himself by punishing the musicians for actual and imaginary infractions. The performers, like the historical Nazi prisoners, cannot anticipate and cannot prepare for the punishments because the decisions about who will be punished when are made during the performance by the actor playing the SS guard. Insofar as possible the musicians do not interrupt their performance, even when required to do strenuous physical exercises or hang from a trapeze. The guard sometimes throws buckets of water on them, requires them to undress, and humiliates them in other ways. For example, he plays with the breasts of one of the women, a man is made to wash his genitals in a bucket of cold water, and the other performers are made to laugh at the man's circumcised penis. The efficacious relationship between the guard and the other performers helps shift the focus from the dramatic illusion of punishment to actual punishment. The performers do not "act" emotional responses; for the most part their reactions are actual responses. They are really out of breath from exercises when they try to sing, they really undergo minor shock when buckets of cold water are thrown on them, it is their actual nudity that is exposed, it is their breasts and penises being ridiculed. Because the audience is partly focused on the actual stage circumstances rather than being absorbed into the fictional world, they are able to think of the actual victims of Nazi concentration camps whose experiences are being demonstrated.

For a century now audiences have accepted the conventional realistic theater as an appropriate expression of our culture, even as an objective depiction of reality. However, anyone who thinks about it knows that realism is no more an objective representation than any other style; each involves abstraction. Although realism was capable of expressing the emotive experience of the late nineteenth century with its belief in science, the style long ago ceased to be capable of expressing the concerns of the changing twentieth-century world. Nevertheless, realism has remained the dominant stylistic convention in this century, despite frequent attempts by experimental theater artists to create new forms to express artistic concepts for which realism was inadequate. The resulting styles—symbolism, dadaism, futurism, constructivism, expressionism, absurdism—broke out of the realistic convention but still depended on an all-encompassing fictional illusion. Beginning in the sixties, however, experimental theater artists were formulating conceptions that could not be expressed by any theatrical form that was purely fictional. These artists, while still making use of illusion, invented a variety of ways to introduce elements of the actual world into their works. From the mid-sixties to the mid-seventies the work of these artists was often aimed at bringing about change in society. From the mid-seventies until the present the focus has tended to be more self-referential.

Some of these experimental artists have found support for their work from established institutions such as the National Endowment for the Arts in the United States and from similar agencies abroad. A few have had their work accepted by prominent arts-presenting organizations. Robert Wilson's work in particular has been presented in major opera houses in Europe and the United States; he has been commissioned by European governments to produce new work, and he was selected to design the celebration opening of the Opéra Bastille in Paris on the eve of the bicentennial of the storming of the Bastille. Many of the experimental companies have performed in the Next Wave Festival of the Brooklyn Academy of Music, in the London International Festival of Theatre, and in a number of other festivals in Europe.

Although very little of the experimental work of these artists has been presented in the established theater, many of the artists have been accepted into mainstream theater, film, and television. Richard Foreman has directed at the Paris Opéra and on Broadway, Emil Wolk of the People Show has received a best actor award for his work at the Royal Shakespeare Company, Lee Breuer has directed on Broadway, Diana Quick of Red Ladder has played leading roles in the West End, Willem Dafoe and Spalding Gray of the Wooster Group have become well-known as film actors, Luis Valdez of El Teatro Campesino has directed films and on Broadway, and Jérôme Savary of le Grand Magic Circus has become director of the Théâtre de Chaillot in Paris.

Still, experimental work is inevitably outside the established institutions, aesthetics, and economics. And there are always a few new companies willing to put up with these hardships. One, at least, has even put its work at the service of the disenfranchised. In 1985 John Malpede in Los Angeles brought together a variety of skid row drifters and people who had experience working with the homeless.

LAPD (Los Angeles Poverty Department) creates productions that attempt to illuminate the forces shaping the lives of those who live in poverty and homelessness. It is one of a few recently formed companies that focuses outward to the conditions of society in hopes of bringing about social change.

BIBLIOGRAPHY

Most of the factual information in this essay is from rehearsals and performances seen by the author and from interviews and conversations with the artists involved. Some of the companies mentioned have been discussed at greater length in the books listed below.

Esslin, Martin. *The Theatre of the Absurd.* Garden City, N.Y.: Anchor Books, 1961.

Kaprow, Allan. *Assemblage, Environments, and Happenings.* New York: Harry H. Abrams, 1966.

Schechner, Richard, "6 Axioms for Environmental Theatre." *Drama Review* 12, no. 3 (Spring 1968): 41–64.

Shank, Theodore. *American Alternative Theatre.* London: Macmillan, 1982; reprint, New York: St. Martin's Press, 1988.

Shank, Theodore. *California Performance: Volume One / San Francisco Bay Area. Interviews and Essays.* Claremont, Calif.: The Mime Journal, 1989.

Shank, Theodore. *Theatre in Real Time; Materiali per uno studio sul Nuovo Teatro. America—Inghilterra dal 1968.* Milano: Studio Forma Editrice, 1980.

The Absurd, To and Fro

BERNARD WEINER

The show onstage was absurd, but I had no idea that it was Absurd. The play was *Waiting for Godot* in its United States premiere in 1956 at, of all unlikely places, the Coconut Grove Playhouse in Coral Gables, Florida, just a few streets from my home. I was sixteen years old and crazy about theater. I understood little of the style and resonance of the play, but I appreciated Bert Lahr's antics and some of the other humor, and I wondered why so many adults walked out, or didn't return after the intermission. I had some sense that something important was happening in the theater, and I wanted to stay and watch it unfold. I never regretted it. Only much later did I realize that I had been "present at the creation" of the absurd in the United States.

Godot and the Beckett/Ionesco/Pinter/Albee productions that I saw in different theaters over the next several years were instrumental in shaping my theater point of view as an audience member and as a budding playwright. One of my early plays, a 1962 one-acter, was entitled "The Usual: Hommage et Réponse à Samuel Beckett." I admired his work and couldn't help imitating it, but his quietism troubled me, and my characters were more active.

Like the famous absurdist playwrights, I too wanted to break down old forms and create new ones in the postwar rubble. True, I hadn't seen any rubble, nor had I suffered through a war that laid waste to countries and philosophies; yet I responded in temperament to postwar existentialism. Although I verbalize it now, I couldn't then articulate an aesthetic or philosophic vision. Then I read a book that made a sweeping diagnosis, that discussed the sources, meaning, and impact of the new theater—and my thoughts took shape, were shaped by this provocative tome.

It was of course *The Theatre of the Absurd*, by Martin Esslin, a name unknown to me. The book analyzed postwar drama, but its sweep was far-reaching. For twenty-one-year old me, and for many of my contemporaries, Esslin's book offered a coherent way of viewing a chaotic, unjust, confusing world. He helped it make sense, or, rather, made the senselessness more comprehensible. The locus was theater, but the focus was the world.

I wasn't the only theater enthusiast touched by this volume. John Lion, a college student in Chicago, realized through Esslin's volume that "absurdism was the last of the useful isms, offering alienated individuals not just an aesthetic but a philosophic system that contained both the means to expand clear boundaries all at once—and I began avidly to read as many of the philosophers and playwrights as I could lay my hands on."

While still in Chicago, Lion began to direct Jarry's *Ubu* plays, along with works of Genet and Ionesco. In 1963 Lion arrived in Berkeley for graduate work in theater. He was attracted by the presence there of Jan Kott, a visiting professor, who, using the same approach as his friend Martin Esslin, was subverting the traditional view of Shakespeare. In the Bay Area new theatrical ground had been broken by the innovative San Francisco Actors' Workshop, directed by Herbert Blau and Jules Irving, who had early produced Beckett, Pinter, and Brecht. Lion then directed other Esslinian figures such as Tzara and Arrabal.

In 1967 Lion founded the Magic Theater, so named because his first Berkeley performance space was a bar, the Steppenwolf. Steeped in the European absurdists, Lion soon produced nontraditional American playwrights—Jeff Wanshell, James Schevill, Nick Kazan, Terrence McNally, Jean-Claude van Itallie, Susan Yankowitz—and premiered the innovative works of Michael McClure and Sam Shepard. In 1970–71 Lion directed Shepard's *La Turista*, which he interpreted in the absurdist tradition. The director quoted Shepard as saying "that what changed his life was reading *Waiting for Godot*."

After Lion obtained a new home for the Magic in San Francisco's Fort Mason, it was the in-house presence of Shepard from the mid-seventies to the early eighties that gave his theater its richly deserved reputation for the premieres of *Inacoma, Angel City, Curse of the Starving Class, True West,* and *Buried Child,* as well as two experimental projects with Joe Chaikin—*Savage/Love* and *Tongues.*

In 1974 I became the drama critic for the *San Francisco Chronicle,* while trying also to keep my hand in theater production. In 1977, these disparate threads of Lion and myself were tied in the knot of Esslin's presence in the Bay Area. Having retired as head of radio drama for the BBC, Esslin began a new career teaching at Stanford University, and Ruby Cohn brought him at once to the Magic Theater, already in San Francisco but not yet at Fort Mason. When she phoned John Lion to announce Esslin's forthcoming presence, he held the curtain until their arrival, and later commented: "It was like having a dream come true: Martin Esslin was in our lobby." Esslin soon became the unpaid dramaturg of the Magic, and Lion said recently:

> Having Martin as our dramaturg has helped keep the Absurdist stream flowing at the Magic, even to this day, even when a good share of our programming began to move in the late 70s toward the new realism of playwrights like David Mamet, Israel Horovitz, and Sam Shepard, along with the experimental, highly visual theater of groups like SOON 3.

Until 1989 Esslin helped Lion shape each season's repertory at the Magic. Over the years Esslin was responsible for bringing such European writers as Austria's Wolfgang Bauer and Poland's Slawomir Mrozek to the Magic, as well as American writers such as Martin Epstein, Lynne Kaufman, and John Robinson. And Esslin was responsible for the belated union of the Magic Theater and Samuel Beckett. Lion had shied away from directing Beckett: "I was only in my early 20s then and simply didn't feel I could do justice to those instant classics." But in the eighties, Esslin convinced the Magic to revive *Godot, Endgame,* and *Happy Days* (with scripts revised by the author), as well as Beckett's late, difficult plays *Ohio Impromptu* and *What Where.*

Esslin and Lion each had a veto over the other's choice of plays, but Esslin's veto apparently carried more weight. For example, if

Esslin objected to a particular script—which did happen occasionally, although neither man will name names—he would threaten to resign. Usually, however, the two very dissimilar men worked harmoniously together, Esslin often introducing Lion to European absurdist or expressionist works, such as Georg Kaiser's *Europa*.

Esslin himself believes his most important dramaturgical function was the positive effect of his naysaying. There is no way of knowing how many poor scripts might have been staged at the Magic, were it not for Esslin's vociferous objections.

My own relationship with Esslin was also marked by such objections. As indicated, Esslin's theory of the absurd was an important formative agent for me. When I was in college, his book helped me understand modern theater in both sociopolitical and aesthetic terms. In my formative years as a critic (*University of Miami Hurricane, Claremont Courier, San Diego Magazine, Northwest Passage*), Esslin's influence made me partial to nonrealistic and experimental drama rather than to the Musty Old Classics. When I began daily reviewing for a major city newspaper, the *San Francisco Chronicle*, I was inspired by Esslin to stand on his strong and strongly grounded opinions.

Esslin was one of my most highly reactive readers. He would not hesitate to let me know if my writing was ill-conceived or badly written. At first these chastisements cut me to the quick: my mentor disapproved. An adverse criticism from Esslin could depress me for days. One painful experience occurred after I wrote an unfriendly review of Richard Nelson's *Between East and West*, directed by Esslin's colleague Carl Weber. However, I gradually grew more secure in my own views, which tended to accept classical and realistic drama produced by Equity companies such as the American Conservatory Theater and Berkeley Repertory Theater, who lean toward Molière, Shaw, and Chekhov.

I do not presume to speak for Esslin, and yet I believe that he sees my writing, and that of American reviewers in general, as woefully deficient when measured against the best European critical writing. His attitude springs in part, I believe, from his never having come to grips with the fact that San Francisco and New York are not Vienna or London, with their huge, homogeneous, classically educated class in the audience.

It took me years to grow comfortable with the fact that I am an American critic, writing for an American audience, from a postwar

American perspective that is a generation away from the world that Esslin grew up in and represents so well. We American critics do not have the cultural background of Esslin's European generation, but what we lack in one area, we hope to make up for in other ways.

While recognizing that we younger American critics have helped create a peculiarly American aesthetic—one more open in the past decade to all sorts of experimentation in theater and performance— we realize that we are primed to do so because of our understanding of absurdism as analyzed by Esslin.

The Oversight of Ceaseless Eyes

HERBERT BLAU

"You're sure you saw me, you won't come tomorrow and tell me that you never saw me!"[1]

That desperate line from *Godot* seems, in the recessive distance, if anything more forlorn and, in the context of recent thought, just about doubly absurd. For even if Didi were seen, as he (dubiously) appears to be, he is after all only an appearance, and what does the seeing amount to—what does it *mean*?—if we can't quite count on an identity, an *I* that goes with the *me*, an autonomous self or ego, as the stable subject of sight. The issue is recurrent in Beckett, explicit in other plays, where in all the rushing words the void keeps pouring in, as with the retrospective subject of *That Time*, which, "never having been" in the first place, is "never the same but the same as what for God's sake did you ever say I to yourself come on now *(Eyes close.)* could you ever say I to yourself in your life. . . ."[2] Well, then *(eyes open)*, should one speak of the object? And even if that were stable, says a more theoretical voice, "exemption from intrinsic flux in a given object does not change the fact that it is the correlative of a subject that does not enjoy such immunity. The observer infects the observed with his own mobility."[3]

This may sound like an echo of Heisenberg in the language of

279

Lacan, but it is once again from Beckett, in the precocious essay on Proust. If the garrulous nothing of *Waiting for Godot* was an aporetic enactment amid the slippage of the signifiers, the slim volume of *Proust*—with its "contempt for the vulgarity of a plausible concatenation" (62)—was an already exhaustive preface to poststructuralist themes and the specular obsessions of the discourse of desire. The loss, the lack, the rupture, all of it is there, the break in origins and the originary trace, and—in the "gaze [that] is no longer the necromancy that sees in each precious object a mirror of the past" (15)—the terror of separation and uncertain signs. "Moreover, when it is a case of human intercourse, we are faced by the problem of an object whose mobility is not merely a function of the subject's," but even more irreparably than the allure of "otherness" implies, "two separate and immanent dynamisms related by no system of synchronisation. So that whatever the object, our thirst for possession is, by definition, insatiable" (6–7). If the desire for possession is bound up with the gaze ("the eyes with gazing fed": from Shakespeare's sonnets to feminist/film criticism), there remains the troubling question—suggested not only by Marcel gazing at the sleeping Albertine, but also by Didi (with the look of being looked at) gazing at the sleeping Gogo—as to *who* is really doing the seeing in the specular play of an absence that is the principle of sight.

"You don't have to look." "You can't help looking." "True." Never mind *who* for the moment; looking at *what*? As the tramps gaze over the forestage in the exchange of ceaseless eyes—veering wildly in their imaginings from "the very beginning" (the primal scene?) to "the last moment" (the one before or yet to come?)—they see "A charnel-house! A charnel-house!" which seems to arise through the maw of the audience from the recursive deadliness of thought itself. "What is terrible is to *have* thought" (*Godot*, 41). And if you think of it it's appalling, the more you *think*, feeling it coming all the same, the end or the beginning ("The very beginning of WHAT?" [42]), as Didi said at the outset, "(With emphasis): AP-PALLED." You can't help looking, true, but any way you look at it, it can't be seen because, as Gogo says after peering into his boot, staring *"sightlessly"* before him, "there's nothing to show" (8). And there's the rub, which leaves us—like the claim of Hamlet to what "passeth show"—with the equally ceaseless problem of interpretation, that estranged enterprise of the mind, somewhere between "the luminous projection of subject desire" (*Proust*, 1) and the desire to make (objective) sense of whatever it is we see, or even more so, what we don't; or what with more or less hysteria, like Gogo waking from his dream, we're not quite sure we saw. In that respect, it is meaning we want to possess (to *have* thought, then, is *not* to have it) and more than that, insatiably, the *meaning* of meaning, an ancient philosophical problem focused radically again in the theater with an incursion of the absurd (returning to the question of *who:* "Do you think God sees me?" [49]), in the now-canonized elusiveness of *Godot.*

Meanwhile, one of the ironies of the postmodern—the theatricalized period that followed upon the absurd—is that what seemed in Beckett infolded, secretive, encrypted, narrowed down to a needle's eye, became in a warp of specularity among the staples of MTV, as if the repressed contents of the unconscious, exploded, were released to the world at large. If that, in theory, mitigated somewhat the existential anxiety (and Beckettian pathos) that came with the absurd, it burdens the question of meaning with almost more than we can possibly see, a virtual pornography of sight that has begun to seem obscene. I want to come to that shortly, along with the repercussions in newer kinds of performance, beyond the perimeters of the scene established as theater. But let's for a narrower moment reflect on that, as it were through the theater (the site of seeing) reflecting on itself. With the minimalism of Beckett in mind, what I am most particularly concerned with is the subtle thing the theater came from before it widened into theatricality, an *excess of theater* that from the very beginning—escaping the desire for "ocular proof"—always threatened to undo the form. It is precisely this excess, inappropriable as meaning, which has been compulsively remembered through the entire history of the drama, as if the paranoia of its major figures, from Sophocles' Oedipus to Genet's Irma, has proved contagious and possessed the dramatic text. It's as if the text itself, distrusting theater, were suffused with a certain anxiety about the prospect of its performance. There are any number of symptoms carrying over to theater practice and the dynamics of the relation between actors, directors, playwrights, critics, and scholars. Each (as Beckett was himself)[4] has been invested in or protecting a certain meaning. As the god of the theater, Dionysus, should have suggested in "his" own nature, whatever the most certain meaning is, it can be right there before your eyes but—because it's essentially *imageless* (as Nietzsche said of Dionysus)—in any event it always escapes.

"The meaning of meaning is Apollonian," says Derrida in his essay "Freud and the Scene of Writing," "by virtue of everything within it that can be seen."[5] As we reflect upon (and within) this Apollonian heritage—switching back and forth between the seer and the scene— we are inevitably drawn into the dialectical wordplay between the visible and the invisible, where in the very sinews of perception the spectacle appears as a trace or decoy, the ghostly, reverberant *surface* of the seen. Theater is made from this play of meaning in a structure of becoming, the passing form of an invisible force, where we lose meaning by finding it, and there is always something *repressed*. So it is, with all its duplicity, in the camera obscura of *Endgame*, which— to the degree that Beckett's theater is a reinterpretation of the form— seems in its spectral beginning like the ontological moment, the *precipitation* of appearance, or the materialization of theater from whatever it is it is *not*.

What meets our gaze is what we do not see. That's what appears to be self-reflexively dramatized in the teasing revelation of the blinded Hamm who, even when unveiled, remains behind his glasses, (un)canny, logorrheic, intertextual, the object (or objective case: the "*Me*" who is going to play)[6] of subjectivity, a signifying presence with no reality except as a *figure of speech*. What we might have seen there, however, is what we have since encountered in the semiotic terms of the newer psychoanalysis: that there is a double articulation to theatrical fantasy, arising from the linguistic structure of the unconscious, that is *founded* in repression. (Here we touch upon what, not only in Beckett, is a truth of theater that is archaic in theater, and that is *the theater's fear of its own presence*, what is both repressed and articulated at certain astonishing moments in its canonical history.) What appears to be theater occurs in the difference between manifest and latent, surface and depth, the "spacious breadth" of the division in "a thing inseparate," as Troilus says in that mad discourse on the scene of betrayal (*Troilus* 5.2.144), the succession of signifiers that constitute performance. The unconscious signified arises from some pitfall of this inseparate thing, the gap or absence in which it resides (with dimensions too fine for

"Ariachne's broken woof" [5.2.148]), the orifice between the signifiers, not in order to express what has to be said, but in order to indicate, *by veiling it*, what needs to be hidden.

Caught up in the strange logic of this succession, what we think of as "living theater" is, in the repetition of its seminal moment, a representational problem. This problem was compounded, after the advent of Beckett (but in a sort of misprision), in the dissidence of the sixties, which, scorning the hidden and wanting nothing repressed, aspired to unveil it, as in the desublimating redundancy of the Living Theatre, which literalized the succession in its signifying bodies—the naked inscription of Paradise Now—and the solipsistic images of the spectacle's excess. The utopian mission of the sixties (sublimated in theory and persisting today in the discourse of desire) was to liberate the unconscious onto the public scene, acting out the imaginary in a perverse romance with the media and the strategy of appropriation of the fantasy machine.

For the audience in those exhilarating days—the old dramaturgy rejected, everybody making the scene—the profusion of images offered a double prospect: that it might become the spectacle, and, as Rousseau projected it in his letter to D'Alembert, that the spectacle would be a community. What it got instead was *commodification*. And never more abundantly so. For there is nothing that carries with it so readily as image that consumable equivalence that is—as Danton perceived on the "thin crust" of the promenade in Büchner's play[7]— the circulatory principle of bourgeois exchange. Today, on the lucrative fringes of what used to be the counterculture, this is by no means an embarrassment, as we can see in the Day-Glo salability of the (new) psychedelic glamour on the periphery of Tomkins Park, passing from the desolation of the East Village to the dazzle of the Palladium. (Given the quick inflation of the art, not to mention the real estate, in the East Village, it has passed, besides, into the mainstream galleries of bourgeois exchange even faster than I have been able to take note of it in the slower movement of this scene of writing.) Whether or not the society of the spectacle is a culture of narcissism, there is nothing more indicative of a commodity-conscious culture, designer-fashioned and hyped on style, than the high performance of high visibility that we see now in the arts, whether the spotlighted neo-abstraction in the disco Kamikaze or the '61 Cadillac, overpainted and supercharged, the Suprema Ultima Deluxa of Kenny Scharf. The circulation of appearance is made all the more spontaneous when replicated by the media, with images of other images and, in the new bohemia or avant-garde, images of the artist-as-image who is, along with the audience-as-spectacle, remaking the scene for somewhat glossier consumption, as if mediation were natural law and—born again in quotation—the sixties were never repressed.

It is a scene in which "the eyes with gazing fed" are glutted by the gaze that, seeping from the unconscious, saturates the world. What is happening in the theater can hardly compete with these newer modes of performance on the spectacular scene of bourgeois exchange. While the solipsism and excess persist, now more than ever as a matter of style, they do so at their best with a no less beguiling and often chastening irony, like the expensive labor in the enchantment of Christo's Parisian epic, a marvel of high fashion, the repackaging of Pont-Neuf. The implication of the conception is that it was already packaged, by the culture of guidebooks and the eroding traffic of ceaseless eyes. Also viewed by multitudes (some of those in Paris for the spring collections), Christo's polyamide spectacle was a semiotic veil over the history into which—stretching and fretting its magic hours upon the bridge, or laving its sides in a watery splendor with light reflected from the Seine—it was committed to disappear. Here, after the sublimity of its little moment, the ordinary monument was restored, with whatever ambiguous residue from the spectacular transformation.

But some of those captivated by the expanse of spectacle in our lives also think of it as an unabating infatuation that threatens to engulf the real, if it has not already done so. This is something else again, not the old fear of deceit in the image, an aversion to appearance, but rather as if the Platonic cave were a breeder reactor whose core was toxic waste: what we're looking at, it appears, is the end of representation that, by runaway reproduction, has at last undone itself. For Jean Baudrillard, there *is* an obscenity in all this, "no longer the hidden, filthy mien of that which can be seen," but rather "the abjection of the visible," its nullity. This arises from a universe of systems and stretches over it, mirroring our technologies, "their sleek and accommodating distances, miniaturized . . . ."[8] In the accommodating spectacle of this reduction, the giant wrappings of Christo, which suggest the engulfment, would be another hapless gesture, the mimicry of redundancy in a network of redundancies. Nor is this anymore the return of the Same. Too attenuated to be the return and insufficient to be the revenge, it is no more than a minor mockery of representation, now bleached, nullified, and liquidated by the information system.

(There is likely to be—as there has been, among some with a theoretical investment in the prospects of mass culture—more or less resistance to this bleak and imploded view. But should it require confirmation, think for a moment of any of those recurrent catastrophic events, out of the realm of pure contingency, that seem to constitute the threshold or outer limit of the system of representation. Recall, for instance, the seeming innocence with which the space shuttle Challenger—carrying the teacher whose pupils were at school watching over television—exploded into the white radiance of eternity or the ultimate communication, the apotheosis of visibility. We all remember the image, with instant replay, parsed and graphed, replicated by the hour, but perhaps have forgotten how it was absorbed by the media and a media-conscious administration into the construct of a national emotion, or some appropriate facsimile, for which only televised disaster seems to be the sufficient cause. Meanwhile, in what has become a national habit, the almost universal urge for image, augmented by the right to information, seemed to be honored over privacy in the supremacy of the networks, which will sometimes exact the image even from a victim like an ethical obligation. More often than not, that we are all there to be imaged is assumed as a reflex that won't refuse.[9] Thus, the watching students and the family, seen viewing the explosion in its horrific instance, or pursued by the cameras after—or even, no doubt, watching their own images later on—were quickly deprived of the continuity of devastation or a pure moment of unmediated grief.[10] Without minimizing the widespread decency that follows disaster or the sensitivity in the commentary that is aware of these ironies, there was one that was sure to go unmentioned as the images of the fireball, relayed by satellite, encircled the globe. While it's obviously in order for all systems to be shut down (as that wasn't) when there's the slightest trace of a malfunction before the launching, when the perfectly imaginable horror does happen in flight, it seems just about inconceivable for all network coverage, that other system—from which, after all, the space program is inseparable—also to be shut down, letting all emotion settle into a nonspectacular interval of national silence. But that quite naturally has to wait—the silence—for the moment of prayer and meditation in the unison of the memorial, when we mourn together over television, with cameras on the grieving families.)

What makes them obscene, in Baudrillard's view, is that the images never cease. Nor do they cease to be commodities (like the pictures in a well-known children's book—called *I Spy*—which my daughter used to insist we look at, over and over). Brought to a pleurisy by reproduction, the tumescence of image virtually exceeds the real, the very boredom of the endless replications inducing a fascination that, so far as we can see, might exist without an image, in the disembodied passion of the look. The trouble is that, thus fascinated by the fetish/image, we can hardly be expected to see anything very far.

It is the paradoxical stupefaction of these mediated spectacles, "the glazed extreme of the body," that crosses into the obscene, an advanced state of the disease of catatonia among the spectators of what Brecht called the *culinary theater*. "True, their eyes are open," he wrote in his notorious description, "but they stare rather than see, just as they listen rather than hear. . . . Seeing and hearing are activities, and can be pleasant ones, but these people seem relieved of activity and like men to whom something is being done."[11] What happens offstage in this audience, Beckett put onstage in *Waiting for Godot*, where in the stunned proceedings nothing happens twice. But in the empty scene that Baudrillard is describing nothing happens again and again and again, filling "the viewfinder," until "we are saturated with it." This evocation of a glutted emptiness is preceded in Baudrillard's essay "What Are You Doing After the Orgy?" by an *outré* form of culinary theater, at the S/M end of the spectrum of performance art, though it also happens to be "real." As the event was reported, a young Japanese dismembers a white and nubile woman with a kitchen knife and, as he eats the "delectable parts," tries to reassemble her *image*. He also takes Polaroids at every stage to be sure that he won't forget (43).

This, to be sure, is the worst possible case of the society of the spectacle, which is also, as the case is made, the termination of the social in the indeterminate Mass. Whether or not the social is ended, this indeterminacy is now something more extensive than an aesthetic of the aleatory on the margins of the avant-garde, worked out by a throw of dice through the Book of Changes, as it once was by John Cage. Since the sixties, art has not only had to navigate the sometimes collapsing, then reappearing, rather indiscernible lines between manifest and latent, surface and depth, nature and culture, but to situate itself between high culture and mass culture, popular culture and subcultures, and the overall diffusion of culture in which we have seen the accumulation of a vast array of spectacles as the most favored commodity of consumer capitalism.

What we encounter in this diffusion are performance events that, like *The Marble Fog* of Robert Longo at the Brooklyn Museum, are seduced by the fascination effect of the world of simulation even as they expose it.[12] The effect is spectacular but not at all specific, as the fog (like history) dissipates, along with whatever remains of the solidity of tradition, the ideological status of recycled forms. The audience may be deliberately confused in such events by the pastiched blurring of the living and nonliving, presented and represented, but it is an audience for the most part born to the specular mania of the postmodern. It grew up in a confusion of genres, consuming the bricolage. The tableaux of Longo—like some doubly glazed and panoramic distension of the art that fascinated Diderot—are very much aware of this. In the performative bravura and monumental borrowings of their oversized theatricality, they are a sight to be beheld. Longo is himself ambiguously entranced with the quotable resources from myth, history, and the media available to the spectacle, but the viewer is also being asked—with more or less factitious terror in the swarm of uncertain signs—to examine the manipulative powers of the signifying apparatus. The combinatory devices of his performances can be mesmeric as they hint at meaning, but they are also concerned with the disarming ways in which alienation and mystification, the seductive staples of commodification, are bound up with spectacle.

There is in such performance a somewhat elusive attitude toward the further release of simulations and the overrehearsed images from a kitsch and archaic repertoire. The argument is that cultural forms and myths are being recycled in order to deconstruct them. There is something discomfiting in the claim that amounts to a double bind since—as in the work of Riefenstahl or Syberberg, or theory's obsession with classical Hollywood films—the persistent glamor of the showing, the embossed past and emblazoned kitsch, the renown of the empty signifiers, keeps the myth attractive. Recent performance art is, however, much less ambiguous about the revealed mechanisms of representation that account for the mystifications. It is also a good deal less embarrassed (aesthetically and sexually) about what we used to call having it both ways, which is not exactly what formalism meant by resolving paradox in ambiguity. In Longo's work, the various arts are not merely overlapped or blended as in the earlier multimedia (though it could be said that the photographic and filmic images are in the most favored, absorptive position).

The resurrected images and iconic forms of Longo are not "fused" into the appearance of an autonomous work in the modernist sense, but rather given the off-the-wall look of an assemblage of appendages hoist by their own petard. Incongruous elements are, simultaneously, kept free-floating and endowed with gratuitous aura, artfully aggregated and hyperbolically juxtaposed, in a sort of elephantiasis of surfaces whose effects are neither an account of history nor, if history's causes are known in its effects, a reliable record of why and by whom. As with the collaborative activity of a movie, Longo often includes his coworkers in a list of credits, but in Aristotelian terms, the formal cause is absent. In the aesthetics of the postmodern, that absence is not without virtue. The ideological dilemma, however, of the Longo spectacle is expropriation of the expropriators, as with Laurie Anderson at the Grammy Awards after recording for Warner Brothers. Like Longo, Anderson is able to include the dilemma with more or less irony, or disarming humor, in her work, as she did in *United States*, but it's as if their technical operations were programmed by and for a supply-side economy. As for the audience, in the rather glamorous means by which we are made aware of the fetishizing attraction of the exchangeable image, we find ourselves consuming, not altogether distastefully, another unliving if upgraded commodity.

It seems to be the inevitable outcome of the postindustrial reification of image that is the reign of representation. In recent theory, the critique of representation is rabid and powerful. As if they'd discovered what always eluded Artaud, a body without organs, certain variants of poststructuralist discourse—polysexual, schizoanalytic, radically feminist—are still engaged in the probably vain anti-oedipal and tautological enterprise that proposes to bring representation to an end. (In somebody like Karen Finley, the gender-busting audacity of her assault on logocentrism amounts, in a sort of apocalyptic delirium that knows it won't end, to shitting on representation or sticking it up her ass.) But so long as there is a spectacle, it may be well to recall the Situationist thesis, formulated by Guy Debord at a time when radical transformation seemed not only urgent but a more likely possibility: "The spectacle in general, as the concrete inversion of life, is the autonomous movement of the non-living."[13] Artaud was enraged by the repetition of this autonomous movement that inhabits the recurrent discourse on repetition in the libidinal economy of deconstruction. As for the articulation of "the living upon the nonliving in general, origin of all repetition,"[14] whose trace is material and immaterial at once, it sounds like a definition of performance that brings us back to the unconscious. As in the stagings of the unconscious—where we are actor/audience to a spectacle whose repetitions may escape us—we are always dealing in performance, the insubstantial pageant, with an (im)palpable signification whose truth is invisible and whose energy is opaque.

The (apparent) truth is that there is always a displacement at work in the form of its vanishing. The drama itself is an extended meditation on the idea that whatever it is we're perceiving has already passed us by. Its subject is *aphanisis*, the movement of disappearance that is, most radically, the manifestation of the subject. (The term was used by Ernest Jones for the disappearance of sexual desire, a fate not identical with castration; thus aphanisis is the object of a fear even more profound than that of castration.) Shakespeare's sonnets are a virtual textbook on that proposition, and the perceptual impasse dramatized in the plays has been taken up anew in the performative nexus between psychoanalysis and deconstruction, as in this passage from Derrida: "The graphic image is not seen; and the acoustic image is not heard. The difference between the full unities of the voice remains unheard. And"—as we may see in the redoubled watching of the duplicitous scene with Troilus, the imperceptible fissure in the identity of Cressida—"the difference in the body of the inscription remains invisible" (*Of Grammatology*, 65). The performance, in its signifying succession (not-signified), conceals and erases itself in the motion of its production.

This is the motion that teases us out of thought. No one sees the motion but the motion, as Ben Jonson wrote in one of his masques.

And that motion—like the exertion of force between breaches which, to avert pain, arouses *resistance*—initiates and contains the problematic of the audience, which gathers around this paradox: that the pleasure of seeing—what Freud called *Schaulust* (seeing, being seen), with its implications of sadomasochism[15]—is constrained by the desire to see what cannot be seen. That is not, as we tend to think, merely the primal scene, the bed of incest, but the seeing of the scene, the scopic drive itself *(the desire to see)*—the object of specularity that is really out of sight, like the ghost in the mother's chamber that only the son can see. Resisting ocular proof, it is the motion producing meaning that, to Apollo's eternal frustration, never lets itself finally mean.

NOTES

1. Samuel Beckett, *Waiting for Godot* (New York: Grove, 1954), 59.

2. Samuel Beckett, *That Time*, in *The Collected Shorter Plays* (New York: Grove, 1984), 230–31.

3. Samuel Beckett, *Proust* (New York: Grove, n.d.), 6–7.

4. If the repetitions of the paranoia are consummately focused in the drama of Beckett, there was until his recent death the double irony of his own protective vigilance over the integrity of his texts and the correct way to stage them. Since his drama has, in a sense, prepared the ground for revisionist performance, his rage over the presumptions of other productions—sometimes shared by reverent scholars—raises any number of theoretical questions about authorship and authenticity and the statute of limitations on the rites of theatricality.

5. Jacques Derrida, "Freud and the Scene of Writing," in *Writing and Difference*, trans. and intro. Alan Bass (Chicago: University of Chicago Press, 1978), 26.

6. Samuel Beckett, *Endgame* (New York: Grove, 1958), 2.

7. *Danton's Death*, in George Büchner, *Complete Plays and Prose*, trans. and intro. Carl Richard Mueller (New York: Mermaid-Hill and Wang, 1963), 31.

8. Jean Baudrillard, "What Are You Doing After the Orgy?" *Artforum* 22, no. 2 (1983): 42.

9. Not only do we live in a time born to be photographed but, as Walter Benjamin remarked in a famous essay, "Any man today can lay claim to being filmed." See "The Work of Art in the Age of Mechanical Reproduction," in *Illuminations*, ed. and intro. Hannah Arendt, trans. Harry Zohn (New York: Schocken, 1977), 233. With the immediate feedback of the electronic media, we can also lay claim to seeing ourselves being filmed.

10. The desire for such an unmediated moment, or the *singularity* of his grief, is what proves so moving in the book on photography written by Roland Barthes after the death of his mother, and which—as it turned out—seemed to be a premonition of

his own death. Determined to be guided in the book only by the consciousness of his own feelings, he is also very conscious—as he approaches the *spectacle* of what-she-was in the photograph—that he has spent a lifetime as "observed subject" and "observing subject" in a world dominated by the visual image and without a "History of Looking" (*Camera Lucida*, trans. Richard Howard [New York: Hill and Wang, 1981], 10, 12).

11. Bertolt Brecht, "A Short Organum for the Theater," in *Brecht on Theater: The Development of an Aesthetic*, ed. and trans. John Willett (New York: Hill and Wang, 1964), 187.

12. If the effect can be experienced, even through boredom, it can also be *produced* quite spectacularly. For a commentary on the calculated estrangement of this ambiguously produced effect in the earlier work of Robert Longo, see Hal Foster, "Contemporary Art and Spectacle," in *Recodings: Art, Spectacle, Cultural Politics* (Port Townsend, Wash.: Bay Press, 1985), 79–96.

13. Guy Debord, *La Societé du spectacle* (Paris: Editions Chamo Libre, 1971), note 2. The book is a virtual formulation of the strategies, with a theoretical base, of the International Situationist group, whose critique of advanced capitalism in the early sixties was inseparable from the critique of representation, which continues in theory with undiminished vigilance. First published in 1967, it was translated as *Society of the Spectacle* (Detroit: Black and Red, 1977).

14. Jacques Derrida, *Of Grammatology*, trans. and intro. Gayatri Chakravorty Spivak (Baltimore: Johns Hopkins University Press, 1976), 65.

15. A discussion of *Schaulust* can be found in Jacques Lacan's seminar "The Partial Drive and Its Circuit," in *The Four Fundamental Concepts of Psychoanalysis*, ed. Jacques-Alain Miller, trans. Alan Sheridan (New York: Norton, 1978), 174–86. After indicating that what is fundamental at the level of each drive is the reflexive movement outward and back by which it is structured, Lacan then says it is remarkable that Freud could designate the two poles of this movement by a slight shift in verb forms that relates sight and pain: "*Beschauen und beschaut werden*, to see and to be seen, *quälen* and *gequält werden*, to torment and to be tormented." The sadomasochism is implied in the circuitry of the two verb forms, Freud having understood from the outset that no part of the distance covered in seeing could be divorced from the circular character of the path of the drive, in which there appears what "*does not appear*," a new subject that is the other. "It is only with its appearance at the level of the other that what there is of the function of the drive may be realized" (178–79).

After the Absurd: Rethinking Realism and a Few Other Isms

ENOCH BRATER

When Martin Esslin published *The Theatre of the Absurd* in 1961, he was among the first to respond to the climate of spontaneity that gave life and bold new energy to the postwar European drama. The conventions of bourgeois realism with its picayune illusionism had previously and vigorously come under attack in the "avant garde /avant guerre" playhouses of the twenties and thirties.[1] The cafés and pocket theaters of Paris, Zurich, and Berlin were celebrated show-cases for Dada and surrealist manifestations questioning the "art" of dramatic art. Such notorious theater practitioners as Tristan Tzara, Jean Cocteau, and Antonin Artaud refused to hold, in O'Neill's phrase, "the family kodak up to ill-nature."[2] They turned their backs on Ibsen and Chekhov and took their inspiration instead from Jarry, Apollinaire, and the Strindberg of the late and luminous chamber plays. Offering us something at once more compelling and more disturbing than a playfulness about the possibilities of dramatic form, this was revolutionary theater: no more art, especially dramatic art, with a capital *D* and a capital *A*.[3] While Europe was quickly becoming a theater of war instead of a theater for artistic exploration, experimental drama was forced to take a long pause. When the spirit of the new reemerged after an armistice was declared, it had been sobered by the Grand Guignol that was to have its most gruesome displays in Auschwitz and Hiroshima. Innocence was gone, but the theater remained. In cities devastated by destruction and pain, it awakened to claim its prewar heritage of dramatic remaking.

Esslin directed our attention not only to drama's invigorated spirit, but also to its dazzling and puzzling forms. Taking his cue from the popular currency of Jean-Paul Sartre and Albert Camus, he began to articulate just how wide the dimensions were to this new "theater of the absurd," a phrase that has proved more durable than any other in describing what the drama of this period was meant to be. *Ab-surd:* not heard. The missing sound was reason.

Formally, the absurdists for the stage set an ambitious agenda for themselves: how to organize a play without using the timeworn conventions of a previously agreed-upon "logical" system, now thoroughly discredited by Beckett, for one, as "solution clapped on problem like a snuffer on a candle."[4] Life—and theater—had to be more resilient than that; both, after all, had miraculously survived the war. Looking back on it now, from the vantage point of the last decade of the twentieth century, Esslin's claim for a theater of the absurd seems modest, even tame, especially in terms of the new ways of thinking about drama that his select but international group of Western playwrights spawned. Pre-performance art, pre-unscripted drama, and certainly pre-theory as something to be equated with the theater event itself, what Esslin tagged the theater of the absurd has shown itself to be a fertile laboratory for much that continues to be innovative and enduring in the theater of our uneasy time.

One begins with Beckett, not because of the privileged status awarded him by several contributors whose work appears in this book, but because that is where Esslin chose to begin. He began not theoretically, but experientially, with the actuality of *Waiting for Godot* in performance. And no mean *Godot*, this: in 1957 Herb Blau brought his San Francisco Actors' Workshop production to San Quentin prison. The event itself, as well as Esslin's telling about it on the very first page of *The Theatre of the Absurd*, has proved legendary. And though Beckett's play was restaged at the same prison as recently as 1988 by the Swedish director Jan Jonson, this time using inmates as the actors, the sad fact remains that what separates the late fifties from the early nineties is that it's now a cliché to observe that you don't have to be a lifer to wait for something to arrive that never comes. *Waiting for Godot*, as the director Alan Schneider observed, is no longer only a play; it has become a condition of life.[5]

Critics like Ruby Cohn, John Russell Brown, and Thomas R. Whitaker have elsewhere addressed the question of Beckett's strong influence on a younger generation of playwrights.[6] The plotless play, the use of discontinuous dialogue, the set empty but filled with mysterious suggestion, the denouement that never comes, the effects of silence and the tension that builds in a pause, the sheer theatricality held by the actor's voice in extended monologue, or the dramatic opportunity that lies in standing stock-still, have become so characteristic of our theater that we hardly notice them at all. Once an audience comes to the theater expecting the devices of the absurd, even more than a little inclined to their charms, the absurd doesn't seem quite so absurd anymore. Instead, "it all" seems quietly reassuring, familiar—almost, one is tempted to say, real. Yesterday's revolutionary techniques have become today's conventions: Sam Shepard's moonscape in *A Lie of the Mind* opens on a blue pay-phone set nowhere in particular on some vast American highway—there's no "there" there, and the second act of Caryl Churchill's *Cloud Nine* makes twenty-five years pass for its characters but more than a hundred for the audience, and we call this realism. Beckett, we now realize—and it was *The Theatre of the Absurd* that first made us realize this—was only one of the more significant players in the wholesale reshaping of Western drama that was taking place all over Europe and America. Something was indeed taking its course—so much so that it was to change forever our notions of what might be made to happen in a performance space, as well as to challenge any preconceptions we might still have concerning what constitutes a performance itself.

Perhaps the movement called the theater of the absurd has left its most direct mark not on those flamboyant plays written in the pure avant-garde tradition (if one can be forgiven for the moment the absurdity of using a term like purity to talk about anything as fluid and spontaneous as the avant-garde), but rather on those works that still pay reluctant tribute to the well-made play within the realistic illusion of looking through a fourth wall. Harold Pinter's dramatic world has so often been scrutinized for its absurdist insinuations that one sometimes forgets that in most of the plays of his most prolific period, from *The Birthday Party* through *No Man's Land*, the audience is almost always looking into a room through just such an imaginary wall. On this stage we can study in miniature what strange things happen to an illusion like Ibsen's once it passes through the theater of the absurd. "If you take the glass," Ruth says to the captive Lenny in *The Homecoming*, "I'll take you." General Gabler's decorative pistols are no longer necessary. Words, however cryptic, can now speak daggers, just as Shakespeare had predicted. The theater of the absurd convinced us that a refrain like "Got any olives?"[8] can be a through-line as rich dramatically as any of the three sisters' haunting cries of "Moscow! Moscow! Moscow!" Whether or not a wasp gets caught in a jar of marmalade provides as much tension and suspense as whether or not Toozenbach, Irena's intended, will be shot in his offstage duel with Solyony. "One Baron more or less," anyway remarks a laconic Chebutykin, "what does it matter?"[9] On the set for *The Caretaker* a statue of Buddha is a detail as incongruous (and therefore as noticeable) as the map of Africa hanging on a wall to which Astrov refers in the fourth act of *Uncle Vanya*. Water dripping into a bucket from Pinter's ceiling in *The Caretaker* resounds in theater space with the same evocative force as those footsteps we hear from John Gabriel Borkman's "upstairs" study during Ella Rentheim's interview with her twin sister, Borkman's wife. The pale light of a noisy Hoover on a darkened set can be just as intimidating as any Natasha catching us off-guard with a single candle. We no longer need any other contrivance to end an act than this: "Listen. You know what it's like when you're in a room with the light on and then suddenly the light goes out? I'll show you. It's like this."[10]

Pinter is perhaps too obvious an example. Esslin had already targeted the early Pinter's mystery and menace well within range of that perhaps too broad category he labelled "parallels and proselytes." (In the third edition of *Theatre of the Absurd* Pinter graduates to a major figure.) To these we might add a few updates: the simultaneous set used to so much advantage in *A Lie of the Mind* or the "buried" children, literally and metaphorically, who seem to be as endemic to Shepard's world as rhinoceroses are to Ionesco's; the busy set for *American Buffalo*, where David Mamet's pawn shop is as cluttered as anything we have seen before in *The Caretaker*, and where Teach's entry line defies and finally exorcises every rule in the game of realistic exposition: "Fuckin' Ruthie, fuckin' Ruthie, fuckin' Ruthie, fuckin' Ruthie, fuckin' Ruthie" (compare, for example, Nora's opening line in *A Doll's House:* "Be sure and hide the Christmas tree carefully, Helene, the children mustn't see it this evening, when it's all decorated"); the loudspeaker installed on Brian Friel's set for *Aristocrats*, through which a dying man calls out to present children and absent friends; or the toilets that flush in unison in Maureen Duffy's *Rites*. (Why does no one go to the bathroom in Ibsen anyway? No one even farts in modern drama until *Waiting for Godot*, though several Dada-surrealist manifestations offer us examples of sketchy characters suffering uncontrollable flatulence: Artaud, for example, was fascinated by Ida's flatulence in Vitrac's *Victor: ou les enfants au pouvoir* (1928). So it goes with "a resounding tinkle," again with the obvious exception of Beckett: "My anger subsides . . . I'd like to pee." Compared to the bourgeois reserve of the so-called realistic style, the Elizabethan playhouse was far less squeamish in employing such gritty naturalistic detail.)

Yet it is not so much on the writing of new scripts that the theater of the absurd has had its most profound effect. What the idiom of absurdity made us realize was that an entirely new attitude toward theater was noisily emerging. Here avant-garde playwrights coerced us into rereading the classics, especially Shakespeare, resulting in our modern preference for *King Lear* over *Hamlet* and our even more recent preference for *Measure for Measure* over both. Lear and Edgar on the heath, as Jan Kott so ably argued in *Shakespeare Our Contemporary*, is *King Lear* and/or *Endgame*. There was suddenly more than one "alternative" Shakespeare.[11] "Our revels now are ended" is *The Tempest*—but is it only that? Rearrange the dialogue, change the accent, and shift the speech from Prospero to Hamm (precisely what Beckett *has* done), and it's *Endgame* once more. The supposed comic relief of the gravedigger's scene in *Hamlet* or the knocking on the gate in *Macbeth* now read like something out of Beckett, the later the better, just as the Viennese brothels in *Measure for Measure* were straight out of Jean Genet. It was only on reflection that we recognized that things were really the other way around.

Nor has the modern repertory itself been immune to such dynamic rethinking about what Bert States called those "great reckonings in little rooms"[12] set on a realistic stage. Charlotta Ivanovna, the eccentric German governess who performs magic tricks as a sideline in *The Cherry Orchard*, now seems like a central figure in the play, as does the young Masha mourning for her life in *The Seagull*, where she poses in bohemian black and takes snuff. "That's disgusting," an impatient Dorn demurs, setting just the right tone here. The theater of the absurd made us understand something fundamental about Chekhov that even the master Stanislavski struggled with: his play was a comedy, in places almost a farce, just as the author always intended it to be. Slice-of-life realism always depends on just who's doing the slicing. Even "papa Ibsen" might be read differently in light of the absurd, especially when we notice such promising figures as the enigmatic Rat Woman in *Little Eyolf* or Old Ekdal in *The Wild Duck*. Ibsen's late symbolic plays, always difficult to categorize, now seemed uniformly accessible, even in a translation as dated as Eva Le Galliene's:

> *Borkman:* What's the matter with your foot? You're limping.
> *Foldal:* Yes. You see—I was run over.
> *Borkman:* Run over?
> *Foldal:* Yes, by a covered sleigh—
> *Borkman:* Aha—. . . .
> *Ella:* They ran over you?
> *Foldal:* They came right down upon me. . . .
> *Borkman:* (*Laughing inwardly*) Do you know who was in the sleigh? . . .
> *Foldal:* No, how should I? . . . But what difference does it make? . . . I'm so happy! So very happy!
> *Borkman:* Happy?
> *Ella:* But didn't you hear him say he had been run over?
> *Borkman:* We are all of us run over sometime or other in life. The thing to do is to pick oneself up again—as though nothing had happened.
> *Foldal:* That's a profound saying, John Gabriel. . . . [13]

Our readings in the dramatic canon have therefore been unmistakably mediated by that knowledge of the absurdist enterprise Esslin first brought to our attention. Sometimes the perspective yields results that could not have been predicted in advance. A production of *Strange Interlude*, originally planned as a vehicle for Glenda Jackson, first on the West End, then on Broadway, tapped O'Neill's darkest undertones for all the absurdity they were worth. Scenes once considered unplayable now held the stage with new and surprising authority. Critics, this one included, left the theater and went home to reread the play. The same "absurdist" perspective can also yield results that are more than a little unsettling. When the Wooster Group under Elizabeth LeCompte's direction incorporated video scenes of *Our Town* into the structure of *Route 1 & 9*, Thornton Wilder's old chestnut seemed oddly moving in this deft, but highly outrageous, context. Absurdity was in the eye of the beholder.

As the examples above should make clear, it is in the life of the drama as performance where the most liberating effects of the theater of the absurd can be most persuasively studied. For what the absurdists gave us, finally, was nothing less than an uninhibited attitude concerning how a play might be written as well as how it might now be produced, particularly in a post-Brechtian age of such adventurous European directors as Peter Stein, Giorgio Strehler, Anatoli Vasiliev, and Ariane Mnouchkine, or an American like Robert Wilson. There would be "no more masterpieces."[14] Although they did not do so systematically, the absurdists laid the foundation for the breakdown between such formally separate entities as "text" and "production" and urged us to concentrate on "performance" instead. Sometimes a performance had a text, sometimes it didn't, sometimes a "script" arrived only after improvisation or through other collaborationist techniques—the new style of "process writing" we associate with Jerzy Grotowski's "poor theatre" in Poland, Joe Chaikin's Open Theatre in New York, Dario Fo and Franca Rame's work in Italy, or the plays engendered by Monstrous Regiment and the Joint Stock Company in London. Besides, in the wake of absurdity, texts, now considered highly unstable and susceptible to a variety of moods and modes, were being hastily rewritten. During rehearsals in Basel, Dürrenmatt became so impatient with that icon of preabsurdist drama, *The Dance of Death*, that he offered *Play Strindberg* in its place. Tom Stoppard became the darling of the Edinburgh Festival in 1966 by writing star turns for Rosencrantz and Guildenstern and banishing Hamlet and his problem to an unenviable minor role. Disrupting conventional notions of stage time as well as stage text, the German theater has performed more radical surgery: letting his imagination range wildly over a royal prince's subscript to the fair Ophelia ("Thine evermore, most dear lady, / whilst this machine is to him, Hamlet"), Heiner Müller has fashioned his own "theater work" by inventing a new *Hamletmachine*.

Compared to these shenanigans, a play with a recognizable beginning, middle, and end can be downright refreshing, especially if it is one of the more "realistic" sort from when walls were walls and men were men. A steady diet of theater in the absurdist vein can make Pinero seem like the latest news, Granville Barker a revelation. That is perhaps the most stunning tribute we can offer to the theater of the absurd. It made us discover, once again—but this time on our own terms—what John Gassner long ago characterized as realism's multivalent personality.[15] The possibilities we now find in that elusive term *realism,* some of which I have tried to outline in this brief conclusion to this volume, are really quite different from those stable qualities we were once told were there. Context is everything. Our own is one in which the theater has been marked forever not only by the techniques, but even more so by the posture firmly established by those visionary muckrakers brought to center stage in *The Theatre of the Absurd.* Playwrights like Beckett now made us see as new things that were always there in front of our eyes, but never before in such sharp relief. They urged us to look backward as well as forward in thinking about what a twentieth-century repertory might be made to be. In doing so, this heady band of theatricians, working mostly on their own and certainly never organized into anything even vaguely resembling a movement, managed against all odds to do what the best "isms" do: "theory" notwithstanding, they widened our perception of the rich potential for representation that lies in that illusionary realm called theater, which is merely human potential *in extremis.* Yes, as my colleague Ruby Cohn observes, "the absurd is around"—I would add here that it is *all* around, even in unexpected corners. There's no *after* after the absurd.

NOTES

1. See J. H. Matthews, *Theatre in Dada and Surrealism* (Syracuse: Syracuse University Press, 1974); and Marjorie Perloff, *The Futurist Moment: Avant Garde, Avant Guerre, and the Language of Rupture* (Chicago: University of Chicago Press, 1986).

2. Eugene O'Neill as quoted by Robert Brustein in *The Theatre of Revolt: An Approach to the Modern Drama* (Boston: Little, Brown, 1962), 338.

3. For a comprehensive study of the origins of the Paris avant-garde, see Roger Shattuck, *The Banquet Years,* rev. ed. (New York: Vintage, 1968).

4. Samuel Beckett, "Denis Devlin," in *Disjecta: Miscellaneous Writings and a Dramatic Fragment,* ed. Ruby Cohn (London: John Calder, 1983), 92.

5. See Alan Schneider, "'Any Way You Like, Alan': Working with Beckett," *Theatre Quarterly* 5, no. 19 (September–November 1975): 27.

6. See the following essays collected in *Beckett at 80 / Beckett in Context*, ed. Enoch Brater (New York: Oxford University Press, 1986): Ruby Cohn, "Growing (Up?) with *Godot*," 13–24; John Russell Brown, "Beckett and the Art of the Nonplus," 25–45; and Thomas R. Whitaker, "'Wham, Bam, Thank You Sam': The Presence of Beckett," 208–29.

7. See Samuel Beckett's *Footfalls*, in *Collected Shorter Plays of Samuel Beckett* (London: Faber and Faber, 1984), 237–43.

8. See *The Collection*, in Harold Pinter, *Three Plays* (New York: Grove, 1962), 51 passim.

9. Citations in my text from Chekhov are taken from *Plays by Anton Chekhov*, trans. Elisaveta Fen (Harmondsworth, Eng.: Penguin, 1959).

10. Harold Pinter, *No Man's Land* (New York: Grove, 1975), 53. For a more thematic approach to the Pinter-Chekhov connection, see John Lahr, "Pinter and Chekhov: The Bond of Naturalism," reprinted in *Pinter: A Collection of Critical Essays*, ed. Arthur Ganz (Englewood Cliffs, N.J.: Prentice-Hall, 1972), 60–71.

11. See Jan Kott, "King Lear or Endgame," in *Shakespeare Our Contemporary* (New York: Norton, 1964), 127–68; and *Alternative Shakespeares*, ed. John Drakakis (London: Methuen, 1985). See also John Elsom, ed., *Is Shakespeare Still Our Contemporary?* (New York: Routledge, 1989).

12. See Bert O. States, *Great Reckonings in Little Rooms: On the Phenomenology of Theater* (Berkeley: University of California Press, 1985).

13. *John Gabriel Borkman*, in *The Wild Duck and Other Plays*, trans. Eva Le Gallienne (New York: Modern Library, 1961), 431–32.

14. See Antonin Artaud, *The Theater and Its Double*, trans. M. C. Richards (New York: Grove, 1958), 74–83.

15. See John Gassner, "Realism in the Modern American Theatre," in *American Theatre*, ed. John Russell Brown and Bernard Harris (London: Edward Arnold, 1967), 11.

Contributors

Ruby Cohn, professor of comparative drama at the University of California, Davis, is the author of *From "Desire" to "Godot"; Just Play: Beckett's Theater; Back to Beckett; Samuel Beckett: The Comic Gamut; Modern Shakespeare Offshoots; Dialogue in American Drama;* and *New American Dramatists, 1960–1990.* Forthcoming is *Retreats from Realism in Recent English Drama.*

Jan Kott, the famous Polish author of *Shakespeare Our Contemporary,* has taught at the University of Warsaw and later at SUNY, Stony Brook. His other writings include *The Eating of the Gods; The Theater of Essence; Theater Notebook, 1947–1967;* and *The Bottom Translation: Marlowe and Shakespeare and the Carnival Tradition.*

Katharine Worth is emeritus professor of drama and theatre studies at the University of London. Her published works include *Revolutions in Modern English Drama; The Irish Drama of Europe: From Yeats to Beckett; Oscar Wilde; Maeterlinck's Plays in Performance;* and the symposium called *Beckett the Shape Changer.* Her critical edition of Yeats's *Where There Is Nothing* (with *The Unicorn and the Stars*) was published in 1987.

Linda Ben-Zvi is the author of *Samuel Beckett* in the Twayne Series and the editor of *Women in Beckett: Performance and Critical Perspectives.* The author of many essays on Pinter, Beckett, and O'Neill, she is professor of English at Colorado State University and is currently writing a critical biography of Susan Glaspell.

James Knowlson, who is writing the authorized biography of Samuel Beckett, has previously published *Light and Darkness in the Theatre of Samuel Beckett* and the editions of *Krapp's Last Tape: Theatre Notebook I* and *Happy*

Days: Samuel Beckett's Production Notebook. He is the coauthor of *Frescoes of the Skull: The Later Prose and Drama of Samuel Beckett* and organizer of the Samuel Beckett International Foundation at the Beckett Archive of the University of Reading in England, where he is professor of French studies.

H. Porter Abbott is professor of English at the University of California, Santa Barbara. He is the author of *Diary Fiction: Writing as Action* and *The Fiction of Samuel Beckett: Form and Effect.*

Charles R. Lyons is the Margery Bailey Professor of English and Dramatic Literature at Stanford University. His work in print includes *Bertolt Brecht: The Despair and the Polemic; Shakespeare and the Ambiguity of Love's Triumph; Heinrich Ibsen: The Divided Consciousness;* and *Samuel Beckett.*

Benedict Nightingale, who has written regularly for *The New Statesman* and the Sunday page of *The New York Times,* is currently the drama critic of *The Times* in London. A former professor of English and theater at the University of Michigan, he is the author of *A Reader's Guide to Fifty Modern British Plays* and *Fifth Row Center.*

Bernard F. Dukore is University Distinguished Professor of Theatre Arts and Humanities at Virginia Polytechnic University. His books include *"Death of a Salesman" and "The Crucible": Text and Interpretation; Harold Pinter; Bernard Shaw: Playwright; The Theatre of Peter Barnes; Where Laughter Stops: Pinter's Tragicomedy;* and the edition entitled *Dramatic Theory and Criticism.* He is preparing the first full edition of Shaw's drama and theater criticism, including cinema, radio, and television.

Hersh Zeifman, the author of many essays on Stoppard, Pinter, and Beckett, teaches in the Department of English at York University in Toronto, where he is also coeditor of *Modern Drama.* He is the editor of *David Hare: A Casebook* and the coeditor of *Essays on Contemporary British Drama, 1970–1985.*

Toby Silverman Zinman is an associate professor at the University of the Arts in Philadelphia. A specialist in the relationship between the literary and the visual arts, her work has most recently appeared in *Theatre Journal, American Theatre,* and *Modern Fiction Studies.*

Rosette C. Lamont, who teaches at Queens College and the graduate center of CUNY, is a frequent contributor to *The New York Times* and several drama periodicals. Her published work includes *The Life and Work of Boris Pasternak; De Vive Voix; Ionesco;* and *Two Faces of Ionesco.*

Theodore Shank is the author of *American Alternative Theatre; The Art of Dramatic Art; Theatre in Real Time; Materiali per uno studio sul Nuovo Teatro. America—Inghilterra dal 1968;* and the exhibition catalogue *Contemporary Experimental Theatre.* He is professor of theater at the University of California, San Diego, and the editor of *500 Plays: Outlines and Production Notes.*

Bernard Weiner, formerly the theater critic for the *San Francisco Chronicle,* has published in *American Theatre; The Drama Review; Yale/Theater; The Village Voice; Sight and Sound;* and *The Nation.* He teaches regularly at San Francisco State University and at the National Critics Institute at the O'Neill Center in Waterford, Connecticut.

Herbert Blau is Distinguished Professor of English at the University of Wisconsin, Milwaukee. He is the author of *The Eye of Prey: Subversions of the Postmodern; Take Up the Bodies: Theater at the Vanishing Point; Blooded Thought: Occasions of Theater; The Impossible Theater: A Manifesto;* and, most recently, *The Audience.* He was cofounder and codirector of the San Francisco Actors' Workshop, codirector of the Repertory Theater of Lincoln Center, and founder and artistic director of KRAKEN.

Enoch Brater is the editor of *Theatre Journal* and professor of English and theater at the University of Michigan. His published work includes *Beyond Minimalism: Beckett's Late Style in the Theater; Why Beckett* (also translated into Spanish and Japanese); and the collections *Beckett at 80 / Beckett in Context* and *Feminine Focus: The New Women Playwrights.* He is the author of two forthcoming books, *The Drama in the Text: Beckett's Late Fiction* and *The Stages of Arthur Miller.* Most recently he has been the coeditor of *Approaches to Teaching Beckett's "Waiting for Godot."*

Index

307